Project Adventure, Inc.

Cowstails and Cobras II

A Guide to Games, Initiatives, Ropes Courses & Adventure Curriculum

by
Karl Rohnke

A Project Adventure Publication in cooperation with
KENDALL/HUNT PUBLISHING COMPANY
4050 Westmark Drive   Dubuque, Iowa 52002

WARNING

Improper use of the adventure activities described herein may result in serious injury. The activities should not be attempted without the supervision of trained and properly qualified leaders.

Neither the author, publisher, seller or any distributor of this publication assumes any liability for loss or damage, direct or consequential to the readers or others resulting from the use of the materials contained herein, whether such loss or damage results from errors, omissions, ambiguities or inaccuracies in the materials contained herein or otherwise. No warranties, express or implied, as to merchantability or as to fitness for any particular use or purpose are intended to arise out of the sale or distribution of this publication and this publication is sold "as is" and 'with all faults.' The liability of the author, publisher, seller, or any distributor of this publication on account of any such errors, omission or ambiguities, shall in any event, be limited to the purchase price of this publication.

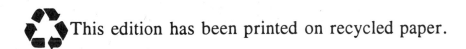This edition has been printed on recycled paper.

Nicki Hall photo

"True Cynea, we cannot fly; but do not excuse your hesitation for lack of wings."

— Clavidicus

Credits

Did you know that Robert Lentz was the first director of Project Adventure? And that he:

- established the initial five learning goals that form the basis for the Project Adventure approach and teaching philosophy.

- was initially responsible for guiding a federally funded small-time operation into what has become the largest non-profit Adventure Education consulting organization in the world.

- has the most indecipherable handwriting in the world.

Bob, this revised edition of *Cowstails and Cobras* is dedicated to you because without your initial leadership, program perspicacity, and frugal sense of what's necessary, Project Adventure would have become just another good idea that didn't make it.

The 1971 Project Adventure staff
Mary Ladd Smith
Robert Lentz
Jim Schoel
Karl Rohnke

Ongoing thanks to the original physical education and administrative staff at Hamilton-Wenham Regional High School, who were, and continue to be, professionally confident enough to try "new stuff."
    *Hammond Young — then superintendent
    *Jerry Pieh — then principal
    *Gary Baker — then curriculum coordinator
    *Sherm Kinney — then athletic director
    *Sally Anderson — then Woodsom
    *Jennifer Simone — then Swisher
    *Cliff Mello
    Mike Jackson
    Chuck Cook
    Doug Hoak

*indicates the original 1971 staff

To quote from the original text in *Cowstails and Cobras*: "Their willingness to try something new, and to continually help refine the program, has been most appreciated by us all."

About this edition
The impressive layout and formatting of *Cowstails II* resulted from the joining of two formidable performers: Conrad Willeman and his mega-byte marvel (the "Mac").

Thanks also to Nicki Hall for use of her many fine Adventure-based photographs.

Additional gratitude is due all the Project Adventure staff and friends who gave so freely of their time and talents to make this "simple rewrite" the BEST Adventure publication so far, deadlines notwithstanding. (Ref. Tom Zierk, Feb. 1987, "…considering that most of the writing is done, we should have this ready by spring.")

Contents

Preface

by Dick Prouty

Cowstails and Cobras II is a major revision of the original *Cowstails and Cobras* published by Project Adventure in 1977. That original text was an overview of the National Model Physical Education curriculum, as evaluated by the federal Office of Education at Hamilton-Wenham School District, in Massachusetts, in 1974. Between 1977 and the summer of 1987, when we stopped publishing that edition, over 44,000 copies were sold. Five to six thousand of those were given to the education and recreation professionals who attended Project Adventure training workshops during that period. The remainder were sold to a wide cross section of persons from the fields of education, counseling and therapy, camping, recreation, and corporate training. Many of these people went on to use some of the ideas from the original text to start a PA type program or to infuse some of the ideas into an already existing Outdoor or Adventure Education program. Several thousand of the texts found their way overseas as purchase orders and requests for the book have come in from over thirty foreign countries, including the Soviet Union, Poland, and Czechoslovakia.

Clearly, the book has had a major impact on the emerging field of Adventure Education. The primary reason for the popularity of the book is that it was founded on a belief that struck a responsive chord in people who work with people. In his introduction to the original text, Bob Lentz stated, "This belief holds that we need to provide room in the development of young people (and probably in the continuing development of other people) for an approach to physical activity which combines a joyful sense of Adventure, a willingness to move beyond previously set limits, and the satisfaction of solving problems together." This belief has been reaffirmed continually in the life of both *Cowstails and Cobras* and Project Adventure, as both have grown together in the decade of the Eighties. Schools, and other adapting institutions that have used the curriculum ideas, have discovered that it is a powerful belief that, when properly implemented, has the potential for changing the educational experience for both student and teacher alike.

A second practical reason for the popularity of the original book was that it was, as its subtitle said, a practical "Guide to Ropes Courses, Initiative Games and other Adventure

Activities." Many people first learned of a ropes course by way of *Cowstails and Cobras*, and many constructed elements using the book's drawings. By 1987, however, the original *Cowstails* was in need of a major overhaul. The growth of the Adventure field had initiated major changes in curriculum design options for physical education and recreation programs, and the advance in the technology of ropes course design and construction had caused significant changes. *Cowstails and Cobras II* is much more of a complete curriculum guide for those implementing an Adventure program in the physical education or recreation field than the original text. The material on leading the experience, both in chapter one and throughout the other chapters, is intended to help the reader get a feel for the important leading skills necessary to implement the program. These skills are, in our training experience, well within the reach of the majority of professionals; but they do need training and thoughtful practice in order to master.

The advice on the construction of ropes course elements contained in the original is not included in the revision. Instead, we have developed a new concept to help those who continue to desire (or need for financial reasons) to construct courses on their own. *Challenge by Choice* is a package available from PA that includes a 95-page detailed construction guide text, an accompanying two-hour video tape, and telephone support time. An on-site safety inspection of the course is also required. This systems approach allows us to continue to help those who wish to construct on their own, yet takes into consideration the new need, caused by the growth of the field, for a more comprehensive approach to safety and construction standards.

A third major reason for the success of the original text was the unique style of the author, Karl Rohnke. It's just plain easy to see or

recapture the necessary fun ingredient in the PA approach when you're reading Karl. Spontaneously creative, dedicated to Adventure and fun in learning, and never happier than when he is sharing these qualities in a workshop setting, Karl has truly unique gifts. Jim Schoel and other PA staff have also written on leadership issues in some parts of the text and are identified where they have contributed. This team approach, we feel, gives the reader a good view of how leadership styles may differ and how the quality of leadership can affect the Adventure experience. Karl and I, and all of us at PA, have one strong desire in common for this book. Please use and enjoy *Cowstails and Cobras II* in the spirit in which it was written: *Learning can be and should be a joyous Adventure!*

Introduction

After 13 years I think the reader is due an explanation of what *Cowstails and Cobras* means. A Cowstail is the frayed end of a rope. A Cobra is a yoga exercise. Juxtaposed, the words are meaningless, the title is pure nonsense. But the curriculum contained herein is no nonsense at all — although paradoxically requiring a level of pedagogic play that belies the serious intent — having been adopted and adapted successfully by literally thousands of professional educators since Project Adventure began in 1971. *Cowstails and Cobras II* (the meaning of Cowstails in this context has not changed — it still has nothing to do with a bovine), is a radical retooling of the original book that boasts substantial deletions (some of the technical data was really out of date), extensive curriculum additions (compulsive lesson planners take note), a humongous amount of rewriting, and preservation of some of the original text that was soooo good I just couldn't bear to change an apostrophe — the FRCBOA* historical society was delighted. I've tried from a don't–knock–success standpoint to maintain the less–than–literary flavor

*Future Ropes Course Builders of America

of *Cowstails and Cobras* and approximately follow the layout format. "When you find a technique that works, stick with it. Don't get bored with success."

Shall we call it *Cowstails and Cobras II*? Call it whatever you want as long as you recognize that ability equates to inherent capability; i.e., Barbra Streisand and I are never going to make a top ten record together.

I almost forgot to mention that the proposed original title of this book was Cowstails and Crabs, but the negative response from the staff and practically everyone else caused the change. Crabs, in context of the deleted title, referred to carabiners — you knew that!

I began my career work in outdoor Adventure education with the personal credo, "Don't take yourself too seriously." Rather than

mellowing with age, responsibility, and repetition, the credo has escalated to, "If you take yourself too seriously, no one else will." Casual competence and a sense of responsible abandon are beneficial attributes and are key toward refining your Adventure Education approach.

The emphasis of a PA approach is expecting a consistent and conscientious attempt at goals that often seem beyond accomplishment. So don't worry about what curriculum events you personally can or can't do, as long as you are willing to occasionally attempt the same things you have been asking the students to do. For years I've pushed the aphorism, "An ounce of image is worth a pound of performance." That's not faking, that's occupational survival with élan.

Nicki Hall photo

Using This Book, A Note to the Teachers

The activities and curriculum covered in *Cowstails II* flesh out the Project Adventure philosophy toward learning, which in essence states that individuals are usually more capable (mentally, emotionally, and physically) than they perceive themselves to be, and if given the opportunity to TRY in a supportive atmosphere, can discover this excellence within themselves.

Use all the material included in this book to add to your repertoire of Adventure activities, but don't just accept the information here as the definitive source of Adventure ideas and scenarios.

Some of the included curriculum material can be easily adapted to your own lesson plan format and that's OK if you recognize the dead end consequence of using one lesson plan ALL

THE TIME. Experiment with ideas of your own or those suggested by students. (Don't expect formal written suggestions — "Hey coach, this game sucks," — is a pretty fair indication that other activities should be considered for that time slot.) Some ideas will work and some won't, but take the chance of trying, and you will eventually get a feel for the functional.

Much of the rationale and justification for this indoor/outdoor Adventure approach to education emerges out of the teacher's and student's positive experiences in trying the various games, stunts, trust activities, and Initiative problems. There are, however, important goals that need to be stated which provide an ongoing philosophical touchstone for invention and implementation, and which tie all the varied activities together. These learning goals are:

1. *To increase the participant's sense of personal confidence.*

The aim of many activities is to allow the students to view themselves as increasingly capable and competent. By attempting a graduated series of activities, which involve physical or emotional risk, and succeeding (or sometimes failing) in a supportive group atmosphere, a student may begin to develop true self-esteem.

The curriculum has been planned to encourage students to try new and different activities — some of which may involve initial anxiety.

It is our belief that as a person matures he/she needs to learn to be familiar with the anxiety that precedes any new venture, cope with that uncertainty, and dare to enter fully into new situations.

2. *To increase mutual support within a group.*

The curriculum is based on the assumption that anyone who conscientiously tries should be respected. Success and failure are less important than making an effort. In many cases, the success or failure of a group depends on the effort of the members. A cooperative, supportive atmosphere tends to encourage participation. The use of teams, points, and timed competition, has been consciously minimized.

3. *To develop an increased level of agility and physical coordination.*

A number of exercises entail the use of balance and smoothly flowing movement. Balance and coordinated movement form the basis for many physical activities ranging from dancing to track and football. A person who perceives himself as physically awkward, often sees himself as inadequate in other ways. Balance activities which can be successfully completed often give a feeling of accomplishment and personal worth to the doer.

4. *To develop an increased joy in one's physical self and in being with others.*

One of the criteria which we have used in assessing various activities is that it must have a substantial element of fun in it. Instructors are not solemnly engaged in building confidence, social cohesion, and agility. Just as people in the program may regularly be anxious and even fearful, so should they even more regularly experience joy, laughter, anticipation.

The program is designed to give the participants many opportunities to come to recognize that they are physical beings and that using one's body can be a joyous, satisfying, exhilarating, and unambiguous experience.

5. To develop an increased familiarity and identification with the natural world.

Young people too often have little experience with sun, rain, dirt, snow, cold, Spring, Fall, and Winter. Because of the activities involved in the program, the students become increasingly comfortable with rolling in the dirt, with the smell of the grass, with the feel of rain of snow or wind of cold or sunlight — in all their various moods. The weather always adds to the unpredictability of the chosen activity.

A Closing Note

The course and the risks involved are in many ways uncompromising. For students, the experience is both stressful and joyous. Ideally, as they dare to try, they begin to experience physical success and recognize that the seemingly difficult is often quite possible. Their struggles are often the beginnings of maturity which we believe entails, in part, having real experience with a wide range of natural human reactions — fear, joy, fatigue, compassion, laughter, pain, and love.

Elements of the Adventure Program

The games, Initiative problems, and trust activities included in this section are easy to like and easy to use. A teacher should recognize, however, that there is a philosophy and approach associated with these activities that is significantly different from more traditional teaching scenarios, and which requires specific training as to presentation, sequencing, and proctoring, to insure optimum and safe results.

There are a lot of do's and don'ts that come to mind, and I was tempted to start listing them, but that's what Project Adventure's training workshops are designed to accomplish. Do's and don'ts presented out of context become another list to peruse and forget. If you plan to use Adventure curriculum material as part of your ongoing program, I strongly recommend that you attend a regularly scheduled residential Project Adventure workshop so that you can try (in a supportive setting) these various experiences that you will eventually be presenting to your own students. I'm not trying to sell you a "bag of goods," just recommending a training sequence that will prove exhilarating, rejuvenating, and programmatically useful.

For example, let's take a look at a specific Initiative problem and see what's involved. Asking a group (10–20) to try and ascend a 12' high wall, represents a classic Initiative situation. An Initiative problem in this context is a situational task presented by an instructor with no solution offered. A good Initiative involves a task requiring group effort (cognitive and psychomotor).

Probably first used by the military, the *Wall* combines all the essentials that you want to see in a problem of this kind; appears initially impossible to some participants, involves fear of failure and physical harm, provides unequivocal feedback on a pass/fail basis, requires a group effort (cannot be accomplished by an individual), indicates leader/follower roles and the value of each, pin-points gender prejudices, encourages spotting (caring) for others, suggests that success is measured by the quality of an attempt rather than achieving a particular physical goal, says that trying is more highly valued than performance level, etc., etc.

Considering the above, it's obvious that an instructor has a wealth of presentation and evaluative material to use with students. However, if that instructor sees the *Wall* as simply a fabricated barrier, and is interested only in physical results (timed attempts), all the "good stuff" mentioned above is either ignored (don't bother me with that psychological junk, can't you see these kids are having a good time?"), or never used because he/she didn't know or recognize that the subtleties exist.

A typical Challenge Ropes Course Wall is 12 feet high. A fall from that height could be damaging. An untrained instructor presenting this Initiative problem (from a book) might not be aware of or remember which areas for spotting are essential, or more disastrously, not be aware that spotting is necessary at all. Further, an instructor who is used to coaching a sport, might feel justified in coaching a group over the *Wall*, not recognizing that his/her good intentioned help reduces the students' feeling of accomplishment.

Finally, a teacher who presents the problem safely and compassionately, then stands aside to provide support and encouragement when necessary, is visibly doing a good job. But if that instructor hurries the same group from activity to activity to "make sure that we cover the curriculum content," students are apt to miss the educationally significant part of the Initiative problem scenario — the spontaneous comments and emotional reactions relating to the experience that are essential for group and individual sharing, and eventual understanding of the experience beyond the vacuous, "I really liked it!" type of non-comment.

All of this disclaimer-type rhetoric is an attempt to convince you that specific training beyond reading the book is necessary to achieve a useful and safe level of functioning as an Adventure curriculum teacher. Anyone unfamiliar with the safety knowledge and facilitation skills necessary to present and process the Initiative tasks outlined in this book, should seek further information or assistance from Project Adventure, Inc.

Other books are available from PA that may be of interest or provide essential curriculum information. A complete list of these publications is provided at the back of this book.

Nicki Hall photo

Chapter 1

Leadership Issues in Adventure Programming

by Jim Schoel

When Project Adventure first began in 1971, one of our tasks was to put together a year-long 10th grade Physical Education curriculum. With vigor we approached that work, starting out with field exercises, going to initiatives, then low ropes, high ropes, winter skills and campcraft. We finished up in the spring with an initiative day where students would practice what they learned by forming small groups and solving a circuit of problems. Many students participated in interdisciplinary camping trips where they would concentrate on academic problems, bringing to bear their new skills of problem solving, trust and risk taking. Sounds good, doesn't it?

But over the years we've learned a lot about what makes our activities and programs hold together. For example, we've found that a group tends to be more productive if time is spent on some kind of goal setting before the activities begin. This is because goal setting helps individuals clarify what they are doing during the activity and what they will carry away from it. We have responded to the "force 'em through it" school by forming a philosophy of Challenge by Choice. Through our experience in leading thousands of hours of ropes course activities, we've found that the ability to choose and to say no is in most cases a sign of strength not weakness. In this sense, we are no longer so activity-oriented that we miss what is going on inside the individuals within the group. The activities are important, but only insofar as how they affect individuals. Failures can be turned into successes because

the participant has had a chance to look at him/herself from the perspective of a supportive group. The kind of good spirit and fun that playing at Adventure produces is extremely productive. We fool 'em into exercising, thinking, cooperating, taking risks, and feeling good about their accomplishments.

Finally, because of our experience, we've removed some activities from our repertoire. These decisions come from many days of coaxing students through certain activities with a gut wrenching feeling of "what if," banging away at our insides. The Flea Leap is a good example. Although it's an excellent activity in terms of group dynamics and risk, the spotting issues were too severe to continue using it. This deletion is a result of an ongoing evolutionary process which involves many hours spent by the safety committee mulling over pro and con issues, consulting the 15-year safety study, and making hard decisions. Any program leader needs to involve himself in such a process. Because each program is site-specific, activities will naturally develop that are unique to that particular setting.

It is our goal here to provide you with some practical suggestions concerning group leadership. This conscious approach is broken down into the following issues:

- Group Formation
- Selecting Appropriate Activities
- Briefing the Group
- Leading the Group
- Debriefing the Group

Group Formation

You may not have much choice as to the group you get. The school system assigns you an adventure class, or the camp gives you a cabin or patrol, and there you are, first thing in the morning, with your bag of tricks, ready to go! Then again, you may be able to interview

potential candidates as part of an intake process where you can carefully measure, help with expectations and fears, and set goals. Whatever the case, it is helpful to look at some group formation considerations. You'll get better mileage out of the experience you are presenting if you do. Some of the considerations we find helpful are:

• Common issues and/or goals.
• Group balance (a good "mix").
• Mental and physical ability.
• Intensity of the experience.

Common Issues and/or Goals

The Adventure experience is a common experience because of the group development that takes place. As students pursue games, trust activities, problem solving, ropes course risk experiences, community service, and academic cooperative learning exercises, they become a group that learns to listen, respect, and care for itself. This shaping of the group is the process of bringing the members to some kind of commonality. The students are simply "buying off" on or accepting what is going on. Various types of groups develop along differing lines of intensity and kinds of goals. For example, physical education classes operate differently than drug treatment counseling groups but they still go through the group formation process. Knowing what you want to achieve with your group, then communicating this to the participants, is what we want you to consider. If there are students who will not or cannot fit into the goals you've laid out, then adjustments need to be made.

Group Balance

A good mix could mean placing strong students with weak, older/younger combinations, or student leaders with followers. Group balance issues are more important when

difficult and disturbed populations are addressed but they always need to be considered. You could involve interested, regular education students with a special needs group. Everyone can benefit from this and motivated students will find that students with problems "aren't so bad after all." Student leaders who have gone through a training process (often, completion of the previous semester's class, along with some skill instruction and discussion of roles), will add a great deal to a green class. The participant/leader position also provides incentive and status.

Mental and Physical Ability

Almost every type of person imaginable has participated in Adventure activities. But understanding the culture and needs of a group is nowhere as important as when dealing with physical and mental impairments or disabilities. The underlying assumption of Adventure, that you can do more than you think you can, continues to apply to disabled students but the assumption requires special thought, and, at times, special apparatus. Having both able-bodied and disabled persons in a Shared Adventures group gives a disabled population the chance to utilize appropriate aid in accomplishing tasks while giving the able bodied students an opportunity to relate to a population that is quite often shoved aside.

Intensity of the Experience

Much of the outdoor education movement has been based on challenge and stress. The assumption has been that if individuals and groups come up against it in terms of extreme difficulty, change and growth will take place. We need to be careful with this. No matter what we do, we must think about the needs and potential responses of each group we work

with. There are simply many times when a stressful situation is not appropriate. It may take weeks, even months of lead-up and group development time in order to get to the more challenging and difficult situations. Group type needs to correspond to the level of intensity you bring to your leadership.

Some sample groups:
- Adventure Physical Education classes ranging from 15–25 students
- Adventure Based Counseling groups ranging from 6–12 clients
- Adventure Experience groups at camps or recreation programs
- Adventure Education classes that are part of a school's regular curriculum
- Adventure Executive or Staff Development groups as part of a corporate or institutional structure

Within a physical education class, you may have a highly functioning group that needs to dive into the activities in such a way that it is always kept on its toes. You may also have a group that requires a great deal of slowed down encouragement and support. An Adventure Based Counseling group, with court-referred clients, may require a dramatic rappel or a high ropes experience on day one, with the intensity geared in such a way that it gets the attention of otherwise turned off clients. But you can't follow the same approach with patients on suicide watch in a mental hospital.

Selecting Appropriate Activities

The buzzword for this in Adventure programming is Sequencing. Sequencing means the correct selection of activities at any given time for any given group. Good sequencing begins with making a list of all activities available, then building your curriculum from this base, remembering that not all activities need be used. Certain activities may not work with your group. You may want to use ropes course elements that most challenged *you* when you were attending a training workshop, but those

Nicki Hall photo

elements may be too much for the groups you teach. Or you may simply need to wait for the right time to use the activity. Sequencing refers to timing as well. That's why it's important to know as much as possible about the group you're going to lead before you begin your work with them.

No matter what activities you choose to begin with, we recommend a thorough run-through of the Trust Fall/Spotting sequence which is detailed in Chapter Two, Warm-Ups. The Trust Fall sequence and the activity of Spotting are basic material for the psychologi-

cal and physical well being of individuals, and the emotional development of a group. The Trust Fall sequence is really part and parcel of the larger issue of spotting and should be presented as such. The spotting issue is one of the important reality bases of Adventure for it gives a larger purpose to the trust activities. It is fundamental to Adventure activities as a whole. We recommend that instructors begin this training with a statement to the effect that "If you want to participate in the low and high ropes experiences, you have to pay attention to this initial training."

The sequential approach to Trust Fall activities provides for the gradual development of trust, thereby encouraging greater participation and more profound relationships. The alignment of Trust Fall activities with Spotting concepts provides for a sound, practical relationship, that results in a combination of physical and emotional safety.

Lead-Up activities help set the stage for what is to come and also give you time to assess and make sequencing decisions. Please note that following these steps exactly is not necessary for every group. What we advocate is the concept of moving gradually, especially in counseling situations. Sequencing and timing decisions are up to the discretion of the leader.

Step #1: Ice Breaker/Acquaintance Activities

Here are some sample activities. Selection depends on the needs of the group and time allotted.
- Warmups and Stretching
- Everybody Up, with the variation of Two-Person "Get Up"
- The Clock
- Add-On Tag
- Moonball
- Toe Tag
- Backwards Relay (two teams race each other in a relay, running backwards)

These activities serve to loosen up a group and get them to touch each other. For many individuals, a simple thing like hand-holding is too much because of either timidity or machismo. The game aspect helps the group reach the goal of physical contact without much conscious thought.

Step #2: Deinhibitizer Activities
• Samurai

• Yells
• Inchworm
• Dogshake
• Lap Game or Circle Sit

Deinhibitizers get the group to let go, do something out of the ordinary, and act silly. Try framing Yells by having participants imagine that they are lost in the woods. Ask the participants either to go into the center of the group, or sit on the perimeter of the circle. Then get them to scream for help as loud as they can. The debriefing can focus on what an inhibition is and why it's difficult to let go in front of a group. The same can be said for the yelling that is demanded in the ritual death of a Samurai Warrior where group members, when "killed" by the gesture of a boffer, must die painfully, dramatically, and loudly (a scream or howl will do).

Step #3: Beginning Trust and Spotting Activities
Spotting is a human safety net provided by other people for the person doing an activity. It is the primary safety system for Initiative problems and low elements. It is also used in limited ways for certain high elements. Basic spotting techniques are taught to participants through introductory activities and then modified or added to as the demands of specific elements require.
• Two-Person Mirroring
• Yurt Circle
• Rolling
• Two-Person Trust Fall
• Circle Pass
• Levitation
• Gauntlet
• Trust-Fall from a Height
• Trust Dive

Falls are to be expected. Proper spotting helps to prevent falls from causing injury. Regardless of the specific spotting technique being used (techniques do vary for different events and elements), the fundamental principle is to protect the participant's head and upper body through physical support.

This sequence takes the group from Ice-breakers, to Deinhibitizers, to the actual Trust Activities so that the group is prepared for the Initiatives. All of them relate to spotting, for spotting requires a connected group that is willing to get involved both physically and mentally. You can use the sequence to kill two birds with one stone: Forming the group in a gradual, non-threatening manner while at the same time preparing the participants to spot for each other on the low elements and during some Initiatives.

Briefing

It's a great temptation to plow right into an Adventure experience without saying much of anything other than what is going to happen on that particular day. After all, you've done a lot of preparation yourself in terms of training and planning. You don't want to waste time either. But stop! Some members of your group may not be clear about what is going on, or what is expected of them, or there may be some group problems that need to be looked at. Time spent briefing, if it is regular and calm, has a cumulative effect. You don't need to say everything in one session. Your brief-ings will gradually build into a solid body of information and expectations. You are provid-ing a space and time for communication.

To brief is to inform. In the briefing discus-sion period, there are two levels of informa-tion: 1.) Instructions that the leader gives the group, much of it non-negotiable safety infor-mation, and 2.) Shared information where there is give and take, goal setting, clarifica-tion, and framing. Briefing in these terms connotes action: what goes on in the briefing relates directly to what goes on during the

Peter Steele photo

upcoming activity. The instructions relate to the particular safety and completion needs of the activity. The safety information cannot be negotiated. The framing of the task, in terms of completing it, can be adjusted according to the needs of the participants (everyone goes back if you touch, or only one person goes back). The shared information draws on some kind of response from the participants. It's here that the participants can voice doubts, talk about goals and contracts, and work on consciously transferring what was learned in the previous activity to the present one. Briefing sessions should be responsive to the needs of the group. In that sense, you may not need much time at all, or then again, you may need a lot of the period.

Goal setting has become an important Adventure activity over the years. The process is generally set in terms of what we call the Full Value Contract. This handy item works for all types of groups — executive programs, standard physical education classes, and intense counseling groups. Its universal application comes from a combination of simplicity, levels of interpretation, and the need for every group to establish some kind of protocol for how members deal with each other. Introduced early on to the group, the FV Contract can be made part of every Adventure experience. There are three commitments that are usually made in terms of the contract:

1. The agreement to work together as a group and to work toward individual and group goals.
2. The agreement to adhere to certain safety and group behavior guidelines.
3. The agreement to give and receive feedback, both positive and negative, and to work toward changing behavior when it is appropriate.

You can choose what you want to emphasize in this contract, but the bottom line needs to be the agreement to work together as a group and to be safe. The acceptance of group behavior guidelines has to do with not only acting out behavior, but the need to agree not to devalue or discount others, or oneself. Any group can come to an agreement on this before the activity begins. This goes for one day groups, or year-long groups. Once this agreement is made, the leader has a more potent voice when it comes to stopping an activity, and in conducting the Debrief (the evaluating time of the Adventure activity). "Did we honor the Full Value Contract?" "Was there any Devaluing going on?"

A deeper level of interpretation is available when you get into individual and group goal setting. Goal setting can take place during a short experience. In fact, we've found that our one-day experience groups are more successful if the participants come with an idea of what it is they want to achieve.

Finally, when you choose to explore the group's acceptance of feedback, and to look at ways of changing behavior, you are entering

the deepest level of the Full Value Contract. This is generally set aside for counseling, though aspects of it can be utilized in other kinds of groups. One should be careful when entering this area, however, for although giving and receiving feedback is fairly common, it can be hurtful if done without the proper supports. A group of twenty-five giving feedback to one member, though truthful, can be a devastating experience. Counseling training is important for these kinds of interactions.

Leading

So we enter into the activity with some important arrows in our quiver: A sense of the group, appropriate activity selection, proper safety training, and a briefing session. This preparation gives us the groundwork for the actual direct leadership of the group. Let's go out now and do it!

Nicki Hall photo

While we're leading Adventure activities, we must be responsive to the group. But responsiveness can be elusive: how do we keep our agenda and still listen to the group's needs? Without an easy answer, let's consider these leadership ideas: Common Ground, Challenge, Instruction/Intervention, Listening, Competition and Cooperation, Co-Leading, and Humor.

Common Ground

The shared experience of Common Ground presupposes that the leader is an active member of the group. Visualize and practice it: helpful, full of the joy of learning and doing,

attentive, willing to try new things, to listen, to get right in there and play. Then add to it adult planning, observation, and control. No line is being crossed over in order to relate to the students. Common Ground brings out a new kind of leader, one who can both lead and experience at the same time.

There are some tactics to this. First, acknowledge that you can get bored repeating things. One way to fight boredom is to look through the eyes of the participants. For them, it's all completely new. But because of their newness, you can experience newness through them! In this respect, the activity itself is no longer at issue, rather, it's the experience of the participants that's important. Second, let yourself play and have fun. If you're able to establish a sense of newness, playing becomes easier and more exciting. Third, your prior experience of doing the activities allows you to identify with the participants. You've been there yourself. You can speak from experience.

Because of Common Ground, you have more of a chance to operate from inside the group — no longer are you the outside expert. And there doesn't have to be any loss of credibility or authority. You can and must step back and operate as the bottom line. The group wouldn't want it any other way. But you still convey the message that you're part of them. You are human, have feelings, get excited, angry, even make mistakes. You become a different kind of role model in the Common Ground because you are allowing yourself to be known, to be vulnerable.

But at the same time you always have charge of the situation, and of yourself. Participants are thirsty for such persons to identify with. There is a line that must be maintained, and we are not naive about that. At the same time, that line can be carefully established in the midst of the group, on common ground. You can't cross that line and ask the group for help with profound difficulties you may have. Nor do you need to hang out with them, or get into their personal raps, to achieve the sense that you belong. And there are many activities that you simply cannot participate in because of your need to keep control of the safety issues.

Challenge

During the briefing, when the leader says, "It's important to be able to say at the end of our Activity today that you challenged yourself in at least one way," he is utilizing one of the most effective tools he has. Challenge means going beyond the old, pushing into new territory, new ways of doing things, dealing with fear and accepting help and support. Challenge also is looking at that part of ourselves that isn't sure what it is able to do, or to be. Challenge has the potential of stripping us

bare, of getting down to the essentials, the nub of things.

But Challenge is a two-edged sword. While it presents an opportunity for change and success, it also lays bare the issues we are afraid of: losing face, failure, and injury. Where there is opportunity for growth, there is also the opportunity for overstepping boundaries, of pushing too far, and thereby retarding the growth we want so badly for our participants. For this reason, the dictum Challenge by Choice is important to us. Karl Rohnke adds some personal reflection on the journey he followed in order to get to Challenge by Choice.

"I've had an extended background in pushing people beyond their perceived capabilities. My role of "program encourager" began officially in 1967 as an Outward Bound instructor, but had been matured over the years by a certain level of physical self-flagellation achieved in sports and a brief stint in the U.S. Army.

Pushing people in a program sense was satisfying because the validity of your presence as an instructor depended upon being recognized as more than capable, and immersing yourself into the same experiential milieu that the student was experiencing (usually a fearful or physically uncomfortable scenario that involved being hungry, lost, fatigued, or bugged).

Then, because of a change in student population, demographic location, and being newly introduced to the public school persona, the approach to 'pushing' practically changed overnight; changed to mellow is probably most descriptive.

What a change! What a revelation that the simple affording of that choice could achieve more toward growth of self-awareness and image than what used to require large doses of performance pressure. What a relief!

With the pressure off (instructor and student), the opportunity for growth was palpably

different. There was a remarkably sentient feel to teaching that had been masked and blunted by years of ego satisfaction and adherence to a one-minded, often glandular approach."

Challenge by Choice offers a participant:
- The chance to try a potentially difficult and/ or frightening challenge in an atmosphere of support and caring.
- The opportunity to "back off" when performance pressures or self-doubt become too strong, knowing that an opportunity for a future attempt will always be available.
- The chance to try difficult tasks, recognizing that the attempt is more significant than performance results.
- Respect for individual ideas and choices.

Respecting the right to choose doesn't mean you can't challenge. The nature of Adventure activities is one big challenging obstacle course: climb over this, let go of that, run around and act stupid, laugh and have fun, solve the problem over here, go over and accomplish those things. There's always a surprise, a monkey wrench to dig out of the machinery, a coat that can't touch the electrified Spider's Web.

Your role as leader must be to continually find ways to offer understandable challenges that can be accepted by the group as it maintains its right to make choices. Sometimes it may be necessary to say, "This is the way it's going to be. Do it!" You may seem like a drill-sergeant, but groups respond to that mentality too. A lot of growth can take place when people have no choice as to whether they are or are not going to do something. Just remember that whenever you make choices for the group, you take an essential power away from it.

At the same time, you can't allow participants to wander off or do other things during an activity. That is not respecting the right to make choices. Challenge by Choice addresses those vulnerable areas where a person honestly feels that he's not able to do something, even if he previously said that he was willing to try it. On the other hand, it deals with a person's right to assess the situation and say, "I want to do the Inclined Log now," or "I want to lead the singing at the rest home this week."

Here are some principles to keep in mind when challenging your group:
- Not everyone needs to do everything. Too often Adventure leaders pridefully boast that each group member did a particularly difficult activity. That may be a good thing, but it misses the point of Challenge by Choice.
- Utilize the activity sequencing information. Proper activity selection goes a long way

toward supporting the Challenge once an activity is in progress. Intensity decisions are an important accompanying factor.

- Time spent setting goals is time well spent when dealing with the Challenge of an event. When the participant is clear about what he/she wants to do, it's much easier for everyone. Remember, goal setting doesn't have to take place only during a briefing session removed from the activity. A person may decide to do something during the session. But the same thing holds: make certain that the person knows what he is doing, and is as clear as possible about what it means. This can involve some Counseling on the Run.

- Group pressure is very real and can be used in a positive way. Participants are aided in this when they're familiar with each other

and aware of each other's goals. That's why it is important, when choosing your activities, to reserve the more intense ones until the group members are more comfortable with each other. Because of the trust that develops in Adventure groups, members are much more likely to respond to positive group pressure. The agreement in the Full Value Contract, to confront and be confronted, comes into play here. As long as we're confronting in a positive manner, group pressure can and should be used. It is then defined as group support. You must be aware, however, that group pressure can go beyond the bounds of caring into aggression and abuse. And it can happen very quickly.

- Trust, to repeat, is a great support of Challenge. Certain challenges require a strong dose of it. If the trust isn't there, perhaps more lead-up is necessary. On the other hand, effective challenging can bring about trust. Sometimes you need to take a calculated risk by pushing ahead at a certain time, counting on the trust to emerge.

- Individualize when necessary. Certain participants just will not do what the others are doing. Take the heat off by finding something supportive or manual for them to do.

- Regularly infuse a sense of fun and fantasy into what can easily become a too serious approach.

Instruction/Intervention

There are skills to be learned for Adventure Programs: step-by-step cognitive work, knots, map and compass, first aid, safety, equipment maintenance, curriculum for student tutors, activities for the old folks' home. Because Adventure is so active, the group readily responds to the need to understand how things work. It is in their interest to tie the knot correctly, to know how a canoe works, or how to use a compass.

Instruction is especially useful when you need to rein in the group, to remind them that you are still the boss. Your intervening to teach directly tells them that now is the time to look at you. There's no Initiative Problem solving to it, where everyone has a say. It is leader-centered, and, because of that, you can change the tempo.

So instruction is practical in terms of leader control as well as transmitting necessary how-to information. The combination of the two elements is important because of safety considerations. There are Adventure items that simply are not negotiable. Each event has its own safety issues which must first be mastered by the leader. The leader then must pass this information down—proper care for the equipment, knots tied correctly, calls gone through in correct sequence, proper helmeting, and no horsing around. Without adequate coverage in this area, the event cannot be practiced. Period.

When instruction is referred to as taking control, it crosses over into an intervention mode. Intervention takes place whenever the instructor sees the group as needing to stop and take a look at itself and what it is doing. The group may be involved in some conflict that needs to be looked at. Or a participant may be doing something that is devaluing, or endangering to the others. It is certainly important to intervene before the problem gets so out of hand that it can only be resolved through drastic means. Intervention, in order to resolve conflicts, and the willingness to spend time on conflict resolution, is not only good for the group, but is good role modeling. There is too often little successful conflict resolution in peoples' lives. To participate in the process is to go a long way toward learning how to do it oneself. Types of intervention include:

Substitute a More Relevant Activity. For example, you are trying to do Elbow Tag with a group of urban high school students. They think it's stupid and don't want to do it. You might choose to intervene with something like the Trolleys. In this way, you can use an activity that is more serious, group-oriented, and causes them to get closer together. It is also an Initiative, although not a very intense one, which moves your group from the game aspect on to something more serious, but still a lot of fun.

Modify the Activity. It's getting late, the group hasn't solved the Spider's Web Initiative (get the whole group through a vertical web of rope), and frustration is running high. Call a time out. Ask them to decide whether or not they want to solve the problem with changed

rules, or whether they want to come back and try again. Or you can have them Freeze Frame their effort. Group members must freeze themselves where they are. They are then asked to listen to each other, going over all the ideas that have been suggested. The way you approach the problem can have a lot to do with the decision they make. If you wait until time runs out before you intervene, there can be no decision. Also, you can use the discusssion time to slip in some suggestions about what they are doing wrong or missing.

Refocus the Group. Some of your participants are seriously trying to solve the Amazon Initiative. The rest of the group is hacking off and not paying attention. It's a typical situation where the temptation for the teacher is to plead: "Come on you guys, you're supposed to do this thing together!" A better tactic might be to call the group off the activity, blindfold those who are serious about the problem, forcing the hackers to continue with the solution. Whatever happens, the solution takes second seat to the debrief and the sudden switch of roles. Or, you may choose to simply take the

group aside and get the members to talk about their process. This gives them a chance to confront each other, and to find a solution to their real problem: working together.

Ask for Group Input in terms of the Full Value Contract. The fact that you've set up this learning contract gives you a framework to negotiate virtually all aspects of your Adventure program. "Are we honoring the full value contract?" can be used again and again. Participants want to be called on their agreements, and indeed get nervous if the contract isn't looked at enough or is being ignored. Therefore, consistent questions about it have the capability of clarifying what could otherwise be a cloudy, confusing situation. Participants' goals can be discussed as well. Of course, the full value contract should not be used like a club. Its use must be timely, not punitive.

Listening

Listening, which is an essential component of observing, provides us with all kinds of important information. Continual repetition of activities, and an over-emphasis on logistics, are two enemies of successful listening. If you're so tied up in the nuts and bolts of making the activity work, you'll miss many important interactions. The key to good listening is the development of empathy. For then,

the critical eye and ear are connected to a sense of caring. Catch yourself if you are beginning to just go through the motions. Take time to prepare for the group in terms of the individuals involved, not just, "what are we going to do today?" Watch them, connect with them, play with them, encourage them. If they know you are really there, through an insight, a perceptive joke, encouragement that is correctly timed, or a connection with another incident, or quandry, or success, then your group will come alive in a much more profound way. This takes time and effort, something not always readily provided by institutional work situations. But, boy, does it help make the Adventure Experience!

Competition and Cooperation

We say that we are cooperative, not competitive and generally this is true. But competition is so ingrained in our culture that it is foolish to pretend it doesn't play a part in Adventure. We like to think that the kind of competition we do practice is aimed at developing strong individuals and group unity, not a continual scenario of winners and losers. If participants can be brought to a point where they decide to go just a little bit further than before, they are learning to compete with themselves. If a group decides that it wants to get everyone through the Spider's Web without

touching, then they are competing with the obstacle before them. If the group works for a world record in the Clock or Group Juggling, everyone knows that the goal is foolish and arbitrary. But they're willing to go along with the competition in order to do better, and besides, it's fun. Here are some helpful suggestions:

- Time the events. Let the group work against the clock, rather than against each other.
- See how many participants you can get on, or over, something.

- See how closely the group can stick to the rules (no touching, don't use the tree).
- Show non-group members (parents, teachers, the community) how well you can do. Be careful with this though. Don't develop an us-vs.-them attitude. It can injure the overall relationship. At the same time, there's nothing wrong with proving that you are good and capable. Everyone likes an underdog. Teaching an underdog to like itself is a good trick.
- Talk about those things that keep us from growing as the things that need to be defeated.
- Make certain that participants experience success. There's nothing like success as an antidote for bad feelings or a self-concept of being defeated.

- Insist on the Full Value Contract. Competition for the attention of the group or of the group leader causes members to work against each other.
- Design games and activities that make a spoof out of competition by changing rules and inventing new ones. Get the participants involved in this. Their ideas can be extremely satisfying to them. This is part of the Initiative aspect of Adventure.
- Use competitive games when they fit in with an overall group feeling. We've used softball, for example, as a way to simply play, everyone getting a chance to run, catch, and hit. The score isn't an issue.

Co-Leading

It's difficult to run an Adventure Program completely alone. Indeed, some Adventure groups, such as Adventure Based Counseling, demand co-leadership. In terms of the leader who has a group by him/herself, regularly seek the counsel of others in your department or your supervisor. Ideally, Adventure leaders should get together to discuss common issues, be they logistical or interpersonal. It is difficult enough doing the work, but doing it alone can create real problems.

When co-leading, leaders must spend time before the group starts getting to know each other and agreeing on goals and approaches. This will establish a commonness or sympatica. The resultant feeling between the leaders will certainly be picked up on by the participants. Regular meeting time throughout the life of the group is also necessary. Leaders should work at complementing each other with their skills, drawing out the best, and teaching what they know to each other. Hence, a team of a counselor and a physical education teacher can work very well together teaching an Adventure class of learning disabled students.

Humor *by Karl Rohnke*

Humerous — The large bone of the upper arm, immediately distal to the scapula. A fairly funny-bone, but not in the same class as the ribs, which are prone to tickle.

Let me be so bold (controversial) as to say, "humor makes the program." Perfunctorily profound at best and not catchy at all, but if you forget to regularly infuse your approach, presentation, and evaluation with some smidgen of humor, don't anticipate enthusiastic student response.

This doesn't mean that you have to memorize applicable jokes, or wear a clown's nose to get a laugh. What you do need to be aware of and work toward blending with your teaching style are the following pedagogic points:

Don't take yourself, and what you are presenting, too seriously. I'm referring specifically to course content and how you perceive yourself. I don't expect to change your approach or outlook by listing a few do's and don'ts, but...who really cares (or should care) if someone runs out of bounds from time to time or changes the rules to fit the occasion. It's the level of participation that's significant; level meaning the percentage of people willingly playing and the measure of joy attained. Obsessive evaluators take note: how do you measure the median joy percentile?

But what about continuity, self-discipline, and adherance to standards, you say? (Rhetorical license to put words in your mouth — sorry.) Games without consistent rules are a travesty, an unlearning of societal standards that borders on recreational anarchy. Don't worry about (it's me talking again) societal sequencing and civil disobedience; there's an intractable guardian of the rules called THE REAL WORLD that regularly and humorlessly hammers the printed rules home. God help you if you pass GO and ask for more than $200.00.

Change the rules of whatever you are doing to fit the situation. Rules in this context are

not made to be written down and certainly not to be consistently reinforced. Remember; if the group likes a certain rule and it makes the game fun and challenging to play, keep it. Try rule variations from time to time to see how the group responds. People have been brought up and taught to adhere to rules, so be aware that there's bound to be some resistance when you suggest making third base first base and

running counterclockwise, (Aussie rules).

Don't use objects that the players are familiar with. If you haul out a basketball, football, or baseball, expect a predictable mind (gut) set about what's going to happen next. Some of the performers, who are predictably adept at ball sports, are going to bubble, "oh boy, let's shoot some hoops, spiral a few passes, make some contact and..." further embellish their inflated self-image. Some of the less developed participants will cringe, and anticipate another embarrassing episode of athletic maladroitness. The rest, (median/mode group), will unenthusiastically participate.

Use balloons, beachballs, deck tennis rings, fleece balls, rubber chickens — something different and fun. As Leo Buscaglia suggests, "...be outrageous!"

Use different and unique names for the games that you play and the play objects, names that are fun to say. If the students ask,

"What are we going to do today?", and you say Volleyball, that's a pretty good indication of what the class will be doing, i.e., predictable. Then it's either "Yippee!", "Oh, no!", or "Who cares?" Tell them that for today only you will be introducing and playing Valloon, an existential version of the REAL game, in which you substitute a balloon for the volleyball and remove the net entirely. (The beauty is you can play anywhere.) Teams try to score a point by _____ , remembering that the balloon cannot be hit at a downward angle. The balloon (valloon actually) is served by _____ after each change of serve. Rotation and number of hits on each side depend upon _____ . You fill in the blanks. Put a little water in the balloon (before you blow it up — I'd like to see you try to get the water into a full balloon!) if it's a windy day, or if you want a little more unpredictable action, or if it's hot and you want to get wet.

Is this weird? Probably, but it's got to make you smile and shake your head, and even laugh. That's different, that's fun, that's humer (i.e., humor).

Debriefing

Debriefing is a blindspot for many Adventure leaders. They may be fine at leading games, Initiatives, camping trips, and ropes activities. But sitting down with a group to talk about "what it all means" tends to be particularly difficult and intimidating. Perhaps because it is so important, or because a lot of people are making a big deal out of it nowadays, the problems leaders have with debriefing are increased. Here are a few thoughts that should help in the struggle to gain skills with this critical tool.

Debriefing should not be looked upon as a separate activity. Rather, it is connected to the whole of the Adventure experience which includes the pre-activity and briefing work, as well as the contents of the Adventure activity itself. This wholeness is represented in the image of the Adventure Wave. The wave is a symbol for the brief-activity-debrief scenario. All during the activity of the wave, the leader scans the group for appropriateness of activities and for substantive information that can be useful during a group discussion.

Bear in mind that it's common for Adventure leaders to come away from an experience feeling that it all worked perfectly, and everyone did everything, only to find a whole set of complications. Missing is the perspective of the student who didn't feel supported, or another who felt railroaded. Often, our scanning will miss these things. The debriefing time allows the group to come forth with their perceptions and conflicts. How much better it is for the group to have these issues emerge in a group talk session than in the hallway, or in a one-on-one discussion with the leader.

Talking things out in the group gives the participants the opportunity to gain strength, and become a more integral part of the change process.

One way to accept the debriefing process is to see it as an initiative. Use the principles of initiatives to talk about initiative oriented experiences. Consider the following elements of initiatives that relate to debriefing:

- Everyone participates.
- Full Value Contract is in effect.
- Safety/trust issues are paramount.
- The leader provides the structure for the activity, but relies on the group to provide the solution.
- The experience is focused on achieving positive outcomes.

- The group focuses on issues it's able to handle.
- Group and individual issues are seen as problems to be solved.
- Leaders and participants are bonded by their experience together.
- Emphasis is on the present experience.
- Debriefing takes place after every group experience or whenever necessary.
- Participants are the agents for their own change, and gradually need to take more responsibility for their learning.

We must learn to be collectors of information, both cognitive and affective: what people do, how they feel, and how the group feels. Ease with leading the activities helps us with being open to these responses. The more

second nature they are, the more thought we can put into our collection. This is an important bedrock issue, freeing us up to see, hear, and feel. Carry a notebook, or make it a habit to sit down at night and go over the day. Think through the work of each of your participants. It's a tough discipline because in Adventure work, it's easy to concentrate on the more dramatic episodes, missing the less obvious, but perhaps more important, interactions. Adhering to the discipline of reviewing each and every person helps you counteract that tendency. Building your collection is better when you can do it in concert with a co-leader. They will see things you don't see, and vice versa. Occasional use of video tape can aid in the collecting. Participants tend to like it — everyone wants to see themselves on the silver screen!

Doing something with what you collect is the next step. The trick is how to fit it into the initiative-oriented debrief. Again, does initiative require that the leader be passive? There's nothing that says the leader can't participate. "Relying on the group to provide the solution," could be construed as that, but in the debrief, especially in some difficult, interpretive situations, the leader must step in. The leader should sit back as long as the group members are providing ample interpretation and feedback. If they aren't, then say something. But don't jump in with both feet! Often we are so excited about the insight we've developed that we can't stop ourselves from dropping the pearl. Give the group the opportunity to come up with it! When it's time for you to say something, try to work it out so that the group says it. Oftentimes a well placed question can crack a deadlock and get the juices flowing better than a wizened monologue. Remember, the group wants you to be the expert, for experts are safe to be with, and they have all the answers. The group doesn't have to think when experts are willing to step in. Much of the

flattery directed towards their leader is the group's method of keeping you on top and itself free from the burden of interpretation and responsibility. It is not that you shouldn't share your knowledge. But you need, in the initiative-oriented debrief, to get participants to do the thinking as much as possible, to dig into their feelings, to build up their own collection of observations, and provide an atmosphere to act on them.

Sequencing the Debrief

A group needs to get warmed up before it can get to the nub of the experience. It's just like playing warm-up games before doing problem solving. That's why it's important to sequence the discussion.

Sequencing of debriefing issues has been addressed by Quinsland and Ginkel (1984, p.8). They relate a familiar debriefing scenario. After facilitating a two-hour series of ropes course activities, the leader has assembled the participants in a circle and begins the processing session:

> *'Well, how do you feel about this experience?..'*
> Silence.
> *'How about you, David?..'*
> *'Uh, I don't know'..*
> *'Paula?'..(shrugs her shoulders)*

We've all been there. We know the students have experienced *something*. We saw it in their expressions, heard it in their exchanges. So why can't they talk about it?"

Examining this interaction, you can see that the leader has jumped right into the most difficult and abstract debriefing topic, that of evaluation and opinion. The leader might have had more interaction if he or she had started at a level appropriate to the group. So often we go right to the heart of things! The lack of group response can come more from an uneasiness with the questioning rather than an inability to discuss what has happened.

To answer this problem, Terry Borton, in Clifford Knapp's *The Art and Science of Processing Experience*, is helpful in structuring an effective debriefing sequence. She presents three tiers: the What?, the So What?, and the Now What?

The What?

The What? helps us ease into the discussion by beginning with the facts. It "pertains to the substance of the group interaction and what happened to the individuals." (Clifford Knapp) Because of the doing in the Adventure experience, there are plenty of facts, occurrences, and interactions to work with. Here are some methods that can help get at these "What?" facts:

- **The Go Around.** Everyone in the group contributes a descriptive sentence. The description can be shortened to one word as well.
- **The Memory Game.** "One person starts, explaining in detail everything that happened. Everyone must listen carefully. If anyone else in the group thinks that the person talking missed something that happened, say, "hold it!"....and then explain what is missed. Then, the speaker who said "hold it" will continue, etc… (p.11, Quinsland and Ginkel, op. Cit.).
- **Talk in the present tense.** "I'm now climbing up the pegs on the tree. My knees are acting like sewing machines!" Because of the present tense, the participants come close to reliving the actual experience.
- **Photographs.** If you take instantly developed pictures, you'll generate a high degree of

What? interest. Video-tape also works and helps to break down nervous resistance.

The What? can be the structure for an entire debrief. Starting with the What? leads naturally into interpretation. In experiential learning, specific well placed What? questions, and the dialogue that follows, helps participants raise their awareness level about those issues and behaviors that should be maintained, and those which they might want to change. Once one phase or time period has been exhausted, use the What? questions to move on, and in so doing, go through everything that happened. This is especially effective with longer experiences where there are many details that need to be worked over. You can bounce ahead, or go back, depending on the needs of the group. You can always come back to the sequence of events as a way to maintain an orientation. The need to keep going can also be used as a way to get the group out of a no-win situation.

The So What?

Active listening presupposes that we do something with what we hear. The interpretive aspects of the So What? provide us with the place to do that. Because we've gotten the group to talk, it's much easier to get into this. According to Borton, it "pertains to the difference the experience made to the individuals, the consequences, and the meaning for them." (Knapp, p.6). It's here that group members abstract and generalize what they're learning from the experience.

You can use the above What? techniques in the So What? by simply shifting from the

Nicki Hall photo

descriptive to the interpretive. For example, use the Go Around as a way to describe how participants feel about the event. You can also ask each group member to come up with a one word or short sentence definition of a key term, such as spotting, discounting, belaying, helping, involvement, leadership, confronting. Perhaps some of those key terms will arise from the Go Around or the Memory Game. You can then build upon what they're already talking about. In addition, try The Whip — a short round robin or a positive non-threatening whip in which each person completes a short statement like, "I'm glad that I...."

We can also ask the group to reflect on goals they've been working on during the So What? phase. The question "did we honor Full Value Contract?" gets us into those group goals. It is a general, non-threatening question, one that can be asked after every experience, and a safe place to start because you're not focusing on any individual behavior. It translates as, "Did we treat each other well, or did we discount each other?; Was there support, or devaluing?; Did we stick to the rules we set up?" The group is seen as an entity that needs to be taken care of, much as we take care of an individual. The group members are both the agents of change and the persons to be changed. We can say "Without a healthy and responsible group, we are greatly diminished."

The Now What?

The Now What? is the process of taking lessons learned from the experience and "reapplying them (those lessons) to other situations." (Rhoades, p.104). We call these "transfer points." It is a standard device at the end of the Debrief to ask a question like, "What lessons did we learn by doing Blindfold Square that we can use when we do Swinging Tires Initiative?" Taking the learning from one activity and carrying it over to the next activity, helps the group connect what they have

been doing to a larger picture. Often you will clearly see what can be carried over, but the group will not have the foggiest notion. It is important to help them make the connections.

The Now What? is a good place to talk about goal setting away from the Adventure experience. Use the energy of the experience to start participants thinking about what they can do in other areas of their lives. For example, the spotting energy that a particular person exhibited during Tire on the Pole could be suggested as a lesson that can be applied to being able to concentrate during an academic class, or the caring that is necessary to hold down a job.

The Debriefing process can be a safe time where the group considers its activities. The leader's confidence in the importance of the

Nicki Hall photo

Debriefing helps the process become a meaningful experience for the group. It is a skill like any other and must be practiced and honed by both leader and group. Debriefing has certain principles that need to be remembered:

- Don't be surprised by resistance.
- Make the Debrief initiative-centered, where the discussion is connected to the group problem-solving experiences so important to Adventure activities.
- Train yourself to listen and observe all activities prior to the Debrief, and utilize that material in an appropriate manner within the Debrief.
- Sequence the Debrief in such a way that it leads up to more gutsy issues.

Conclusion

Conscious leadership is a worthy endeavor. Adventure activities provoke such profound interactions that you must be able to plan, observe, and respond to them. The Adventure Wave can be a powerful experiential force when the three elements — Briefing, Leading, and Debriefing are taken seriously. But it should not cause you to tighten up and lose your spontaneity and your sense of humor.

We hope these considerations will help your wave resonate in positive ways as you learn about, and practice, the activities in this book.

References

Knapp, Clifford C., 1972, *"The Art and Science of Processing Experience."*

Quinsland, Larry K. and Van Ginkel, Ann, 1984, *Association of Experiential Education Journal.*

Rhoades, John, 1972, *"The Problem of Individual Change in Outward Bound: An Application of Change and Transfer Theory,"* unpublished Ed.D. dissertation, U. of Mass., Amherst.

Chapter 2
Getting Started

Nicki Hall photo

An Adventure course curriculum attempts to introduce new, unique, and relevant activities to supplant the older and less acceptable ones. The message conveyed to the student is "Try something new within this supportive atmosphere; you have little to lose, and may gain something from trying...you might even like it!" The activities are geared toward success through consistent and conscientious effort. Success breeds success and to malinger is no longer an accepted goal, but a recognized cop-out.

Coordination and Cardio-Vascular Movements

In the first ten or fifteen minutes of each class period, a session of exercises can be used to "get the blood moving" and set the tone for the somewhat less physical but more emotionally demanding requirements of the curriculum.

These movement activities get away from the tried, tested, and, ofttimes boring warm-up exercises that the students have been doing (or not doing) for years; i.e., push-ups, jumping jacks, etc.

It is not necessary for the group to arrange themselves systematically or geographically for these activities. Just indicate that "You need some room to move freely."

Warm-Ups

Indicate that the warm-up for today is going to be some simple hopping and that you want them (students) to follow your lead.

Start your demo/leader hopping with a simple, ultra-relaxed, barely-clearing-the-ground two-footed hop-hop-hop; concurrently maintaining a constant supportive patter. "All I want you to do is follow me. Here we go, that's it...just a nice simple hop. Since we're going to be doing this for awhile I want you to be comfortable, so do the hops any way that's easy for you to maintain, as long as you're all clearing the ground with both feet." Demonstrate various casual foot manipulations that get away from piston-like up and down movements.

"What we are now doing is called RELAX-ING, so whenever we finish a sequence I'll say RELAX, then just continue doing what you are doing now. Looks good, keep it up...now try this...."

Demonstrate different movements that require varying the simple up and down hopping action. Start with movements that are familiar and gradually introduce dance steps or whatever bizarre body kinetics that you have in mind. Here are some examples:

Crow hop from side to side attempting to gradually increase the length of each lateral hop until no more distance can be added. Say, "Try this, but don't jump in time with me; set your own pace. Our object is to keep the C/V pump working and get some stretching in at the same time. You'll know when you reach your lateral distance limit, then just RELAX, you remember what that means, right?"

Criss-cross your legs on each hop, again trying to increase the length of each lateral movement until a limit is reached. Say, "Recognize this movement? Right, it's the lower

half of a jumping jack, but we're stretching to your maximum with this exercise. Set your own pace as before and stretch until the RE-LAX point is reached."

Ski hopping. Say, "Keep hopping and lock your legs together. Hop side to side now, as if you were jumping over a log. Kinda like skiing, eh? You're right, this is a downhill ski exercise. Keep your legs together and hop front to back. Great stuff, I can just feel the moguls flying under me. Now, RELAX..."

The group will be breathing harder by this time and your quickened banter also will be punctuated by deep breaths. Tell them what a good job they are doing and that if anyone needs to stop, that it's OK, as long as they start again as soon as their heart and lungs allow. Be good natured in your tone, but, at the same time, subtly challenging in your wording.

Listed are a number of other hopping-type movements. But don't feel compelled to hop your students into the ground just to prove how aerobically conditioned they aren't. Emphasize fitness, but also the fun and frolic available in doing something different together. If you are demonstrating (actually hopping) with 3–5 classes each day, remember what the 5th class is going to be like — pace yourself.

Heel Clicker. Perform a heel-clicker hop for demonstration purposes and ask the students to join you. A heel-clicker is a dance step that involves alternating heel kicks laterally to the left and then to the right. There is a crow hop and change of feet between kicks. Look at the dapper fellow with top hat to the far left of the cartoon below; he's doing a heel click to the left.

Entrechat. Since we're into dance steps, how about an entrechat? A proper entrechat step is difficult to perform correctly and aesthetically, but you can come close enough to provide an alternate hop sequence that is physical and funny. (Here's one of the first opportunities for the group to do something together that they all can laugh about — together, not at each other.)

Look at this foot diagram to see the steps required. Repeat the 1–2, 1–2 sequence over and over until it's time to RELAX.

After the participants are more or less performing the step, say, "Very nice, and now let's add a bit of hand positioning to make this dance step just right." Put both arms overhead with fingertips touching, so that your arms look as if you were making a circle, (two parentheses touching). Surely an inaccurate and ludicrous representation of what a ballet dancer should look like, but on the whole, humorous and useful. (See photo, pg. 32.)

Hop and swing the feet as indicated by the arrows to the #2 position.

Hop on one leg, holding the other bent leg from behind and then change legs after 20–30 repetitions.

Hop 'n Spin. Hop on one leg while spinning, letting the other leg centrifuge up into an "L" position in front of you. Use your arms for balance.

Heel and toe touch. While two-footed hopping, *lock your knees together* and then alternate touching your toes then heels together — a very odd exercise to perform and observe.

Jump and lift your feet and legs as far laterally as possible and attempt to touch your toes with outstretched fingers. Alternate this straddle hop with attempts to touch fingers to heels as the legs bend and heels are brought up to the buttock level. Mention that they all look like cheerleaders — another chance for laughter and becoming less self-conscious.

360° Spin. Hop and try to spin 360 degrees in either direction and then try a 360 degree spin in the other direction. Do this on grass or a mat — falls are not uncommon as the result of an attempted full circle spin.

Scissor kick-hop to the front and then to the rear. Emphasize making the kicks as high as possible.

Slopenhoppen. For variety and conditioning ask the students to do some of the above hops up and down a grassy hill.

Duo hopping. Indicate that, "if hopping can be done as an individual, then we can try doing some hopping as pairs." Hop over to a smiling person who looks like a volunteer and grasp his/her right hand with your right hand.

Dance hopping. Keep hopping together, but on one leg (right) and spinning around together in opposite directions, holding hands tightly to avoid centrifuging apart. (There must be a square dancing term for this movement. Make one up! Call it a Buck-Si-Buck; you know, like Doe-Si-Doe...never mind.) When everyone is more or less involved, yell, "Switch, " and quickly change hands, legs (same person), and spinning direction.

Hook ankles together and attempt the same spinning hops as above using your arms for balance. This will often result in people falling down or spinning apart and that's OK, because I'm getting tired.

Troika hop. While the group is still breathing hard (you, too), ask for volunteers and then pick two smiling participants (I've never had a smiling face say, "no"). Put your arms around their waists, as you stand side-to-side, and ask them to do the same. Indicate that you three are going to hop together and that after the hop is sequencing well (no alternating piston-like action), that you will all begin kicking simultaneously together, alternating kicks in sets of three from side-to-side, starting with the left leg, kicking to the right. Sound confusing? It's supposed to be, but learning by doing is the lesson and it happens fast and efficiently.

Group hopping. As soon as your set of three is hopping and kicking well together, stop the hopping and invite the rest of the group to join in. Indicate that you want two flanking lines with equal numbers facing one another about 6 feet apart — everyone arm-in-arm. Suggest that after the hopping starts and the kicks look good (all in the same direction, alternating left to right in sets of three — like the Rockettes!),

for the ends of the lines to join together forming a circle. Say, "Here is where the trust factor comes in, because if we don't all cooperate and work together, then someone is going to get smacked in the shins." This consequence is apparent as the hopping and kicking begins, and as a result there is an impressive level of attention to the task at hand.

Choreography. As the group hops and kicks, yell out the directions, "Ready, kick right 1-2-3, etc. Kick high everyone, remember this is a stretching exercise also. Try to kick over your own head, stretch those legs, lean on your partners. OK, here comes the finale — three more kicks on each side; make 'em good. Now kick — high, high, high! Smile, or we'll never reach the finals!" Finish with much applause for your own fine efforts.

You are now warmed up, physically and emotionally. If not, repeat the above sequence until you agree with me.

Obviously, any prolonged physical effort is going to result in a certain amount of physiological discomfort. Asking a group of students to purposefully enter into an activity that involves any amount of pain is asking for quite a commitment. These activities increase both a willingness to try something new, without fear

TC3 Staff photo

of failure, and also escalate a student's awareness of his/her own capabilities. I suspect there might even be an eventual increase in C/V efficiency.

Realistic knowledge (self-acquired) of individual, decided-upon physical limits, is an important aspect of self-concept and building confidence.

Occasionally, include a warm-up (work-out) that involves strict hopping only, where the only variation is which leg and how many. This type of routine will produce obvious discomfort, but presented later in the conditioning program, may also allow a type of self-evaluation, and genuine satisfaction resulting from an increased fitness level.

There are obviously more hopping sequences and movements than can be utilized. Your imagination is the storehouse.

If you meet each class with the announcement that, "We'll be hopping again today for warm-up," hopping, or anything akin to it, will soon be avoided and rightly so. I don't care how new or exciting something is, if that's all you do, to the exclusion of other alternatives, then that activity will become tedious and eventually disliked. That's why some students don't like volleyball, or archery, or golf, or whatever activity is offered too many days in a row.

I asked an old acquaintance why he had given up skydiving, thinking that his answer would involve increased danger, close calls, etc., and was surprised by the response that he was simply tired of doing it and wanted to spend some time learning a new activity — he was getting into canoeing as I remember. He was a veteran of over 1,500 jumps and was *bored.* Keep your approach and curriculum content fresh. This is a very important point.

Pedagogic Caveat: *I have known more than one turned-on teacher who said, "I wish I could teach PA classes all day." Big mistake. Again, doing the same thing all the time will*

result in staleness and discontent. There are more than enough curriculum ideas available now to allow presentation of fresh material on a regular basis, but even so, having the occupational opportunity of teaching a variety of subjects is the best way to avoid staleness and burnout.

Nicki Hall, photo

In my role as an Adventure Education consultant for Project Adventure, I frequently find myself suggesting to new PA teachers that they slow down and not try to jam so much curriculum material into a day, week, etc. The idea is to let the group achieve as much as possible from a game or Initiative problem, rather than constantly bombarding a group with new "stuff." From what I'm trying to suggest (somewhat paradoxically), I hope it's clear that there is a fine line and difference between curriculum excess and curriculum repetition. Experience helps to define this line, but being aware of the difference will prevent drifting too far in either direction.

Example: Most students can complete more than one or two low ropes course elements in a class period, and that's OK, because efficient completion of a task is satisfying and noteworthy. But there is also additional benefit to be had by attempting the elements again to see how well they can be done, rather than just how quickly. Many of the low balance events can be tried in a variety of ways, producing a sequential series of physical and mental challenges that would be lost if the event were presented on a one-shot, can-you-do-it basis.

Jim Schoel introduced the Brief/Debrief sequence in the preceding chapter. Be aware in your planning that time must be set aside for this most important aspect of Adventure programming. There is much to do and accomplish and the happy circumstance proves that the doing is fun and satisfying for almost everyone, including teacher and student. Debriefing these intense fun/fear situations will allow student responses to surface that might otherwise be lost.

Other warm-up activities might include:
- Tag games as detailed in *Silver Bullets*, pgs. 153–155.
- *Invisible Jump Rope*, *Silver Bullets*, pg. 157.
- Providing frisbees, aerobies or deck tennis rings to toss around; at least one throwing implement per 2 people.
- Asking a group to try competitive walking (striding) for 1/4 mile. Be prepared to demonstrate.
- Ask the group to follow-the-leader on a 3–5 minute Fun Run. Change leaders every 30 seconds or every minute. Begin the run as leader to establish a pace that a group can maintain for that amount of time, and also to run up, over, and through a few obstacles to demonstrate what can be fun and also challenging.
- Use a game of *Aerobic Tag* as an extended warm-up activity when the temperature suggests staying inside. At 20 degrees, coats will begin coming off after a couple of minutes of playing this very active game. See the write-up for *Aerobic Tag*, Chapter 3.

After the group has spent 5 minutes or so warming up (remember that you only have about 30 minutes actual class time, considering the 10 minutes at each end for changing, showering, etc.), introduce a few warm-down activities that emphasize **limberness and flexibility.**

Warm-Down

The following activities involve a series of slow, deliberate movements to develop limberness and flexibility. It seems appropriate to include these stretching exercises after the cardio-vascular hopping sequences in order to ready the muscles, ligaments, and mind, for maneuvering on the ropes course, or participating in a game or Initiative problem.

It is easy to underestimate the value of these exercises. They are not simply another fairly useful time filler. Such movement exercises, either performed alone or with a partner, often result in a positive attitude toward participation that is difficult to achieve otherwise, and helps to establish fitness habits that will hopefully continue beyond the extent of Project Adventure's influence. There are a number of books available now extolling the beneficial results of regular stretching. Use these books to add to your collection of exercises. If, after reading and trying some of these exercises, you enjoy the movement and student response, try coming up with some ideas of your own based on the more conventional exercises which you normally use.

At the beginning of a program that emphasizes unique and enjoyable exercise, it is useful for the student to begin to anticipate and enjoy the unexpected — particularly when the unexpected can be fun and in clear contrast to the usual routine.

Some of the following activities are a bit off-the-wall, so be aware in sequencing your activity choices that you do not present something semi-bizarre to a group too soon or you may end up turning off the more conservative participant.

It's OK to be outrageous. But let the students get to know you and begin to appreciate that it is allowed to be "kooky-in-context" before you demonstrate the *Dog Shake* or ask them to *Return to the Soil.* Imagine slogging through 9–10 years of traditional PE, and then being asked to hop over an invisible jump rope.

Most of these warm-down exercises emphasize slow movement, stretching, and awareness of the body parts being used. Spend some time during each exercise emphasizing deliberate movement and what muscle groups are being targeted.

After the group has completed whatever cardio-vascular activity you introduced at the class onset, move directly into trying 2–3 minutes of the following stretching exercises (includes mind stretching). Demonstrate each exercise and then ask the students to join you.

The Angel

With your feet about shoulder width apart, and with your legs kept straight, bend slowly at the waist and attempt to touch your palms to the ground (or as far down as possible). Hold that down position for about 5 seconds and then slowly begin to rise into an arms-up, *Angel* position. Take in air as your upper body lifts until your lungs fill and you reach the

arms-extended, palms-up, on-your-toes, head-back, arched position. This final position is very difficult to hold on your toes and rightly so because you are pushing beyond a balance point. As you lose your balance, don't fight it, let out your breath as a balloon would lose its air (flopping slobbery lips if necessary). Slow movements, deep breathing, and attention to the muscle groups involved, add to the relaxing quality of this exercise. Repeat once or twice letting the students set their own pace.

Side Bender

Beginning position — feet are about shoulder width apart and arms are extended to the side, palms up. Rotate slowly from front to back inhaling as you do this. Twist the trunk, keeping your feet flat on the ground. As you begin turning to the front, let your breath out slowly so that you are deflated as you reach the starting position. Continue this stretching-breathing sequence from side to side for a total of three rotations.

5-5-5 Duo Stretching

Include stretching and limberness movements for the individual, but also work toward including a few exercises that involve working as pairs or groups. The following isometric/stretching sequence is an example of a unique one-on-one activity.

1. Facing one another with arms extended, ask the students to put both hands on each other's shoulders. (Try this exercise with a partner of near equal height.) Partners gradually begin trying to push each other into the ground. Increase pressure over a 5-second time span, maintain full pressure for about 5 seconds, and then gradually decrease pressure for about 5 seconds until back to normal. Ask one of the partners to count aloud in order to regulate and coordinate pressure applied. If this psyche contact is too "heavy" — delete the audio ploy.

2. Facing one another, have the students extend one hand forward as if they were going to shake their partner's hand. Keeping hands open and flat (not clasped) and with each arm fully extended, begin to exert lateral pressure on a partner's arm using the 5-5-5-second counting pattern as in (1). This is not a contest, so don't allow students to twist their bodies to gain a leverage advantage. Partners should remain laterally parallel to each other at all times. If done well, both students' hands should not move from side-to-side more than an inch. The increased, maintained, and decreasing pressure, with no movement, is a satisfying feeling of shared struggle.

There are numerous spatial variations to this cooperative exercise sequence. Ask the students to use their imaginations to come up with other 5-5-5 isometric exercise positions. Don't forget the use of legs.

Red Baron Stretch

Most people have the right (and left) props on hand for this solo stretching-into-fantasy exercise. Pretend that each of your hands is an airplane (WW I vintage) engaging in an aerial dogfight. The planes can chase each other anywhere that your body and arm movements allow, aerodynamically possible or not. Keep your feet comfortably separated and stationary.

Don't forget to add the "sounds of combat," dredging up those salivary sounds of gunfire and oral engines that you did so well in the third grade. To end your contest, or as a respite from the intensity of combat, have one of your planes dive into a cloud bank; i.e., under *your* shirt.

If the students enjoy this bit of whimsical stretching, ask them to pair up and, standing face to face, continue the dogfighting with one person's hand (Sopwith Camel) following the other player's hand (Fockwulf), emphasizing that fair play dictates ultra slow motions. Don't forget to reciprocate being the aggressor. This is a mirror image exercise, and if done well, opens the door to more intense sharing scenarios.

Ask the group to sit down on the ground without using either hand for support and to try standing the same way. Then ask if they can sit using only one leg and no hands. This is offered as a quick grab-your-interest stunt that gets everyone where you want them — sitting on the ground.

From a sitting position on the ground, ask the students to perform (following your demonstration) the following exercises:

Grab Your Toes

With their legs extended and separated on the ground, ask students to grab their toes (or ankles, or shins, or kneecaps, depending on individual flexibility), and lean backward into the illustrated position, trying to hold a bal-

ance point on their coccyx (that anatomical point immediately distal to the final sacral vertebrae). The ease of this task is proportional to the degree of Adipose tissue covering that portion of your anatomy. Did you perform this task easily? Then you are "well covered." From this stylized, balanced posture, try rolling over backward while holding onto your toes. No reason really, it's just fun.

Reach and Grab

Sitting spread-legged, try to reach as far forward as possible (without bending the knees), grabbing some grass or fingering the floor for friction. Then try to grab some grass a little bit farther away, etc., etc. Sit up, relax a bit, and try again. Don't throw grass at each other — it itches.

Karate Stretch *(the name sells the exercise)*

While seated, bring your feet together so that the soles meet. Reach forward to grasp both of your feet at the toe end and pull your heels toward your crotch; hold for 15 seconds. In this stretch position your elbows are bent with forearms above and about parallel to your feet

— well…mine are. If you don't feel anything stretching, lean forward and bend your elbows more. Release your feet and sit up, breathing slowly and deeply. Re-grasp your feet and once again pull them toward your crotch, but this time orient your bent elbows outside your shins. Continue pulling toward your body and hold.

Inch Worm

Sit on the turf facing your partner. Inch toward one another until you and he or she are close enough to sit on each other's feet. Big

feet offer an advantage, or at least a certain comfort factor. Grasp your partner's elbows or upper arms with each hand.

Now, decide which direction you two would like to travel. Lateral movement is out, so it's either north or south, east or west or...you know what I mean. After deciding, the partner (in whose direction you're headed) lifts her/his derriere off the ground and moves 12 inches or so toward whatever goal you have in mind (be reasonable). The second partner now lifts off the ground and in a cooperative 1-2, 1-2 bug-like movement, duplicates the step above, and moves toward his/her partner. A natural exercise for impromptu, disjointed competition.

Bottoms Up

A one-on-one warm-up exercise that combines strength, balance, and a very odd position.

Nicki Hall, photo

Sit on the turf facing one another and place the bottom of your feet against the bottom of your partner's feet (sole sharing). Legs should be bent, feet held high, and posteriors skootched fairly close to one another. Then, attempt to push against your partner's feet (while putting all your weight on your arms), until both of your derrieres come off the ground. You will notice (poignantly) a tightening of the tricep muscles in your arms, consid-

erable laughter, and not much vertical movement on the first couple of tries.

If your bottom remains permanently welded to the ground, blame it on your partner, and find someone more your size to blame the next time.

Row Boat Stretch

Sit facing your partner (someone about your height) and put your soles together (very intense exercise). Grasp hands and take turns pulling (gently) one another back and forth, ostensibly to stretch the hamstring muscles but more usefully to give reason for instinctive, compassionate sharing — the instinct in this case is survival of the hamstrings.

Some pairs (because of tight muscles, tight psyche, heredity) will find that one person will have to bend his/her knees in order to grab hold of his partner's hands.

After each partner has found his stretching limit, and some compassionate sharing has occurred, try the duo-stand-up exercise called:

Everybody Up

Using this Initiative exercise is a useful way to introduce the concept of group cooperation.

Ask two people of approximately the same size to sit on the ground (gym floor) facing one another so that the bottoms of their feet are opposed, knees bent, and hands are tightly grasped. From this stylized sitting position, ask the duo to try to pull themselves into an upright, standing position. If the pair is successful (most are), ask them to seek another partner and try standing up with three people, then four, etc., until the entire group eventually makes an attempt. Criteria for a successful attempt are: 1.) Hands grasped so that an electrical current could pass through the group, 2.) Foot contact with the same electrical set-up, 3.) All derrieres off the ground at the same time.

Something that began as a simple cooperative stunt becomes an Initiative problem that includes the entire group; a significant accomplishment.

An expanding group will soon find that the seemingly logical circular configuration of bodies cannot be continued beyond 8 or so. A change of thinking (Initiative) must be employed to come up with a solution that allows large numbers (50 people or more) to complete the problem.

If an adrenaline-pumped group of 8 or 10 jogs over to you, after having stumbled and jerked to a tenuous standing position, and breathlessly asks, "Did we do it right?" — need I say what your answer should be? Are they high? Yes. Do they feel good about their effort and themselves? Yes. Did they do it right?

An alternate or additional way to present this problem, is to ask the participants to sit

back-to-back and try to stand as a pair, a trio, etc. Do not allow interlocked arms for safety reasons (shoulder dislocation possibilities).

Atypicality: *I'm sure you will notice, as you read through this book (and* Silver Bullets*), that the activity paraphernalia and the defining vocabulary are studiously different from traditional physical education and recreation models. And purposefully so, because we are trying to provide a unique experience that will not be approached with dread or apathy as the result of previous negative experiences, nor be eagerly anticipated by those adept players who want to renew their mastery over a practiced activity, including those individuals not so practiced or skilled as themselves.*

A multicolored 20" beach ball is a good example of a useful atypical object of play. It's

hard to react negatively to a beach ball, particularly if you call it a Moon Ball *and play odd games with it. What do you think of when you see an inflated beach ball? Beaches. Summer fun. Non-directive activity. Competition? Tell your group that you are going to play* Moon Ball, *explain the rules (30 sec. max), and have at it. Everyone's attention is riveted on the ball and little significance is placed on the quality of ball strikes or even who hits (misses) the ball. Every player is on the same team with the same goal in mind, and the fact that Pete missed a shot, or Connie made a great save, are of passing interest only to Pete and Connie, as play itself maintains the intensity of the experience. If you bring out a football, baseball, volleyball, etc., at the beginning of the activity time, there will be those individuals who will grin and verbally express their pleasure at the thought of playing with an object that allows them to display their prowess and superiority; and then others who groan, shrink a little, and woefully anticipate the inevitable bad pass, dropped ball, or poor play that signifies and regularly re-establishes their low self-image. I recognize that there are those students who revel in superior physical performance for its own sake, and they should have a vehicle to express their proficiency. Additionally, some won't like or try anything that is offered, no matter how attractive the activity seems. And, finally, there is a majority of middle ground folks who participate with no protest and limited enthusiasm. To all these players (and non-players), I'll offer the gem of something new and neutral with a chance for common ground participation — no pre-sensitivity to failure, minimum rules, supportive instruction on basic skills, and little or no emphasis on winning or losing. We'll play* Moon Ball *once, maybe twice, but not nearly long enough or often enough to establish recognized teams (or uniformed leagues). Then it's on to some other atypical game, activity, or*

stunt that everyone can share and experience together, and where the best player is often the one who thinks best or fastest. There's no secret to this approach, it's child's play.

Comfortable Position

Preliminary to attaining a *Return to the Earth* position, verbally prepare your students with a serious-fade-to-smiles presentation of how to assume the *Comfortable Position*. With a no-nonsense demeanor (antithetical to your real intent), declare that you want the students to pay close attention to your detailed instructions and ongoing demonstration. Ask them to assume the following body position in a military by-the-numbers fashion because their somatic orientation so intricately involves the anatomy, that participants commonly become spatially confused and disoriented, resulting in nausea, recurrent hives, and more rarely, incidental drooling.

First kneel — keep up a running patter about how important it is to follow your lead exactly — then incline your body slowly forward to a push-up position. Then, even more slowly, continue down to a prone position on the ground. Keep babbling, it's your only smoke screen at this juncture.

Lay one hand on top of the other on the ground, point your toes, put your chin on your hands, and smilingly announce THIS as the *Comfortable Position*. The students will feel slightly "had" but will also feel relieved that the intricacy that they worried about was tongue-in-cheek. As all the prone participants glance from side to side, and see their classmates glancing and grinning back at them, a useful feeling of shared nonsense is established. (Not an entirely easy thing to accomplish — nice going.)

If you are a beginning teacher seeking tenure, this simple but effective exercise might be the one you want to demonstrate to your master teacher or administrator toward establishing credibility as an innovative and effective educator. Twenty to thirty students assuming the *Comfortable Position* in a fizz-ed class, is an impressive sight indeed.

From this horizontal (Cheshire Cat) position, it's only natural to further the commitment and go for a *Return to the Earth* juxtaposing of your physiognomy and whatever piece of terra firma you have chosen to be comfortable on. To make sure you completely understand this face-to-earth position, pick your chin up off your hands, separate your hands, and sweep both arms to your side while simultaneously, and with great care, lowering your face directly into the turf. As you sit comfortably now (wherever you are), close your eyes and conjure up a picture of 20–30 students in this au naturel position — awesome! (Photo below.)

If you choose your reclining area with aesthetic forethought, a few deep breaths (nasal inhalation) of the luxuriant turf underface provides a nostalgic return to younger days of more frequent grass contact via games,

wrestling, or just-for-fun encounters with the environment — also, sometimes getting beat up after school and having your face jammed into the ground, which wasn't so much fun, come to think of it.

The *entire* purpose (other than the aesthetic one mentioned above) for performing these two ritualistic and nonsensical movements is to allow people (a group) to try something beyond their own expectation level, and set an experimental/experiential stage which invites further, and often somewhat bizarre, activities that evoke the key anticipatory question — "What are we going to do next?"

To even appreciate what I'm referring to in a curriculum context, you must, as an educator, recognize that there is more to Adventure programming than C/V efficiency and physical skill development. To wit, it's useful to be able to perform a physical task without anticipating shortness of breath or muscle soreness, but also useful to be open to new ideas and not be reluctant to "try them on for size."

The Cobra

Defined — a large poisonous snake indigenous to India and one half the title of a now out-of-print book on Adventure Education Curriculum.

But in the guise of "warming up" a group, the *Cobra* is a useful yoga stretching exercise.

If you have gone all out and tried *Returning*

to the Earth, the *Cobra* provides a fairly rational exercise to try after having buried your schnoz in the turf. If you have conservatively put off *Earth Returning* for the next couple of years, simply begin the *Cobra* from a ventral prone "push-up" position on the ground.

The physical objective of this exercise is to combine stretching, slow breathing, and feeling better. Here's how:

From your horizontal position, raise the top half of your body, head up (as far up as you can), and hold that Cobra-like position for five seconds. As your head and torso rise up, slowly inhale, attempting to fill your lungs at the same time you reach a maximum stretched cobra position. As your body lowers, after five seconds of somewhat resembling a Cobra, release the inhaled air in much the same way a balloon looses its air. Repeat two to three times — don't continue until it's no fun.

If you want to extend your arms in front, that's certainly OK, (HEY, you can do anything you want) but it detracts from the Cobra image.

A double *Cobra* is accomplished by simply raising your head and legs simultaneously, trying to touch your fingers to your heels. If you accomplish this feat, you're CHEATING — stop bending your legs!

Python Pentathlon

It's programmatically useful to have an activity that begins as a simple can-you-do-this stunt and progress humorously to a full group bash. The *Python Pentathlon* provides both the stunt and the humor — it goes like this:

With the group seated on a gym floor or a grassy field (if your Mom doesn't like grass stains you better stick to the gym floor for this one), demonstrate a coccyx balance position which is accomplished simply by picking your feet up off the ground and leaning back onto your coccygeal area (that balance point just distal to the sacrum; i.e., the altered spinal site — a.s.s.). Most people can do this, so the next step is to try and make forward progress from this "L" shaped balance position. This is done by alternating positions of your gluteus (ref. to a.s.s. above) in a 1-2, 1-2, 1-2 manner. This means of locomotion is certainly not swift, but most people can do it. Let's practice, because this alternating action is transferrable to a group situation, which we are soon going to try out. Ask each student to try and make forward and backward progress. They are, of course, going to want to see your demo first. I'll show you mine, if you'll show me yours!

Now that everyone is familiar with this movement (called the glute walk), ask for three or four volunteers to sit facing you so that they are shoulder to shoulder with about two feet between. These intrepid volunteers represent the captains of your *Python Pentathlon* teams. Everyone else on the field (try to have 5 people per team) chooses a captain to sit behind. Each person sits with his/her feet in the lap of the person immediately in front (like a toboggan). Only the captains are allowed to have foot and hand contact with the ground; everyone else

must have only glute contact — feet on laps and hands on shoulders. (See photo above.)

Stand about 15 feet in front of the captains after the teams are set. Spread your legs wider than shoulder width and announce that your feet are the finish line for this great race. When a captain touches one of your feet with one of his/her feet, that team's race is over.

Be liberal with whatever rules you want to enforce, or forget, remembering that you are trying to get the group to do something that is potentially embarrassing and have fun at the same time. This "game" is a one or two time only activity. If the students participate and have a good time, move on to something perhaps more meaningful, like *The Balance Broom*.

Before we leave the field, check out the mega-grass stains on those designer pockets. These gluteal green pants would serve well on a TV clothes detergent commercial. Hey, I told you earlier to wear OLD clothes...not my fault.

The Balance Broom

The *Balance Broom* is an activity that is mostly fun, but also results in subtle improvements in student commitment, and a willingness to appear inept in front of others. How many students miss out on available learning situations because they don't want to appear foolish before their peers?

Procedure: Have the student hold a broom vertically (a foam sword will work as well...better actually) with the handle directly over his/her head and look up at the very top of the broom. Ask the participant to turn around (360 degree turns) fifteen times and then put the broom down and step over it. While turning, the student must keep his/her eyes open and fixed at the top of the broom which is held upright at arm's length.

Most students will fall before reaching fifteen turns and the remainder will have trouble stepping over the broom handle.

The value of the exercise lies mainly in two areas: 1.) It is an exercise that most people will have trouble completing and thus they expose themselves to failure in view of their peers. This potentially negative exposure lessens their normal sensitivity to failure because the activity is fun and the group, engrossed in the enjoyment of the moment, is laughingly supportive of any effort, no matter how inept. The exercise can be kept from degenerating into a negative experience by the control that the instructor has on the event and the people involved. 2.) Successful completion does require concentration and a concerted effort. Dizziness can be controlled by most people.

This exercise can also be performed in pairs. If you are having trouble getting a particular person to try, indicate that the experience can be attempted by a pair. Have one person hold the broom overhead while the other person places both hands on the partner's shoulders, and, both looking up, they begin to rotate

together. Both must step over the broom together. Use spotters.

Because participants become so disoriented
as the result of playing tricks on their middle
ear, it's important to assign at least 4 spotters
(standing North, South, East, and West) to each
spinner. One of the spotters can act as a
counter for the hapless broom wielder, and
each spotter recognizes their responsibility to
prevent out-of-control trips to the turf. This
care is extended beyond the spinning action to
the attempted step over the broom handle, as
the whirling inner ear fluid manifests itself in
an out-of-body disorientation. It's hard to
explain, but the spastic results are predictable.

Have at least 2–3 students try this stunt
individually in front of the entire group. Then,
to save time, a large class can be broken up
into smaller groups for participating and observing. This is an exercise that proves valuable if used once or twice, but can rapidly
dissolve into drudgery and dissatisfaction if
routinely continued.

*Caveat: Recognize that dizziness can trigger
an epileptic attack. Announce this and also
grant a blanket excuse for all those who suspect that spinning may cause them to become
nauseated.*

Yelling

File this activity under OFF THE WALL,
and don't even think about presenting it before
the second or third week of the program, or
until the students get a chance to figure you
out. If you don't heed this curriculum caveat
you will, 1.)...lose student confidence, 2.)...lose
students physically; i.e., walk (sneak) out of
class, 3.)...get letters from home wondering
what's going on.

Knowing when and when not to present
various activities is part of the skill integral to
being an effective Adventure curriculum
teacher. I certainly don't want to alter your
personal style, but...

So, being awash in warnings, here's the
scoop on a useful individual/group activity.

This simple presentation patter lends some
credence to a seemingly useless and potentially embarrassing task. You have to say
something at this juncture to get started, and
following this woodsy scenario will generate
some interest and make what you're about to
do somewhat credible.

"While hiking with a group in a wilderness
area, you may, for whatever reason, become
separated (lost). To get back together, a sound
signal is commonly used to alert other members of your plight; a whistle, sequenced
gunfire, perhaps even the use of a radio re-
ceiver. However, if it's just you lost in the
woods (no noise-maker), try using your vocal
cords to produce a projected identifiable
sound that will travel beyond the vocal shriek
of a panicked hiker. Try to produce and project
a long vocal sound, as this type of yell has
been proven to carry over the greatest distance.
Let me offer a demonstration shout to give you
an idea of what I mean."

At this juncture, without hesitating, take a
deep breath, throw your head back, and give
vent to the longest, loudest, and most round
sound you can produce. The audience response is predictable — nervous laughter,
incredulous glances toward one another, wide
eyed, and fidgeting. There will be no lack of

attention or interest in what your next words will be (or how loud). With confidence and barely controlled enthusiasm, express that you would like each student to attempt a duplication (recognizing individual differences) of your YOOOOOO sound. Indicate that rather than yelling in a sequenced manner around the circle, that you will point to people randomly for their attempt. Also, emphasize that anyone who feels too uptight or embarrassed today has the option to pass until another time. Offering an honest OUT is important to maintain Project Adventure's promise that participation is always optional. The expectation, however, is that a student will eventually make a conscientious attempt at whatever activity is being offered.

Begin by pointing to an individual who you think will attempt a yell without too much hesitation. Comment positively on whatever effort is forthcoming in order to establish a comfortable and enjoyable atmosphere that encourages trying. For example, if the student's attempt is short and squeaky say, "I hope I don't get lost with you," and if the shout is clear toned and extended say enviously, "She/he should think of a musical career." If a student opts out, simply pass on, indicating that he/she can have a chance later on.

Part of the significance of this event and its useability is how the students see themselves as they react to waiting for their turn, and how they eventually handle that stress. The yell itself seems anticlimactic to the fear of the unknown (wondering what you will sound like and how people will react to you). The realization becomes that the object of their fear is manifested more in their mind than, in this case, their throat. A significant carry-over pattern can result, allowing a student to handle more mundane stress-producing scenarios — job interviews, asking someone for a date, choosing a wardrobe, etc. Even if the

physical attempt is not up to their expectation (yelling, running, acting, whatever), the support of the instructor and the group can result in a positive feeling about future attempts at other intimidating activities. Constantly emphasize support rather than criticism.

Why yell? As emotionally cathartic as a good ole lung ripper can be, yelling in this context is most useful to:

- Establish trust within the group — trust that the group will not ridicule your efforts no matter how inept the vocal results.
- Allow an individual to experience, understand, and control stress in a "sit down" situation.
- Establish an atypical curriculum format for future "what's next" presentations and participation.

Some Useful Skills: Mystique and Practicality

Falling Down Without Going BOOM

There are several reasons for including how-to-fall instructions as part of growing up, not the least of which is achieving that goal. Learning to fall is basic training that should be required learning for children, because most people (children and adults) don't know how to handle a fall effectively in order to minimize or eliminate injury. Unfortunately many children grow up in such a protected sphere that the chance to learn day-to-day survival skills never materializes. "Be careful!" "Don't get hurt!", have become less of a mother's hopeful entreaty and more of a not-to-be-ignored parental demand.

Learning to fall:
1. Increases the safety margin for participants in risk-oriented activities, such as soccer, bicycle riding, ropes courses, and walking to school.
2. Decreases the possibility of injury as the result of a fall.
3. Develops increased confidence in one's physical and psychological ability to overcome problem situations.

Injury resulting from forward or backward moving falls, usually is caused by friction on the palms and body (abrasions), or by the sudden absorption of the shock with the hands (sprained or broken wrists).

The falling and rolling technique described here reduces the potential for injury. Confidence that a fall can be handled safely also results in an increased personal commitment to attempt tasks or games where there is some risk of a moving fall.

A proven way to escape or minimize injury in a moving fall is to use a modified forward or backward shoulder roll. The shoulder roll is spontaneously initiated as the result of a fall combined with some forward or backward movement (trip, push, jump), otherwise the roll aspect is comically superfluous. A direct jump down from a height can be accomplished safely (depending upon the height, of course) if the shock of the fall is taken with the legs, and a lesser amount by the hands and arms.

Front Roll

Begin rolling forward from a standing (or squatting) position and continue into a roll. The roll can be initiated to either the right or left side depending upon the force causing the fall, or the side which is most comfortable for the faller.

If a roll on the right shoulder is initiated, the

left hand is put out as a guide (not a brace). The right hand is extended palm down in front of the individual. The right elbow is bent slightly as the forearm provides a surface for the beginning of the roll. The performer looks under his left armpit (thus ensuring that the head is in the proper position), and continues a forward rolling movement onto the right shoulder in a tuck position, and finally into a squat position. Do not land on the point of the shoulder or injury may result.

The actual roll is neither straight over (somersault) nor a completely lateral roll, but rather, a forty-five degree combination. Either of the former rolls increases the possibility of injury.

Back Roll

The legs begin to bend as the body turns slightly toward the hip that is going to have first contact with the ground. The hands guide the now-tucked body over as the roll is completed over the shoulder on the same side as the hip mentioned above.

The front and back roll can be practiced first from a standing (or squatting) position and eventually from a jog. Practice can also be attempted with the participant jumping from gradual increases in height, up to a height of about six feet. The backward jumps should be limited to heights of about three feet. These jumps can be attempted off stumps, benches, platforms, or anything handy.

Group Falling Exercises

1. Have the students form a semi-circle facing the instructor, and in turn, demonstrate a forward or backward fall and roll. The demonstration roll should occur before any practice is allowed because students understandably want to look good before their peers. Having them try something brand new, with no practice, lowers that sensitivity to "looking bad." Also, having the students demonstrate individually allows the instructor to provide individual attention (albeit brief), and to make comments from which all can benefit concerning individual performances.

2. The group lines up on the goal line of a football field facing toward the other goal. About 6–8 feet between students is necessary. On a signal, the participants begin a series of forward falls and rolls up to the 25 yard stripe. After attempting this two or three times in consecutive class sessions, ask students to see how few rolls it requires to reach the 25 yard marker.

   The above exercises can be extended by having the students perform back rolls for the next 25 yard distance. Also, front and back rolls can be alternated for this distance; i.e., front roll, pivot, back roll, pivot, front roll, etc.

3. Have one half the group line up facing the other half at approximately arm's length. Explain that a more spontaneous fall and roll can be accomplished if the fall is initiated by someone other than the falling person. A two-handed shove at the shoulders (partners alternating shoves) will accomplish this. The force of the shoves is gradually increased for about five repetitions.

   To alleviate foolishness and possible injury from too forceful a shove, require that the shoves be delivered on command. More control of the group is thus possible. Demonstrate what you mean by a compassionately forceful shove.

4. Jumping and rolling from a height can be attempted after the roll itself is mastered. The jumps are attempted at gradually increasing heights (one foot increments if possible) until a height of five or six feet is reached. Critique the rolls carefully, and, if necessary, limit some students from increasing height until their technique is improved. The psych value of this exercise can be increased if a voluntary limit is set at about four feet. No one is required to progress past this height; however, almost all will because of the Challenge afforded.

5. *Frog Leap*

   If a less intimidating fall and roll is indicated, have the student assume a squat position and lean forward into a shoulder roll. After accomplishing this movement with some sense of agility, suggest that the student frog-leap forward from this squat position, and shoulder roll into another identical squat position. This physically pleasing movement sequence can be strung together to produce a leap-roll-leap-roll exercise.

6. This exercise can serve as a culmination of the fall and roll training:

   • Ask the group to form a line facing away from you with their eyes closed. Require a lateral distance of about five feet between students. Indicate that you are going to walk behind them and initiate a fall by delivering a push on their backs. Any students who do not want to participate are free to stand aside (although very few will at this point).

   • Walk quietly and deliver controlled pushes to shoulder blades. The students, of course, are anticipating the shove, so little pressure is actually required to initiate the fall. Shove randomly so that the students don't know when their turn to fall is coming.

   • There is a paradoxical and gleeful "push me/don't push me" feeling associated with this exercise. Admittedly, the results are more fun than functional.

Spotting

In situations where the students are attempting a ropes course element or an Initiative problem at less than 6–8 feet off the ground, spotting becomes essential.

The term catching is often used in both the teaching and function of spotting. While spotters usually need to be in position to catch a participant in the event of a fall, it is dangerous to literally catch a falling body from even a short height. Spotters and participants need to understand that catching means to support the upper body and head in a fall so that these vital areas are protected. Understanding of this concept of body catching, along with a grasp of

the real meaning and function of spotting, can prevent deterioration of initially fragile feelings of trust. Participants should understand that a spotter who breaks their fall, even though either or both end up on the ground, has indeed performed his/her role responsibly and in a trustworthy manner. Falls, along with minor scrapes and bruises, come with the territory.

Teaching spotting is perhaps one of the most difficult tasks in any pre-ropes course experience, not because of the complex motor skill requirements, but because potential spotters oftentimes do not recognize their importance until they actually have to support a falling body. Here are some key aspects to remember when teaching spotting to a group:

• Effective spotters should mimic the movements of the participant on the activity — especially in the case of traversing elements; i.e., *Fidget Ladder, Tension Traverse, Mohawk Walk, Swinging Log*, etc. The spotter duplicates the movements of the participant and positions him/herself to move with any falling action.

- Spotters need to be able to move in and dampen any motion in a swinging activity; i.e., moving onto a *Swinging Log*, landing on the *Seagull Perch*, falling off a *Rope Swing*.

- It is important to have a teaching sequence developed for spotting. The following example is the sequence used by Stony Acres Outdoor Center, East Stroudsburg, Pennsylvania:

1. Explain concept/meaning of spotting.
2. Demonstrate and emphasize relationship of good spotting to trust.
3. Practice spotting in a controlled, contained context using activities such as *Two Person Trust Fall, Trust Fall, Willow in the Wind, and Two Line Trust Fall* (spotters are kneeling).
4. Distinguish between spotting and assisting or helping.
5. Engender pride in becoming a good spotter. Actively promote the attitude and behavior that teasing and joking about not catching someone, has no place in Adventure activities.
6. Supervise spotters closely, reminding them of proper techniques as needed.
7. Rotate spotters so all have a chance to catch someone and so all are used to spot appropriate sizes (the big people should not end up doing all the spotting).
8. Two spotters is the minimum number necessary for any element. Certain elements require more than two. Size, strength, weight, and fatigue also affect these minimums. Do not hesitate to require more than the stated minimums in particular situations. Do bear in mind that an overabundance of spotters, trying to spot for the same situation, can lead to the problem of no one taking their job seriously enough because of the feeling that their role is not important. Make sure that each spotter is essential to the task at hand. If there are more than enough, rotate positions and responsibilities.

9. The reason for spotting is to offer protection to the individual participating in an activity. But it is important to remember that because of unique aspects of ropes course design, Initiative problems, and the variety of the terrain on which the activities take place, certain activities may require subtle differences in spotting techniques. These differences should always be carefully explained.
10. The spotter should be willing to put him or herself in a potentially risky situation in order to eliminate or minimize injury to another.
11. The spotter should be willing to share responsibility in cooperative spotting situations, not trying to do individually what is more easily and safely accomplished by two or more working together.

The psychomotor aspects of spotting are:

Stance: Balanced, centered, knees flexed to absorb impact, hands up and ready.

Position and Location (relative to participant): Varies with specific elements.

Focus: Eyes constantly on the participant.

Absorbing Force: "Give" with the body, moving or rolling in the direction of force.

Sample Spotting Activities: Part of the Trust Fall/Spotting Sequence

Two-Person Mirroring

As one person moves, the partner duplicates or shadows every move. This can be expanded so that the whole group duplicates the moves of the lead person. Unexpected moves should be explained and illustrated in the framing of this activity. This is the beginning point of "Spotter's Knowledge," which is essentially a connection to the climber in terms of concentration, empathy, and movement. Duplicating the movement of the participant forces the spotter to pay attention to what the participant is doing and positions the spotter to move with any falling action. Instruction regarding which parts of the body should be protected (the head first, then the chest, stomach, and genitals) can be given when presenting mirroring.

Yurt Circle (see chapter 3, Games)

Melisa Webster photo

Two-Person Trust Fall

This activity adds verbal communication, which provides the initial one-on-one contracting for spotting (low ropes) and belaying (high ropes and rock climbing). The calls are initiated by the faller and completed by the catcher. A typical sequence might look like this:

> *Faller: "Are you ready to catch?"*
> *Catcher: "Ready to catch."*
> *Faller: "I'm ready to fall."*
> *Catcher: "Fall away."*

The faller should be reminded to secure his arms across his chest to ensure not throwing out arms and elbows. The falling person should also keep knees and body straight, falling directly backwards. Following the *Two-Person Trust Fall* you can attempt these more advanced trust sequences:

Willow in the Wind

This trust-pass exercise is used effectively as a warm-up activity for the more dramatic falling sequence of *The Tust Fall*. The set-up and sequence can be accomplished one of two ways:

1. Ten to fifteen people stand shoulder to shoulder in a circle with one person (the faller) standing rigid and trusting in the center. Remaining rigid, the center person falls slowly in any direction. Before he/she moves very far off plumb, the circle people redirect the faller's impetus to another arc of the circle. This fall-catch-shove sequence continues in a gentle fashion until it becomes obvious that the center person is relaxing (but remaining rigid) and that the circle people have gained confidence in their ability to work together toward handling the occasional weight shift of the faller.

   Change people in the center until everyone who wants to has had an opportunity to be "shoved around."

2. The second trust-pass sequence represents essentially the same micro-falling scenario as above, with a different set-up.

The circumference people sit down so that they are arranged hip to hip; i.e., closely scooched together. With the center person already set in a standing position (as above), the circle people all put their feet on top of the faller's feet, locking that person in place. This is done not to insure the positive participation of that person, but to provide a firm base for the swaying "willow." The central person then initiates movement from side to side and is consistently and compassionately redirected by the sitting catchers. It is important that the catchers keep their hands up in anticipation of the faller's body unexpectedly heading in their direction. This is not to say that each person must catch the faller by themselves: this is, after all, a cooperative trust situation. If the center person does indeed fall too far in any direction, he/she will find themselves comfortably situated in one of the catcher's laps, or combination thereof, depending on lap size — which is not a useful debriefing topic.

Levitation (with a little help from your friends)

You know what levitation is, right? It's the fake flying sequence that better-than-average magicians can fool you into thinking is really happening. You *know* that if anyone could really levitate, NASA would already have permanent possession of their flight schedule. Anyway, it's fun to be fooled.

But we can all levitate. Not "stripped of the bonds of earthly ties," but making full use of a friendly group's hands-on offer of fleeting zero G's. More succinctly, having a group slowly lift your prone bod from the ground, to a well overhead position, is a dandy way to build trust and feel good.

Just get lots of people to kneel around the body to be lifted, and on a signal, the volunteer

space cadet is gently lifted a couple feet up, moved laterally back and forth and eventually levitated up to a maximum height (about 6–7') and then, sooo slowly, down to a safe non-friction landing. From lift-off to landing takes about 30 seconds.

Levitation may put you in touch with astral vibrations or initiate a career in aeronautics, or maybe you'll just like it… (See photo this page, and also on pg. 28.)

Gauntlet

The faller walks between two lines of catchers who are lined up facing each other. The catchers should be at the "ready" position. The faller can then surprise group members by falling in their direction at any time. This forces the group to be on their guard, and simulates spotting situations that take place on low cable events such as *Tension Traverse, Criss Cross, Wild Woosey, and Mohawk Traverse.* These activities are included in chapters 4 and 5.

Trust Fall

An effective trust exercise can be accomplished by asking a student to stand upon a stump, platform, ladder rung, etc. approximately 5 feet off the ground, and fall backward into the arms of the group (see photo next page). There should be at least ten to twelve individuals standing on level ground to act as catchers.

To increase the commitment of the person falling, ask the faller to close his/her eyes before and during the fall. The faller should keep his/her arms close to the side of the body (hands grasping pants or crossed securely on the chest) and fall with the body held rigid; i.e., not bending at the waist. If the falling person bends at the waist, it concentrates the force of the fall in one area (the derrière) and makes the spotting catch more difficult.

The two lines of catchers stand shoulder to

shoulder, facing one another, with hands extended palms up so that hands are alternated and closely juxtaposed (zippered) to form a safe landing area.

Do not allow catchers facing one another to grasp hands. Knocked heads will result.

Ask fallers to remove all objects from their pockets (pens and pencils, keys, knives, etc.), that may injure themselves or the catchers. Ask the catchers to remove all watches and wrist jewelry.

As instructor, do not succumb to the temptation of being the first volunteer to fall. The smiling, apparently confident group below you, has never caught anyone and the sight of a falling "TEACHER" coupled with a novice's prerogative of doing everything wrong, might be enough to result in a very hard landing: not speculation, fact!

Place yourself in the catching line so that if everything goes wrong you can either catch the falling volunteer by yourself, or do a good job of slowing him/her down. After the students have caught a few fallers, remove yourself from the line, keeping a close eye on what is happening.

Before any fall occurs, establish a communication code between catchers and fallers so that a nervous student does not initiate a fall before the catchers are ready. The following exchange may serve as an example:

The faller initiates the signals by saying: "Are you ready to catch me?"

The catchers respond, "We're ready, _____ _____ (insert faller's name)

Faller says, "Falling!", and the sequence concludes with a safe catch.

If the students eventually ask, "How come you haven't tried this yet, don't you trust us?" then it's time for your show of calculated confidence. If you are not planning to fall, because you don't trust the students, then don't use this exercise. However, if you have a class of elementary age students, and you are clearly too heavy for them to catch, it's obvious that your decision not to fall has nothing to do with trusting or not trusting the students.

Try to have the students change their position in the spotting line as things progress so

that all can experience the responsibility of being a catcher. If you have a large group (20–40), it's clear that only a few students will actually be doing the catching. To further utilize the entire group (i.e., the end of the line), ask the falling person to continue holding his body rigid after falling so that he or she can be passed hand to hand down the entire line of catchers. As the faller is being lifted and passed along the line, locate a lateral spotter on each side of the line.

Be aware that trust can be diminished as easily during this passage as in the fall itself. If a student is dropped *at any time*, it will be a long time before that student will display any trust toward you or the group.

Have someone at the end of the line be responsible for holding the student's torso up while his feet are being lowered to the ground. Reversing this action is not met with much humor. Expect to spend more than one class period on this activity. Make an attempt to achieve 100% participation, even if participation means simply standing on the platform and looking at the line of catchers. From this point it's usually easier to fall than climb down. Gotcha!

There is a danger in beginning this activity from too high a platform. If the head and shoulders of the falling participant reach the line of catchers before the feet, the platform is too high. A height of 6–7 feet will produce this result.

Things to be aware of and watch out for:
- Beware of flying elbows. Ask fallers to put their hands in their pockets, tightly grasp their pants, or cross their arms on their chest.
- Line up the faller each time to prevent badly angled falls.
- Don't let enthusiasm diminish attention to the task. Re-emphasize the catchers' responsibilities.

Trust Dive

From a height of about 2–4 feet, ask a student to dive forward into the arms of 8–10 spotters. Ensure that the diving platform (stump, bleacher) is solid enough to preclude

what we learned in Physics 101 — the old "equal and opposite reaction to every action"...trick, namely that the platform, if not well secured, moves quickly away from the force applied by the jumper.

Indicate to the diver that he/she should aim for an invisible trapeze above the heads of the catchers in order to land in an easily handled position; flat out, arms extended. Discourage dives "into the pool" and pike position landings.

As in the *Trust Fall,* ask divers to remove any objects from their person that may injure themselves or a catcher. Ask catchers to remove watches and jewelry from their wrists.

A set of bleachers provides a variable and usually solid take-off area. The diver can choose height and distance by moving up or down the bleacher steps. Use the end of the bleachers, not the seats themselves. Other usable take-offs include the back of a truck, a cut off tree stump, a low porch, and a large, well-positioned rock.

Arrange the catchers so that there is some Challenge to the dive, but not so close that the diver's movements are restricted by well-intentioned spotters. The position of the catchers is about the same as in the *Trust Fall* activity with the exception that the spotters' bodies are turned halfway toward the diver with one foot moved toward the center of the catching line. This oblique body orientation provides more ability to absorb the momentum of the diver.

To increase the commitment of the diver, remove the first two spotters; i.e., increase the distance from the diver to the spotters. Let this be a choice that the diver makes. Choosing to remove the first, and sometimes second pair of spotters, is not as dramatic a move as it seems initially. A diver will probably not make such a decision unless he is sure of the outcome, and even if the dive comes up short, only the diver's feet will drag on the ground.

Rappelling

Ah rappelling...the programmatic answer for Adventure-oriented programs that seek a sure-fire, grabby, comparatively inexpensive, easily protected, sometimes spiritual, gutsy, enjoyable, physical commitment activity that provides good copy, positive parental reaction, excellent photographic possibilities, enthusiastic administrative support, and a sense of personal achievement that transcends validity.

Is it any wonder that everyone wants a rappel as an integral part of their program? I mean, can you afford *not* to rappel? "Have you rappelled?", becomes less a question of interest and more an opening statement of fraternal affiliation.

The opportunity to rappel within a school curriculum depends upon, and in approximate order, the following:
1. The administration's support.
2. The availability of an accessible area which is high enough from which to rappel.

3. Having someone trained in setting up and running a safe rappel.
4. Having enough money to purchase the necessary equipment.

Item one is seldom a problem with an on-going program unless the rappel area includes a sacrosanct portion of a building or involves possible damage to the roof (resulting in leakage and revocation to the roofing water-seal guarantee).

For item two, buildings, telephone poles, or tree platforms provide good rappel areas. Anything less than 15' isn't very exciting.

Item three: It requires a premeditated effort to get hurt on a properly set up rappel. However, one way to dramatically increase the chance for injury is to have an inexperienced person set up and run the rappel. Anyone who

If you have little or no experience rappelling, **DO NOT** perform any type of rappel without having a mature, experienced climber with you. Many people have been hurt rappelling on clothesline or without a belay or by omitting a simple step that experience would have included.

is unsure about where to tie the anchor point, where to clip in, how to tie the knots, which hand goes where, **should not** be running the rappel.

Item four: What can I say?

Face-First Rappel

This rappel has been performed on slopes, vertical faces, overhangs, and off bridges into water. Hundreds of students have been safely put "over the side" using this method. It appears bizarre, and can be frightening (looking straight down 100' to where you're headed rather than up toward the comforting smile of your belayer can be disconcerting), but with a proper belay, it is as safe as any other rappel. Try it!

Chapter 3

Games

A game can be an end in itself. I have no doubt, from having played and led many games as an adult, that the justification for participating in game activities can be for personal enjoyment only. Notice the period at the end of the last sentence. That's it — that's the reason — period. No validity hassles, or attempting to manipulate the cognitive, affective, psychomotor triumvirate — just flat-out fun.

If your ongoing program needs a boost because of scheduling problems, personality conflicts, or activity repetition, try playing a couple of these games. Games presented in a lighthearted manner can provide the morale growth that facilitates group cohesion and enthusiasm for the program. De-emphasize competition and try to present the activities in such an attractive way that everyone will want to participate. It's hard to turn your back on obvious fun.

Play Pointers

1. Don't just explain; involve yourself in the activity. You don't have to play every game, but be ready to personalize the game with your person; get in there and mix it up with the players.
2. Keep the rules to a minimum. Wordy explanations lead to pre-game boredom.
3. Bend some rules occasionally or change a few as fits the players and the situations.
4. Don't run a good game into the ground. Three straight class periods of any game in this section is boring. That's why some students don't like archery, or badminton, or anything else required too many weeks in a row.
5. Keep the players playing. Don't include or involve rules that permanently eliminate participants.
6. Pick teams that are fair. Don't use the disastrous sociogram method for choosing sides; i.e., asking two students to pick their own teams.
7. Play games that allow as much of a 50/50 male-female split as possible. Organized sports generally demand a sex split and there's enough of that. These games can be played as well by either sex.
8. Emphasize competition against self when competition seems natural. Trying to beat a time established by your own team or attempting to smash a nebulous WORLD RECORD is great fun with none of the second place, next time symptoms of the loser syndrome.

Moon Ball

I'll tell you something honestly: *Moon Ball* has programmatically saved my bacon on a couple occasions when I needed a quickly explained, moderately active game for people standing around at the beginning of a session wondering why they were there. (That last sentence seems a bit run-on, but I'm talking now, not writing...and anyway, you know what I mean.)

Moon Ball is an excellent one-prop-game that develops coordination, fast reactions, and unselfconscious participation. Play becomes intensely competitive as a group competes against its last best effort.

Scatter your group (any size, but use two or more balls as the group size demands) on a basketball court or a field. Use a well-inflated beach ball as the object of play. The group's objective is to hit the ball aloft as many times as possible before the ball strikes the ground. Depending upon the group, set a goal of 30–100 hits to add incentive. The tension and expectation builds as each "world record" is approached.

A Couple of Rules

1. A player cannot hit the ball twice in succession.
2. Count one point for each hit and two points for a kick.

Not too complicated, eh? *Moon Ball* is popular with all ages because it's so simple to understand, requires little skill, and involves everyone. As you hit the ball up to start a round, there's no doubt where everyone's eyes are fixed: on the ball. Watch the players' eyes as the ball bounces from person to person; you'll see what I mean. With everyone zeroed in on the ball, good and bad hits aren't related to any one person, and play continues.

Beach balls (aka Moon Balls) give vent to flights of curricular imagination, because what else are you going to do with a gaily colored balloon-like ball that doesn't pass or bounce worth beans, or kick with any predictability? After you've messed around with the basics, here are a couple of variations.

Ask the group, after playing basic hit-the-ball-37-times, to see how many times the group (6–60+) can hit the ball in sequence through all the players without: 1.) Letting the ball hit the ground or 2.) Missing a sequenced player. Alternately, see how fast the ball can travel from player to player in sequence; i.e., through the whole group. If the ball touches the ground, assign a time penalty — say 5 seconds. The ball must be hit, not simply passed.

Set up a regular *Moon Ball* game and record the most number of ball strikes (hands only) during a one-minute time limit. Only count those hits that are not preceded by a ground bounce. The ball must touch each player sequentially. Allow the group to arrange themselves in whatever position they decide is best to achieve the greatest number of hits.

When the ball begins to leak air (it's bound to happen eventually — these things only cost about a dollar), try a quick round of *Five-a-Side Flatball.*

Aerobic Tag

An active game that requires little explanation, a group of up to 30, a large unobstructed area for running, and provides a nostalgic return to a when-I-was growing-up game that is playfully competitive with minimum emphasis on who wins or loses.

Object: For a team (1/2 the group) to maintain possession of the object of play (frisbee, bean bag, deck tennis ring) for 30, 45, 60 seconds, depending upon the size of the playing field and the age/ability/patience level of the group.

Equipment: A frisbee works well for this game if a strong wind is not blowing and you are playing on a large field. Otherwise, try playing with a rubber deck tennis ring — very comfortable to catch and not affected by the wind.

Being hit by a gliding frisbee can be painful if not injurious, but a blind-side hit by a rubber ring is only embarrassing. You will also need a watch.

Note to Football Coaches: This is a great conditioning game that involves running and catching. Use a football as the keep-away object; no pads, no contact.

Play & Rules
1. The object of play (OOP) is thrown randomly into the air at about mid-field by the timekeeper (you) and timing begins. A player grabs the OOP and by using speed, guile, and strategy, attempts to keep the OOP away from the clutches of the other team.
2. If the person in possession is tagged by a person from the other team (one hand below the neck), he/she must stop running and get rid of the OOP *immediately*. If the tagged person holds onto the OOP for more than one second after being tagged, the other team automatically gets possession and a free throw.
3. If a member of the same team catches or picks up the thrown OOP, time continues for that team. If a member of the other team takes possession of the OOP, the timekeeper yells SWITCH and begins timing once again from zero. The OOP may be caught either in

the air or picked up off the ground — no difference.

4. If two opposing players grab the OOP and a tugging match begins, the timekeeper takes possession and once again throws the OOP randomly up in the air.

5. When a team has maintained possession for the designated time period, the timekeeper counts down the last 5 seconds and shouts SCORE.

6. Play begins again as before allowing some time for shedding coats and discussing strategy.

Considerations:

• No purposeful body contact is allowed except compassionate tagging.

• Limit the playing area (boundaries) or the game may end up somewhere else.

• It will be necessary for players to wear pinnies or distinguish themselves as a team in some way so that you are able to ascertain which team currently has the OOP. Ask the group how they would like to establish their team colors. Suggestions — color of pants or shirts, rolled up pant leg, hats or no hats.

• If you use frisbees on a very cold day, they are apt to crack if they hit the frozen ground.

• Don't hesitate to play this game on a snow-covered field.

Anaerobic Tag

As referee for the previous game of *Aerobic Tag,* you have a considerable amount of control over the outcome of the game. (How many of you who have reffed this game actually kept an accurate measure of how long a team had possession of the ring, frisbee, etc.? I'm lucky to remember which team has control, which I think re-emphasizes the group's potential for F&G — fun and games — in contrast to who gets the trophy.) As ref for *Anaerobic Tag,* all you have to do is count consecutive throws to establish a score. Here are the basic rules and a few considerations.

Set up the game situation as in *Aerobic Tag.* Throw a rubber ring (OOP) somewhere on the field of play. Whoever catches it, or picks it up, may run until tagged or has thrown the OOP to another member of his/her team. The object is to pass the OOP 15 times amongst the members of the group before the OOP is intercepted by the other team.

Rules:

1. Throws may be made to any team member, but not to the same person twice in a row.

2. If a person is tagged (two hands below the clavicle), that person MUST throw the OOP to a teammate immediately (2 seconds or less).

3. If two players grab the OOP simultaneously, require a throw straight up by one of the players: count starts again from zero.

4. When a team reaches 15, they score a point. The OOP then goes immediately to the other team so that a restart isn't necessary.

5. Another way to keep things moving: when a team reaches 15 consecutive throws, they start again immediately, from zero, to try and score another point. The onus continues to be on the other team to tag a runner and intercept the OOP.

6. If the use of numbers by both teams is confusing, assign letters to one of the teams. When the letter team completes sequential throws from, A to O (1–15), a point is scored.

7. If you want the game to last a bit longer (like six hours), ask the teams to number themselves sequentially and pass the OOP in sequence from player to player in order to score a point. A game to last the semester for sure.

Hooper

The game Hooper is a team-oriented extension of *Aerobic Tag.* To play Hooper you must use a deck tennis ring as the OOP. You will also need 4 hula hoops (or 4 sections of rope to form circles on the field). Rules of play for *Hooper* are identical to *Aerobic Tag* with the following exceptions and additions:

1. The four hula hoops are placed on the field of play to form the corners of an imaginary square. They should be at least 20 yards away from one another.

2. A team must keep possession of a rubber ring for 15 seconds, at which juncture the timekeeper yells, "HOOP."

3. To score a point, a player whose team has maintained possession for 15 seconds and hears HOOP, must place him/herself inside one of the hula hoops and catch the rubber ring by having it actually "ring" his/her hand. This catch is most easily accomplished by bringing all the fingers of the hand together and overlapped (not the thumb) to form a "spear."

4. No offensive player may stay inside a Hoop for more than 5 seconds. Both feet must be inside the Hoop for the point to count. Defensive players may not enter the hoop at all.

5. Some boundaries are necessary to prevent cross-country runners from dominating play, but keep the lines far enough apart to allow unrestricted running.

6. Particularly offensive players must shower at the end of class.

Speed Rabbit

You may recognize this stand-in-a-circle activity as an old beer-drinking game because that's exactly what it is. I've changed the rules slightly so that rule infractions result in people switching rather than mandatory beer-quaffing. The fast and ludicrous action, however, remains the same, so chug away for nostalgia's sake (better use soft drinks for a student group — I have a feeling that parents may complain otherwise).

Ask the game initiator to stand in the center of the circle. His/her job is to point to a person in the circle and say either: 1.) Elephant, 2.) Rabbit, or 3.) Cow. The signified individual, and the two people to that person's immediate right and left, must perform a ritualized and symbolic pantomime sequence before the center person can count to 10. If the sequence is not done correctly or in time, then the offending person (one of the three) must take the place of the initiator in the circle. If the sequence is performed correctly, the initiator points to another person until someone eventually makes a mistake, or doesn't complete the sequence within the allotted time — count 1–10.

The animal sequences are as follows and, of course, can be (should be) amended, or added to, as play continues.

Elephant — The person pointed to: 1.) Extends his/her right arm forward, palm down, hand lightly cupped. 2.) Brings the left hand under the arm and up to pinch the nose. 3.) Flaps the right arm up and down, as in flapping their trunk. 4.) The two players to the right and left of the flapping trunk must flap their "ears" by waving their hands next to their ears.

All this happens simultaneously before the count reaches 10.

Rabbit — 1.) Center person hops up and down. 2.) Person to the right stomps his/her foot — person to left stomps his/her foot.

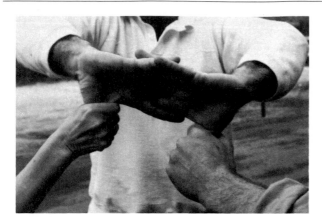

Cow — 1.) Center person interlaces fingers of both hands and presses both palms out away from his/her body, resulting in both thumbs pointing to the ground. 2.) Side people must grab a thumb and mime a milking motion.

Make up your own series of sounds and motions for a Dog (lifting leg?), Skunk, etc.

Five-a-Side Flatball

This is one of those "spontaneous generation" games that occurs full blown as the result of some serendipity and more than a dollop of PGE (playful group energy). *Five-a-Side* also plays better than it reads, so give it a try when group energy is high and air pressure is low — after a heady game of *Striker*, perhaps.

Deflate a Moon Ball (aka beach ball) to about 66-2/3 maximum to provide the object-of-play.

Ten players make up the official roster for this fast-moving game with five players arranging themselves on each side as opposing teams. Use the basketball lines near the end of the court that are parallel to one another and about 6' apart to act as boundary designators. The two teams line up facing one another. Team players should be about arm's length away from one another and facing the members of the opposite team. The suggested lateral boundary lines are 20' apart, measured from side to side.

Object: To smack the flattish ball past the opponent's line using only the front or back of an open hand.

Rules:
1. Players must stand with their toes on the line while waiting for a playable hit.
2. When the ball approaches, a player may pivot one step forward to smack the ball, but may not make purposeful physical contact with an opposing player.
3. A point is scored if the ball completely crosses the player's line. If the ball sails over that player's reach, no point is scored.
4. Play begins with a back-handed hit of the ball being held by a fellow player (called a backy). When a team scores, the opposite team immediately initiates a backy to begin play again. There are no timeouts.
5. The ball may not be picked up, held, or carried.
6. Five consecutive hits of the ball per side is maximum before the ball must be touched by someone on the other team.
7. Kneeling is not allowed — only foot contact with the floor.
8. Penalties are judged and assessed by the players.

What Goes Where?

This simple set-up could become a classic in communication confusion. The object of the exercise is to see if a group member can communicate to the remainder of the group (pencil and paper in hand) the geometrical abstraction (see illustrations) that has been given to them.

Four separate pictorial attempts are made with four separate abstractions, following these guidelines:

1. The presenter vocalizes the abstract illustration with his/her back to the group.
2. Again, verbalize a different abstract figure, but this time facing the audience. Gestures are allowed by the communicator, but no questions may be asked or answered.
3. Now, face the audience and use gestures only: no talking or making any sounds (except laughter, which is hard to stifle at this point).
4. And finally — facing the audience, gesticulating to your heart's content, and responding to the group's questions.

After each attempt, allow the group to compare their separate drawings with one another and with the master abstraction. Note which attempt produces the most accurate representations, and discuss why you think this is so.

These illustrated abstractions are examples that have been used successfully in the past, but they do not represent any holistic, spiritual, religious, or secular anything. Make up your own configurations and I suspect you will get the same humorously insightful results.

The Wave, or Butt-Off

Everybody needs a chair. Flimsy chairs do not work well for this highly active game that involves moving your posterior rapidly from one chair to another.

Sit in a circle with the chairs fairly close together. Don't play with less than 15 moving posteriors. Designate (ask for a volunteer — maybe you) a person to leave his/her chair empty and stand within the circle of seated bodies. As soon as the IT person moves toward an empty chair, that chair must be filled by the person sitting next to it that will result in a clockwise movement of people. As one person moves, the next person must be in motion, etc., etc., in order to fill the rapidly vacating seat. When this game gets moving, the rapid seat changing results in a flow of people that looks impossibly choreographed.

When the IT person finally gets her/his posterior into the appearing/disappearing empty chair, the displaced person must immediately look for and pursue the elusive empty chair. There are no timeouts. If someone becomes too exhausted to continue, let the IT person designate his/her own replacement.

Change directions (from clockwise) occasionally in order to confuse and confound a floundering IT — you'll know when. Play until quivering quadriceps plead for relief (or you run out of replacement chairs). This is one of those games that has to be played to appreciate the potential for, 1.) fast, physical action, 2.) unselfconscious touching, 3.) copious laughter and a sense of abandon that borders on chaos. Get into it; i.e., onto it.

4-Letter Word

A thinking, fast-action game for large groups (30–50+).

This catchy title, approached by the timid teacher with a veiled shudder, has nothing to do with THE four letter words, but the anticipation and harmless titillation is worth a soupçon of unease.

As an interesting aside, I have, on occasion, accused workshop participants of trying to get me to say *the* F word as the result of their weak participation efforts (or complete lack thereof). Incensed, they say, "What do you mean?" My reply includes references to their proclivity for non-success; i.e., the 4-letter F word —FAIL. It's a sometime tool for the right group, and it's yours to use appropriately and humorously.

Back to the game — which I've said nothing about so far via asides and beating about the bush — also a four letter word. Note how many 4-letter words there are just in these few sentences.

Before introducing *4-Letter Word,* obtain a pack of 3"x5" blank file cards. Using a felt pen, print the alphabet — one letter per card — on the cards. Print additional cards for those letters used most often in word makeup. If you have a Scrabble game, you'll get a good indica-

tion of which letters are used most often by their assigned point value. For example, AEIOU should have at least 3 cards per letter; X and Z, only one.

Ask each person in the group to take a card. If the group is small (25–30), have each person take two cards. Mark the corners of a J card and use it as a joker (wild card).

Announce that the task is for each lettered person to get together with other people in the group (on a signal), and form a proper 4-letter word within 45 seconds. If card-carrying players are still fumbling at the end of that time, or are simply without letter partners, they and the other fumblers become observers.

Continue until only the last four *4-letter Word* participants remain — the champs.

Alternate 3, 5, and 6 letter word requirements, occasionally, to add variety. The rules are up to you, but using Scrabble guidelines for allowable words is acceptable to most players. Real you-know-what-I-mean 4-letter words are obviously not allowed.

Janepaulsuefrediradavepeggy, or Hustle Handle

This is a name game that doesn't accomplish much of anything that's measurable: it's just fun. If you time the upcoming attempt, I think you will spark a competitive interest and perhaps generate enough enthusiasm for "one more try." Include this game as part of the impulse genre.

Arrange everyone in a circle, including yourself. Stand by the ubiquitous Casio stopwatch, announcing this as a timed event. Say your name and start the watch. The person next to you (either way) says his/her name, then the next person says his/hers, etc., etc., as fast as possible until the whole circle is finished; i.e., back to you — stop the watch.

This speed-slurring of what used to be a series of distinct names works best with a larger group, but even a smaller number can have some fun with the competitive nonsense. It is impressive how much faster a group can say their names when they start getting competitive with themselves.

If the group is small, go around the circle two or three times. As a variation (that's hard to justify except for the level of laughter) start the name sequence to the left and right simultaneously. Watch the expression and eventual reaction of that person on the opposite side of the circle.

Editor's Note: This is *not* a good game for learning names.

Italian Golf

The hidden agenda of *Italian Golf* is to offer a game that teaches by example the rules, vocabulary, and etiquette of actual golf combined with a format that is low-key enough to encourage 100% participation.

You will need about a dozen rubber deck tennis rings. These soft rings are obtainable from Project Adventure and various physical education catalog suppliers (Snitz, Things From Bell). As far as I know, deck tennis rings are used on the deck of a ship to play a game that resembles tennis, when hitting tennis balls off the court (overboard) doesn't make economical sense. Anyway, the rings are soft to the hit but substantial enough to allow a good long throw. People seem to like holding and throwing the rings, just for the sake of doing it — I suspect dogs like them, too.

The Game: Break up into small groups of 2, 3, or 4. Four players together designates the classic golf FOURSOME. As you stand where you are, look around and try to envision a playable golf hole — something in the 100–300 yd. category with perhaps a DOGLEG and a couple of obstacles (trees, pond, car). Declare, "This HOLE looks like a PAR 8," or however many throws you think it will take your team to HOLE OUT. The first person in your group to DRIVE (throw a ring) gets set on the estab-

lished TEE and throws to another person in the FOURSOME that has assumed a catching position some distance toward the HOLE (final destination).

To legally "catch" the rubber ring, the catcher must extend a hand with fingers and thumb held together so that the incoming ring will encircle the hand and pass over the wrist to the forearm (see photo above). Anything less is a miss, and the STROKE (throw) must be taken again. Once the catcher establishes a position, that person must return to his/her initial position after a miss. The catcher may, however, move toward the ring after the throw is in the air. Only 5 throws (misses) are allowed in each position, at which point the next thrower in the FOURSOME sequence takes over at the point of the last miss and play continues. Each throw is counted as a STROKE.

The FOURSOME continues throwing and catching in sequence until the HOLE is reached. The SCORE is recorded on the SCORE CARD, then the next HOLE is conceptualized and attempted.

Spend some time letting the players throw and catch before the game is explained. The throw/catch sequence is an enjoyable preliminary to the game and gives the players a better idea of how far they can throw accurately and also how well they can't catch.

Be inventive in establishing holes, taking advantage of natural WATER HAZARDS, and other OUT OF BOUNDS obstacles. Particularly intense HOLES include brief sojourns into and out of buildings or up and down stairwells.

Keep score over a series of HOLES so that FOURSOMES can compete against one another. If two FOURSOMES are playing consecutive HOLES, golf vocabulary that fits the occasion includes: PLAY THROUGH, LET OUT SOME SHAFT, NEVER UP, NEVER IN, BIRDIE — EAGLE (or more likely DOUBLE BOGEY), NICE HIT, HOW MANY DO YOU LIE, YOU'RE AWAY, and ...SEE YOU AT THE 19th HOLE!

Have you figured out the Italian connection? Hold up your hand, palm facing you, in the approved finger together catching position. Shake your hand and arm in the position 3 or 4 times to alert your thrower that you are ready. Get it? Maybe you have to be there.

Note: The following games and activities are part of the old *Cowstails and Cobras* publication which did not make it into the book *Silver Bullets*. As the result of overwhelming popular demand (the staff, friends, and even a few readers), they are being rejuvenated in *Cowstails II*. So, here are some old favorites, recently rescued, polished up a bit, and as full of physical fun as before.

Impulse

Ask a group of 8–10 students to arrange themselves in a circle and to hold hands. The circle should be of such a diameter that the participants' arms are neither extended nor too loose.

Put yourself somewhere in the group while explaining how a wave impulse can be transmitted along a flexible connector (rope, wire, spring). Actually begin an impulse within the circle by moderately whipping the person's arm to either your right or left. If the proper arm tension has been reached by the group, and with a little subconscious help, the impulse will travel from person to person and finally back to the initiator — you.

You can also begin two impulses simultaneously by shaking the arms of the individuals on your right and left. The interesting result is trying to let both impulses pass through one person somewhere in the circle and end at the initiator. An alternate strategy for a group is to try transmitting one or more impulses with all eyes closed except the leader's. Observe and describe the effect that this technique has on speed and accuracy. Whether accurate transmission is physically possible with a group of people isn't really important — the fun of trying something unique and challenging as a group is reason enough.

Impulse, as explained above, may or may not "work" depending upon your group. (If a group wants it to work, it will.) Since you have already broken some ice by getting them to hold hands briefly, try to break some more by introducing:

Impulse II

Standing in a circle holding hands, a group of 10–50 tries to send a hand squeeze impulse around the circle as fast as possible — a timed event.

Try doing this both with eyes open and closed and compare the times. As a low key finale to your various attempts, ask one person to start a hand squeeze impulse using both hands so that two impulses are sent racing around the circle in both directions. See if the impulses can cross and continue. See if cheating is necessary to make this happen. See if anyone cares.

Use the impulse idea to send whatever type of action, or sound you can think of around the circle. Try clapping, finger snapping, sticking your tongue out, etc., as the impulse impetus.

Gimmee

On a *snowy* winter day, when spirits are as low as the barometer, a game of *Gimmee* provides a fine physical outlet — and it's fun. The rules for this non-game are few and studiously different. The game format resembles Rugby; the results resemble something else.

Object: To kick, punch, strike, or slide the ball through the opponent's goal.

Equipment: A soccer ball and a soft snowy field (at least 6" deep).

Procedure: Divide the class into two teams and have each team choose a goalie who then stands in the goal area as play begins.

Rules:
1. An unlimited number of people may play on each side, co-ed or otherwise.
2. A football field is used but there are no boundaries and thus no stopping of play.
3. Play begins by grouping everyone (except the goalie) near the middle of the field

where the ball has been placed. A designated player shouts the word GIMMEE three times in any cadence or timing he/she chooses. On the third shout of GIMMEE, anyone is free to try and advance the ball toward the opponent's goal.

4. If a player inadvertently, or in an attempt to gain unfair advantage, strikes the ball before the third GIMMEE, the other team is awarded a goal — serious rule infraction; heavy lumps.

5. The ball may be advanced by kicking or striking it with any part of the body. The ball may not be picked up, caught, or thrown.

6. The goalie is the only team member who may pick up the ball and throw it or run with it. A goalie who chooses to run may be tackled. When tackled (no forward movement) he must throw or release the ball. All tackles must be made above the waist. The goalie may play anywhere on the field.

7. Any team member, at any time, may tackle or grab any opposing player for any reason. Tackling must be done above the waist.

8. A goal is scored by either kicking or striking the ball through the area between the goal posts or by having the goalie run the ball over the goal line within this area. The ball must pass through the field side of the goal.

9. Losing one's temper is temporarily allowed, but punching, scratching, or pulling hair is prohibited. Laughing, shouting, and labored breathing are allowed and expected.

10. Play is stopped only after a goal is scored. Another GIMMEE huddle is then initiated. If desired, a change of goalie can be made at this time.

11. Play continues until the end of the class period. All rules are self-enforced as there are no referees. Teachers, coaches, instructors, etc., act as participants or observers.

Caveats: Gimmee can be an exhilarating game, but if played too roughly and competitively, can become a detriment to what you are trying to accomplish. Use the game late in the program rather than during the first few weeks. Let the students begin to develop some trust in one another and an idea of what's hoped to be accomplished within this strangely cooperative curriculum format.

Do not play this game unless there is fresh snow 6" deep on the turf.

Clubs Royale

A fast-moving co-ed game in which only females are allowed to score goals.

Object: Two co-ed teams of any reasonable size try to forward a slightly deflated soccer ball through a goal area with the use of soccer tactics and field hockey sticks.

Equipment: A partly-deflated soccer ball or a dense foam nerf-type ball, and 10–14 field-hockey sticks.

Play:

- About 5–7 field hockey sticks are given to each team. Only female members of the team are allowed to utilize these weapons (playing implements), and for a goal to be scored, the ball must come off a stick; i.e., only the ladies may score.

- The ball may be moved in only two ways; either by soccer rules or by use of the sticks. Girls using field hockey sticks may also kick the ball, but not to score a goal.

- Play can be conducted on any convenient open area. Include no boundaries except the goals, which may be scored through in either direction.

- Play begins by placing the ball about in the middle of the field with each team lined up at their respective goals. Two males from each team race toward the ball at the GO signal. The remainder of the team can move when contact is made with the ball by either of the two males on that team. Or vary the start as fits the situation or your inclination.

Considerations: *The sticks are potentially dangerous.* Do not allow high swings, *or someone will eventually sustain a leg, head, or groin injury.*

Unnecessary roughness by males is seldom a problem as the girls quickly find ways to subdue such shenanigans with the sticks. There may even be something behavioraly profound in such australopithecinetic actions.

Frisalevio

For you "street game" aficionados, this running game may provide another nostalgic and aerobic twinge.

Object: For a team of approximately 15 people to "capture" another group of equal size and place them in an outlined jail area. This effort is timed by whoever has a watch. The teams then switch roles and the time is measured again. The team which takes the least amount of time to capture the opposing team is declared WORLD CHAMPIONS (or whatever) for that day.

Equipment: Four 26' sling ropes. Frisbees or fleece balls for 1/2 of the team.

Play:
- A "jail" is constructed in the middle of a large field (or middle of a parking lot) by using the four 26' ropes to form a square.
- Provide frisbees for half the number of people on a side. Give these (frisbees) to the jailers and tell them all to wait inside the jail until the word is given: GO! The potential inmates are to avail themselves of whatever anonymity can be found in an open area as they try to appear as inconspicuous as possible while waiting to be chased.
- Play begins as the jailers attempt to capture the members of the inmates' team by throwing frisbees at them. If a hit below the waist is made, the captured inmate must put both hands over his head (and keep them there) to indicate that he has been caught and jog to the jail where he must stay unless released by a teammate. An uncaught inmate may at any time attempt to touch both feet inside the jail area before being hit with a frisbee, and shout FRISALEVIO in order to release all jailed inmates.
- Time is stopped as soon as the last person is caught.

Rules:
1. Frisbees may be thrown over and over by the jailers. A frisbee may not be touched by an inmate.
2. A frisbee has to leave the thrower's hand to count as a hit.
3. Reasonable boundaries are necessary to keep runners from turning the game into a one-on-one, cross-country race.
4. Time how long it takes a team to catch all the other team members, then switch roles and start the clock again to see which team is fastest, and most efficient.
5. Use flexible frisbees (softies) if players complain of painful hits.

Rope Jousting

Object: To cause your partner to fall from on top of a low box or stump by pulling or releasing the rope. Losing your end of the rope is tantamount to a fall.

Equipment:
- Two strong boxes of equal size. The boxes can be ammunition, milk, or wooden packing crates.
- One 50' length of kind-to-the-hands rope for each pair of jousters.

Procedure: Place the boxes about 30' apart. Give both of the participants the end of a 50' length of retired climbing rope, and ask them both to stand on one of the boxes.

Considerations: *Do not set up the boxes on a hard surface; set up on grass or mats.*

The rope lengths can be cut considerably shorter for faster contests.

Use of boxes for this contest are not necessary. Use foot movement as the criteria for a win/lose situation.

Commitment to stay on the boxes can be dramatically increased by placing the boxes in a muddy area with access to a box made by a plank. Exit from the box top is then made via the action or reaction of the participants.

Rat Tail

A good game for cool weather; i.e., this game produces metabolic heat, which translates to lots of fast running. It's also an opportunity to practice with knots and carabiners.

Object: For half the group (cats) to capture the other half (rats) by clipping a carabiner through the loop dangling from their Studebaker Wrap.

Procedure:
- Half the class ties on a proper Studebaker Wrap. From the pile of "rattails" (pretied sections of retired climbing rope — figure 8 loop in each end), a tail is selected and clipped in behind on the Wrap; i.e., dorsal clip. The dangling figure 8 loop should be about 12" off the ground — adjust if necessary by tying overhand knots in the rope.
- This dangling rope arrangement designates the rat; the slippery, fleet-footed person to be chased. The chaser (cat) holds a single carabiner in hand (locking or not — it doesn't matter) and attempts to catch the rat by clipping his/her crab through the dangling loop of the rat's tail. Once so clipped, the rat is eliminated. The cat retrieves the crab and, oxygen uptake well in hand, takes off after another dirty rat.
- The play area should be limited to half a football field or smaller. Once all the rats have been caught, have the cats and rats reverse roles.

Rules: (To prevent arguments and hard blows to the head).
1. The rat may not grab his/her dangling rope and pull it about with the intention of keeping it from the attack cat. Any type of hip gyration, however, is ok.
2. The cat may grab the rat's tail to aid clip-in, but may not use the rope-in-hand to pull, slow down, or drag the hapless rat.

Yurt Circle

Ask the students to join hands and expand their people circle outward until everyone feels some pull on their arms from the people to their left and right. Starting with any convenient student, ask the group to count off by two's all the way around the circle; i.e., 1-2, 1-2, etc.

Encouraging the group to move slowly and deliberately, ask all the #1's to lean in toward the center of the circle, and all the #2's to lean out (without bending at the waist).

Each person should have their feet placed at about shoulder width and in line with the circumference of the circle.

If the group cooperates with one another, each person can exert quite a strong pull on their supporting partners and accomplish a remarkable forward or backward lean.

After some practice and increased proficiency, ask the #1's and #2's to try and reverse position (backward to forward or vice versa) upon command. This is not easy to do and will require a few attempts. Even if the group never completely succeeds, it's good for a few laughs, some unselfconscious hand-holding, and a good natured anticipation of the next activity.

Walt Tompkins, photo

Parachute Sailing

I'd like to admit something to the reader. I'm sitting here in a comfortable chair, going over what should be kept, changed, or deleted from the old *Cowstails and Cobras* book. I nostalgically looked at the picture on pg. 108 of a student riding a parachute-pulled sled, and reluctantly pushed the delete button (that's a bit of electronic fantasy that might be possible on a computer, but all I have is pen-in-hand; my ball point delete button). Then, I retro-read a few paragraphs, saw the following sentence and felt abashed at my own temerity. "Use good judgement, keeping in mind the need for a change of pace, some comic relief, and a few well-chosen thrills." I was about to "erase" a proven, curricular thrill-oriented activity because I thought it was outdated or it might be misused. Well, here's a rewrite of *Parachute Sailing* that looks awfully familiar to something that I wrote fifteen years ago. Thank goodness.

Combining a surplus personnel chute* (complete with 32' diameter canopy and cords), a triangular snow sled (not plastic), and a hefty wind (15–25 knots) produces a thrilling (albeit bumpy) ride over snow, grass, sand, unavoidable mud, and even shallow rain puddles.

*Each state has a federally assigned GSA (Government Surplus Agency) from which non-profit groups can obtain surplus properties from the government. Surplus chutes of many sizes can be obtained for very reasonable prices. The phone # for the Massachusetts Agency for Surplus Property is (617) 727-5774. Call them for information about the surplus agency in your state.

A wind-filled canopy generates a tremendous amount of pulling power. A group of students in a physics class would gain insight and respect for wind power by trying to control a parachute on a windy day.

Speeds of over 20 mph on the sled can be reached on a gusty day. It's a strange feeling both to be pulled at that speed or to be running at top speed and be overtaken by what looks like a huge marshmallow. Two sleds can be clipped together with a carabiner to provide more resistance when the winds gust powerfully. A 1/2" diameter drill bit makes the holes fore and aft on the sled for this attachment capability.

Ready for a ride? Attach the risers (heavy webbing to which the cords are stitched) via the included alloy D ring to the front of a drilled sled using a carabiner. Have the volunteer rider sit on the sled, firmly holding onto the two handles at each side of the sled. Two other students spread the canopy downwind so that all the cords are untangled, and together, simultaneously lift the top skirt of the chute, allowing the wind to enter the canopy.

See that the remainder of the class locate themselves downfield/downwind so that they are able to stop the chute before it goes into the trees, road, fence, etc. They do this by simply putting themselves in the path of the chute and jumping onto/into it — a gleeful and exciting moment.

The rider is simply that — a rider. He/she has practically no control over the direction or speed of the chute. It may seem tempting to grab a handfull of taut cords and try to steer the chute, but cord burns will probably result with little change of direction. If the sled begins travelling too fast, or if the chute leaves the ground and begins to pull the front of the sled up (wheelie position) shout for the rider to "bail out" — an odd command if you think about it. A great visual moment can be experienced at this juncture by watching the airborne

sled (with the rider's weight removed, the sled acts as a stabilizer for the chute — now a kite — and literally takes off). I've only lost one sled-chute combination this way, but the scenario was unforgettably exciting. We never did retrieve that parachute. Maybe you better put your name on the chute with a felt tipped pen. Maybe you better not, considering where it might come down.

Do not allow the chute to blow into trees, as branches will invariably puncture the panels, and small holes get bigger fast. Small holes can be patched with rip-stop nylon swatches and a sewing machine.

After the ride, you will want to transport the chute back upwind for another start. To "fool" the wind, grasp the hole in the center of the canopy and walk upwind to the start, letting the sled trail behind.

When finished sailing for the day, carefully wind the cords around a 2'x4' board to prevent tangling. Parachute cord spaghetti is no fun to deal with and cuts severely into sailing time.

On one dreary occasion, the cords became so snarled, that in a fit of frustration I cut all the cords near the risers, then serendipitously found that I could pull each cord individually out of the Gordian mess and simply retie it with a square knot. Maybe not a great idea for jumping out of planes, but sufficient for terra firma sailing.

These next two sentences are quoted directly from *Cowstails and Cobras* and are **required reading**:

*"If someone in the group with a keen sense of adventure, a flare for inventiveness, and questionable spontaneity, makes the suggestion that it might be fun and exciting to use the parachute as a kite with someone clipped into the chute — **DON'T**. The potential for getting hurt (really hurt) is well beyond a fun & games criteria."* I was the spontaneously creative person clipped into the chute. What happened makes a great war story because I

escaped without serious injury, but the potential for tragedy was there. Remind me to tell you the story sometime.

These types of offbeat activities are becoming more acceptable now within a P.E. curriculum, but the question is still asked, "What does this (parachute sailing, diving for a trapeze, swinging over poisoned peanut butter, etc.) have to do with physical education, or for that matter any kind of education?"

Whenever an innovative program starts up, parents are characteristically concerned about the safety and value of the course. A letter home to explain the goals and requirements is often a useful way to answer questions and assuage fears. Interest and understanding can also be generated by an open house demonstration on the ropes course. The students are understandably proud of their accomplishments, and while their descriptions of what they've been doing are puzzling at the dinner table, they seem to make more sense on a sunny Saturday morning.

Rationale for Participation in Adventure Activities

Why should my son/daughter participate in potentially dangerous and ofttimes fabricated activities? What possible favorable result can be expected by encouraging a student to attempt risky and functionally useless tasks?

Why does my daughter have to get over a 12' wall when it is obvious that a few steps around the wall is an easier and safer means of reaching the same goal?

Why does my son have to perform the questionable task of swinging across a pit of nonexistent poisoned peanut butter?

No student is coerced into attempting any activity. The staff requests a conscientious TRY from all students in the hope that all will participate. The final choice of performance is left entirely up to the student.

As a staff, we are convinced that "real adventure" is becoming more difficult for young people to find and participate in. Adventures of this type often have their own intrinsic rewards; i.e., they're fun and exciting. Beyond these immediate rewards, programs which incorporate Adventure, within a context of mutual support and encouragement from one's peers, seem to increase a student's willingness to enter more fully and enthusiastically into the process of living.

Few activities afford the adolescent an opportunity to become involved in high-risk/high-reward activities. Too often, the high-risk/low-reward course of action (drugs, illicit sex) or the low-risk/low-reward (passive non-involvement) is followed for lack of an attractive and accepted substitute.

To be real, there can be no adventure without uncertainty of results and in good adventure there is also an element of risk and even danger. The adventurer, therefore, has not only to know and observe the rules of safety, but must adhere to another set of values which involve the larger issues of commitment, reasonable risk-taking, and compassion.

Yes, yes I understand all that, but what is the value of my daughter climbing a wall and my son mucking about in ersatz sandwich spread?

Specifically:
1. It is a thrilling and fun thing to do.
2. Commitment to perform, where there is uncertainty of results, is a healthy decision-making process.

3. Proving to oneself that a seemingly insurmountable problem can be overcome is enlightening and satisfying.
4. There is evidence that significant positive carry-over results from the experience of successfully completing a demanding, fabricated problem, as compared to overcoming everyday problems (academic tests, personal relationships).

Programmatic Caution *Games, Initiative problems, or ropes course elements are not a panacea for less defined or not easily mentioned program ills. "Throwing out the ropes or games" as a replacement for "throwing out the balls" is obviously not an answer or even a safe alternative.*

Chapter 4
Initiative Problems

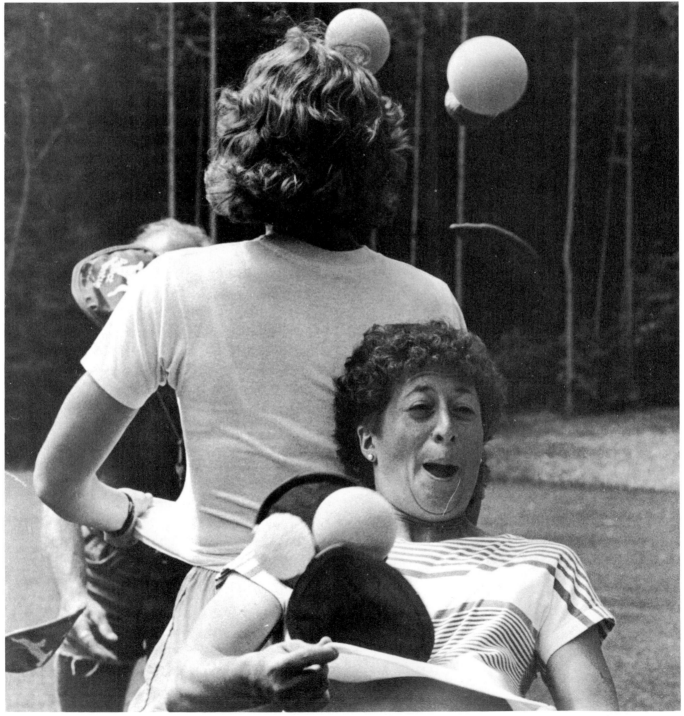

Nicki Hall photo

The following Initiative problem presentation has been excerpted in toto from the book *Silver Bullets* — the author's wife's husband said it was OK.

Initiative exercises offer a series of clearly and often fancifully defined problems. Each task is designed so that a group must employ cooperation and some physical effort to gain a solution. Some problems are more cognitive than physical and vice-versa. This problem-oriented approach to learning can be useful in developing each individual's awareness of decision-making, leadership, and the obligations and strengths of each member within a group. Participants engage the problem in groups to take advantage of the combined physical and mental strengths of a team. These Initiative problems can also be employed to promote an individual's sense of his own competence and serve to help break down some of the stereotypes which exist so comfortably in our social network. Finally, Initiative problems are a nonpareil for building morale and a sense of camaraderie.

Presenting Group Initiative Problems

Teachers and instructors should be familiar with these basic guidelines for Initiative problem presentation:

1. Choose a problem suited to the age and physical ability of the group. An older group is easily turned off by a childish situation, and any group quickly becomes frustrated by problems that require a physical or mental level beyond their capabilities.
2. Find a safe and convenient place to set up the problem and make use of existing materials and supports (trees, poles, etc.) whenever possible.
3. Make all the rules and procedures clear to the participants before they attempt the problem. Avoid overwordiness and too many rules.
4. Present the situation and rules, then step back and allow the group to work (and sometimes stumble) through the problem. While the instructor sets up the problem, and probably knows the best way to solve it, little good will come from interrupting the problem-solving process by giving hints or indicating to the participants a more efficient or "right" way. Interaction is the important process which takes place during an Initiative problem, and not necessarily how well the participants are performing physically under the established guidelines.
5. Initiative problems may be presented in as many different ways as instructor personalities and intuition allow. Some leaders present a highly fanciful situation (the

poisoned peanut butter crowd), while others present the situation just as it is. Select a method of presentation that is comfortable for you and suitable for the particular group.

6. As the group attempts to complete the

Initiative problem, situations may arise when a participant will (usually inadvertently) break a ground rule, thus making the completion of the problem a fairly easy matter. The penalty for such an infraction can be either a time penalty or starting the problem over. Whether to employ penalties, and the extent to which they are used, depends upon the instructor's approach. Be strict in administering the rules of the problem. If the group suspects that you don't care about following the rules (the framework of these fabrications), the problem will dissolve into horseplay and become functionally meaningless.

7. For variety, Initiative problems may occasionally be presented as a timed competitive exercise in order to increase interest and individual effort. Such competition usually takes one of two forms: A.) having the group members compete against themselves in order to improve on a previous record, B.) setting up a competition against other

groups or against a time limit.

Timed competition, against a nebulous group from a school in Western Wherever, seems to work well toward providing a goal to shoot for. Negative competition, within this framework of positive cooperative effort, results from the old redbird vs. bluebird situations where there must be an obvious winner and loser.

8. If you are working with a group of about 25–30, it will probably make sense to split the group in half for participation in games or Initiative problems. If too many people are involved, ideas and good intentions may be shunted aside in favor of loudness and individual popularity.

9. After a group has completed (or tried to complete) a problem, the details should be discussed by all who were involved. The discussion should focus on the process the students have just experienced. They can examine what decisions were made and by whom; who has ideas that were not expressed, or that were expressed but not heard or listened to. The discussion also may focus on the roles of males and females, students and adults, athletes and scholars, etc. The conversations may move naturally into a comparison of the cooperative processes which characterize school life or of our society in general. Verbalization of the group's experience, and reaction to a common task, is often enlightening to the group and to the instructor.

As instructor, you were obliged during the problem-solving process to be silent. Now, in your role as facilitator, you get the chance to carefully pick and choose your comments and those moments when an insightful word or two are best offered. Keep the conversations flowing with pertinent remarks, topics of discussion, and well-chosen humorous vignettes. Use the following list of debriefing topics. These discussion topics offer lead-in keys in order to get the most from a group sharing session.

Initiative Problem Debriefing Topics

• Leadership and Followership: Chiefs & Indians, how many and what's necessary?
• Group Support: What is it? Where does it come from?
• Peer Pressure: Negative or positive effect?
• Negativism/Hostility: How do you handle it? Why is it there?
• Efficiency: The step beyond just doing it.
• Competition: Against self, teams, a nebulous record.
• Spotting: Why essential?
• Sexism: Who plays what role?
• Carry-Over: Do these fabricated problems have real life significance?
• Fear — Physical & Psychological: Fear of height? Failure? Looking bad?
• Joy/Pleasure: At the heart of it all — the raison d'être.

When leading a discussion, it is a good idea to have the students sit so that they can see everyone in the group. Ask the students to agree not to interrupt the speaker, and not to put down or to ridicule anyone else's ideas or comments (upholding the Full Value Contract). Make sure everyone knows that he/she has the right to pass (remain silent) in any

discussion. The teacher's goal is to establish a supportive group rapport so that individuals won't feel intimidated or frightened to say what's on their minds. Refer back to chapter one for a more detailed write-up on the debrief process and rationale.

Initiatives

Some Initiative problems (*Wall, Beam, King's Finger*) require substantial props and are covered in chapter five; some require a few tactile toys (*Warp Speed, Blind Polygon*); a few simplistic games stand on their own.

Blind Polygon *a.k.a.* Blindfold Square

This simple Initiative problem is a gem to include in your personal bag of tricks. It requires a minimum of props, it's simple to explain (remember), and is invariably well received by participants. Don't forget to spend some time talking about blindfolds and trust.

Objective I: For a blindfolded group, standing in a circle holding a rope, to form a square or triangle configuration using the rope to establish the boundaries.

Objective I Rules:
- No one may let the rope leave their hands for more than 5 seconds at a time.
- The group must decide when they think the figure is correct, at which point they may remove their blindfolds.

Objective II: For a blindfolded group to find the rope before proceeding with Objective I. After blindfolding the group, simply wad up the rope and set it 10' or so away from the group.

Consideration:

Keep your (instructor) comments to an absolute minimum during the attempt.

If no rope is available, have the students hold hands in order to form the requested polygon.

#10 Tin Shoe

Tin shoe indeed! The name gives away the most efficient way to use the props — but don't tell them that.

Props Needed:
- 5 — #10 tin cans (the large type used in the school cafeteria, usually filled with corn, carrots, fruit cocktail, and other non-delectables).
- 2 — 6' saplings or poles
- 2 — 8' sections of 2"x6" boards

Objective I: To move a group across a 30' section of turf using only the props provided above.

Rules:
- If a player touches the turf (grass), he/she must return and begin again.
- All of the props are resistant to whatever noxious substance is on the ground.

Considerations:

Putting your feet into the cans is allowed. Note to the instructor — resist the temptation to suggest this idea. Remember, it's their problem and the solution(s) should come from the group.

Try to set this problem up on a grassy area because of the tumbles frequently experienced.

Objective II: Sitting in a circle, see how fast the group can pass a #10 can from foot to foot all the way around the circle. Try two cans going in opposite directions. Try passing one can per person (each can is initialed or numbered) around the circle, and see how long it takes for each person to get his/her can back. In this case, count each can-to-ground contact as a penalty, and add penalties to achieve a final score. Starting over is not necessary.

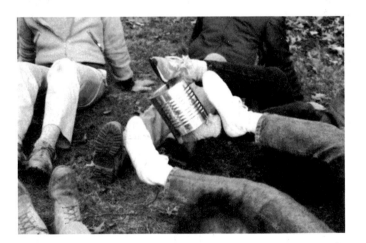

Warp Speed Leading to Group Juggling

This is a highly useable coupling of events. A presentation of *Group Juggling* is offered on pg. 112 of *Silver Bullets,* but you will find this juxtaposing of events even more entertaining and useful.

Warp Speed

Ask your group to circle-up — include your-self in the circle. I've attempted this Initiative game with a group of 32 people, but that's about the largest I'd recommend, and smaller's better.

Announce that you are going to throw a ball (nerf, fleece, etc.) to a person across the circle, and that person will then throw the ball to another person on the other side of the circle. This throw and catch action continues until everyone in the circle has thrown and caught the ball.

Emphasize that each person has to remember who they threw the ball to and who they received it from. To facilitate this throwing/receiving process, ask each person who has *not yet* received the ball to hold both hands up in a receiving position. Once this person-to-person sequence is established, ask them to pass the ball through the established sequence for time. Ask someone who is wearing a digital watch to be the official timer.

After an initial time is established (usually about 1.2 sec. per person average on the first attempt), ask them to see if they can reduce that time by working together more closely as a team. The next couple of sequenced attempts usually show more cooperation, teamwork, etc., and completion time correspondingly drops appreciably. If the first time through is established at 28 seconds, and they eventually drop that time to 20 seconds, indicate that you think (considering their high level of group prowess) that 15 seconds is not out of the question. Amidst groans of "NO WAY," and confident shouts of "GO FOR IT," allow time for some spontaneous brainstorming. If too many ideas are forthcoming, suggest that they try one idea at a time.

The times will continue to drop, in fact well below what they would have thought was

initially possible. Don't be too strict with the "rules," allowing just about any idea that the group feels good about using.

Sample ideas: "Let's rearrange the circle so that the person standing next to you is the one you throw the ball to." "How about arranging the palms of our hands as a ramp so that the ball rolls from start to finish?" These high-energy attempts will eventually reduce their time to less than five seconds — a substantial and impressive drop from the original 28 seconds. They will be impressed and pleased with themselves — smile and agree that they are a very special group. Strange things happen at *Warp Speed*.

Group Juggling

For klutzes and non-klutzes alike.

Now, ask the group to re-establish the initial sequenced throw and catch circle. It never ceases to amaze me that groups can do this with little hesitation and seldom a mistake. As an experiment on one occasion, I asked a group to re-establish the *Warp Speed* circle 24 hrs. later. No problem. I'm sure a behavioral scientist has a ready explanation, but I'm still regularly impressed.

Once re-established, indicate that you are going to start a ball in the familiar sequence and continue to add similar balls in a metronome 1-2-3 throwing pattern until there are almost as many balls in motion as there are people in the group. Whether this is actually accomplished or not is of little consequence. The important thing is the cooperation, fun, and satisfaction resulting from the various (usually chaotic) attempts.

After a couple attempts, ask each thrower to make a unique sound when they throw the ball and a different sound when a catch is made. The "symphony" of sound and movement is beyond explanation.

If you have access to a video camera, try to video a *Group Juggling* sequence — very visual, colorful, and funny.

Squash Balls

This Initiative game set-up lends itself to a variety of approaches. It can be accomplished with or without props, in pairs, as a group, and even by your lonesome. And in addition to all this good curriculum stuff, you get a spontaneous foot massage as you participate.*

---

*Ann Smolowe, Director of Project Adventure's Executive Reach program, and part-time professional masseuse, says that walking on tennis balls stimulates many (I forget exactly, but lots) nerve endings on the bottom of the foot which positively affect other parts of the body, your body. So get walking (rolling), and get stimulated.

Object: You, or you and your partner, try to cross an outlined area of noxious content (let's say puce colored radio-active play dough), by stepping sequentially on a supplied number of tennis balls, which are, of course, resistant to every noxious substance known to woman and man.

Rules and Procedures:

1. Each person is given four tennis balls.
2. The area to be crossed should be a hard surface; asphalt — yes, grass — no.
3. Each individual or pair is offered the use of a stout 6' pole.
4. If someone blatantly touches the floor with any part of their shoe or anatomy, they must return to the start. (Tip — stepping on the ball of the foot, rather than the arch, makes it easier to balance and avoid contact with the floor.)

5. Establish the crossing to be approximately 25'. Mark the start and finish with strips of masking tape.
6. The tennis balls can be shared and placed anywhere on the floor. The balls can be moved and used again.

Variations:

1. To increase the difficulty for one person, don't offer the use of a pole. Spotting may be required for less adept participants.
2. Have pairs or troikas hold hands to increase stability.

The Great Egg Drop

This is a very simple Initiative task to set up and one from which you can expect considerable participant feedback during the debrief. AND, people like it.

Objective: For a small group, 3–5, to design a delivery system that will protect a raw egg dropped from a height of eight feet onto a hard surface. Success and failure is unequivocal; the egg shell either cracks or it doesn't.

Materials Needed:

- Enough raw eggs so that each group can have one — and a couple extras because...
- A roll of half-inch masking tape
- A box of plastic drinking straws (250)
- A plastic garbage bag

Each group is given the following materials:
- 1 raw egg (check for cracks)
- 30" masking tape
- 20 straws

And these instructions: "Your group represents one of many business groups that are vying for a very lucrative construction contract. The contract will be awarded to that HI-TECH group who develops a fail-safe delivery system for the egg, using the least amount of materials and the least amount of time. The essential and final criteria for success, however, is an intact egg at the end of the test. This is particularly significant when you realize that your successful design will establish the structural guidelines for NASA's manned space egg to Mars."

Each group will have 20 minutes to complete their planning and construction. At the end of that time, a spokesperson from each group must make an oral presentation extolling the virtues of their product. The delivery package must also be given a commercial name.

The final decision by the distinguished judges (you), as to which group gets the contract, will be made after each group makes their presentation and the *Egg Drop* is completed.

Breaking of the egg shell does not necessarily eliminate your group, but one of the judges is a Martian trip astronaut....

From a practical standpoint, perform all the drops on top of the plastic garbage bag. It makes discarding of the failed (and slimy) projects considerably easier.

If this Initiative problem is being presented during a class period, be sure to leave some time at the end of class, or at the beginning of the next class, to allow the participants an opportunity to express their feelings about the process, one another, how they felt, etc.

Object Retrieval a.k.a. Chuck-a-Hunk

This splendid Initiative problem involves all the good stuff — thinking, imagination, action, fantasy, risk, and an attractive solution.

The object is for a group to retrieve a fairly heavy (10 lbs.) object that is located near the center of an outlined diameter of approximately 30'.

You will need the following props and geographical set-up:
- One 2' section of 2" diameter hard wood log
- A length of retired belay rope that is longer than 50'
- A length of 9 mm sling rope or 1" webbing that measures 18'–26' long
- One locking carabiner
- One ammo can or bucket with bail
- A substantial hardwood tree located near the center of your 30' diameter outlined

area. This tree must stand alone within this circle and display a trunk/limb bifurcation (crotch) at a height of 12'–15'.

Rules:
- Only the props listed can be used to retrieve the object.
- If *anyone* touches the ground inside the circle, the person closest to the object must start again from outside the circle.
- Set a time limit — 20–30 minutes is reasonable.

The Meuse

If you own a copy of the old *Cowstails and Cobras* (early issue, black cover), look under "Board Stretcher" (pg. 75) for an early presentation of this event. If you're not interested, that's OK, too.

Goal: In search of rare pink porpoise eggs, your expedition team must safely cross the bogs of Lost Swamp. Surprisingly, you have discovered that the boggish water of the swamp is still inhabited by saber-toothed beavers, sneaker-snapping turtles, and the leather-liking Great White Bog-Water Shark. Careful study by your team seems to indicate that their continued existence is directly dependent upon eating whatever fast-food is available in the swamp. Your precise calculations suggest that you have only _____ minutes

to safely cross the swamp before the feeding frenzy will begin again. Time allowed is a function of group size and perceived prowess. Twenty minutes for a group of 10 is about average.

Porpoise eggs aside, you are setting up a series of cinder blocks on a no-touch piece of real estate and asking a group to cross this taboo area using only the provided props, which include a few boards that are measured *not* to fit between some of the cinder blocks. Cruel? Not really, this is meant to be a problem after all.

Prop Tips:
- 4 — 4"x4"x8' boards work well for the crossing planks. 2"x4"x8' boards nailed together will also serve this function, and are actually stronger than the 4x4's.
- Use cinder blocks for the "islands."
- Allow use of a 12'(±) section of 9mm rope.

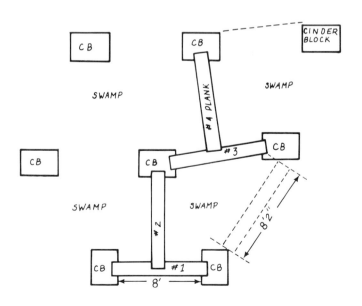

Remember, placement of the cinder blocks is key to making this Initiative problem work. Spend some time before the students show up making sure that the "islands" are in a functional position. Refer to the illustration.

Rules:

1. All team members must start from the same departure point using only the 4 boards and rope provided.
2. Passage can only be made by staying on high ground and avoiding all contact with the swamp's water.
3. Should team members or props come in contact with the water, you must return to the departure point and start over.
4. Subtract one board to make the eventual solution more difficult.
5. If you want to shorten the time necessary to finish the problem, count each swamp touch as a penalty and allow the group to continue.

Leadership Issues — *Jim Schoel*

Going from can to can (*Tin Shoe*), stump to stump (*Zig Zag*), traversing cables (*Mohawk*), getting across the boiling blueberry yogurt lake with large paper rollers (*Jelly Roll*) — all these crossing games have certain similarities. *The Meuse*, however, offers some special opportunities. Using 12 cinder blocks, the task is for the group to move across the sea of "relapse," to the other side where "recovery" is the goal. Framing the event in terms of Alcoholics Anonymous gives focus to their 12 steps of recovery. The lesson is not only available for persons in treatment for their addiction, but applies to prevention thinking, which needs to start out at an early and hopefully untested age.

Spotting is minimal and only needs to occur when great stretches are being made. Perhaps the greatest danger comes from overzealous participants swinging the traversing boards. Unsuspecting group members can get clobbered in the head.

You can add some twists to the Initiative by blindfolding one of the participants and making them an initiate needing sponsorship by the group. This person is essentially helpless and totally dependent. Observe the group to see how well they do with their caring. *The Meuse* can also be timed. The reality hanging over the group is that very few alcoholics, or substance abusers, ever make it into recovery. And for them, relapse is the most common experience. A time limit, set with severe difficulty, can become a metaphor for reality rearing its ugly head. Both of these scenarios provide excellent debriefing topics.

Much of the thinking for this AA application goes to the people at The Institute of Pennsylvania Hospital, and to Chuck Court and Liz Jambour at Parkside Lodge Hospital, Katy, Texas.

All Screwed Up

This screwy event makes up part of a larger and more elaborate Initiative problem (*Macro-Micro Challenge*), but it has proven to be a worthy end in itself.

Props:
- One 6' length of 5/8" diameter threaded rod (approximate cost — $8.25 as of August 1988) per 4–6 participants.
- One nut to fit the rod per participant — 5 players, 5 nuts.

Objective: To see how fast the groups can spin their nuts the full length of the rod. Specifically: at the start, all the players stand with nuts in hand waiting for the *Go* signal. All nuts must be threaded onto the rod, twirled the full length of the rod, and removed before the watch stops. The best time for four nuts on a six foot rod is 2:15. Can you beat that? Do you want to?

Considerations:
- Do not allow use of any lubricant.
- Make sure the rod is well threaded (no strips or crushes) and does not have any burrs.
- Allow sufficient time before the event begins so that the players (team) can discuss strategy.
- Be sure to repeat the event so that the teams can try to better their own times or, more significantly, go for the World Record (as above).

Macro-Micro Challenge

You have already been introduced to the Macro part of this group Challenge; i.e., threading nuts the length of a rod. Here is the follow-up task that represents the Micro Challenge.

You will notice that after having spun four or five nuts the length of a six foot threaded rod, the members of your team will be breathing fairly hard and might make casual mention of pumped-up arms. As soon as the last nut comes off the rod, hand four size 18 tapestry needles to the team, and ask them to thread each needle with a four foot section of size 30 crochet cord. Tie an overhand knot to secure the two loose cord ends. Stop the watch.

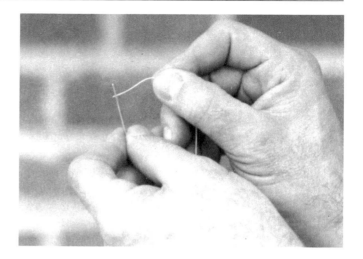

This self-control Challenge scenario is akin to the Nordic event of biathlon in which a participant must cross country ski around a measured course and also fire a rifle accurately during that tour. In this case the events are somewhat different, but the self-control aspects are identical. Who knows, maybe this mini Challenge will be an Olympic demonstration sport in '92.

If there are any aspects of the above Initiative problem that you don't understand, change the rules or wording until you do.

Initiative Run

At first I was not going to include this multi-Initiative tidbit, but the *Initiative Run* was the first "ropes course" building I ever tried at the North Carolina Outward Bound School back in 1969, so my sense of nostalgia wins and here it is — I'm not really apologizing; it's a good series of activities.

Objective: To provide a series of group and individual Initiative problems to be solved in sequence and in such a way that participants must complete a problem before beginning the next.

Procedure and Rules:
1. The group begins at a starting line that is a few yards away from the first Initiative problem. At a signal (this event can be

timed), the group must solve the immediate problem, then continue along an outlined trail, solving and completing each problem.

2. Each problem must have a sheet of instructions on location. The instructor is available to clarify or interpret the rules.

3. An alternate procedure to the above is to provide a compass heading at each site that directs the group to the next problem location.

4. The group finishes when they have *all* crossed a finish line after completing 6–10 tasks.

Considerations:

The course should be designed so that it normally takes a group longer than one class period before they become proficient enough to complete all the elements within the allotted time.

This type of sequential set-up is appealing to all age groups if the problems are geared to a group's capabilities. Business executives will respond well to a series of subtle and somewhat physical problems, while a high school group will react best to a get-over-the-wall type of situation. I'm emphasizing both ends of the performance spectrum — there are obviously in-between levels that apply to almost all groups.

The following list of problems have been chosen because: 1.) people like them and, 2.) they are fairly easy to set up — easy as compared to building a wall.

Problem I

Stretch two sections of 1/4" bunji (shock) cord between two trees or poles at 12" and 48" elevations.

The group objective is either go over or under the cords as quickly and efficiently as possible and without touching the cords. If a touch is made, that person attempting the passage must return and try again, or a one minute penalty may be accepted. Each person gets to make his/her own choice as to whether to attempt a high or low passage, or any passage at all.

Obviously, the open area bounded by the high and low cords is not available for entry because of the deadly shock waves in evidence. (The shock waves originate from the shock cords — you knew that.)

Safety Consideration:

Do not allow students to throw one another over the high cord. Emphasize spotting. Make sure that all rocks and stumps are removed from potential landing areas both in front of and behind the cords. The emphasis in solving these problems is speed and efficiency, but the not-so-hidden agenda is to encourage group cooperation and cohesiveness. Emphasize that a group is not allowed to leave a problem site until everyone has completed their task. Do not allow individuals to leave for the next problem until everyone has gone over or under.

Problem II

Set up a series of hurdles along the path (in a clear area — no roots or rocks) leading to the next problem; six to eight hurdles should be sufficient.

Cut saplings to act as hurdles and use cut 6"–8" diameter logs (vary the lengths) as the hurdle supports. The saplings should measure at least 8' long, and should be light enough to fall off easily if kicked, but not so flimsy that they can blow off the supports.

Arrange the spacing between the support logs so that it's difficult for a runner to establish a smooth stride over the hurdles. And, of course, vary the height of the hurdles for the same reason.

If a hurdle is knocked off, the offender must replace it and begin again at the first hurdle.

A participant may accept help from the group in navigating any of the hurdles; i.e., being lifted or carried over. A minute penalty can be accepted after a conscientious attempt has been made.

Problem III

Standing on a 3'–4' buried stump, a participant is handed a swing rope, and from there must swing over a taboo section of ground and clear a 16" high hurdle at the end of the swing. Distances depend upon the length of the swing rope (pendulum arc), but should be such that an awareness of swing dynamics (pushing off the stump backwards rather than pushing forward) will help achieve the goal of greater distance.

Splice an ample foot loop in the end of the rope allowing those people without much upper body strength a chance at making the swing.

As with all the events, spotting and physical assistance is always encouraged.

If a student touches the taboo turf during an attempt, the swing must be tried again. If a hurdle is knocked off, the student at fault, and the student who last made it successfully, must return and try again.

Problem IV

The entire group must get up and over a large (5'–6' diameter) cable spool. The spool is supported about 5' off the ground, between two supports, by a horizontally lashed section of 2-1/2"–3" OD pipe.

Once an individual has passed over the spool and has touched the ground on the far side, he/she cannot return to the other side (beginning) and physically help anyone. Participants who have not yet gone over can, of course, assist. Spotting is essential for each person on the spool and particularly for the last individual.

Problem V

All participants must make it over a 4'6" high beam without touching it with any part of their body. The 6" diameter beam should be lashed or bolted between two tree supports. Provide a stout (try it yourself) 6'–7' pole for students who think they can vault over the beam.

Spot all vaulting attempts and watch out for the released pole. Be sure to loosen the soil on both sides of the beam and remove any rocks or stumps within a 6' radius of the action.

Do not include this event for younger students who may not have anyone in their group with the strength/coordination to vault.

Problem VI

Set up a length of KMIII (or any such strong static rope) between two trees 20'± apart. With the rope tautly suspended about 10' off the ground, the group must make their way over this swamp of Gram Negative Diplococcus without touching any of the mucoid residue. Anyone so careless as to be slimed must return to the start of this event where a copious collection of Kleenex is kept.

Two 18' sling ropes and two carabiners are offered for those who need assistance and have the prerequisite imagination.

Problem VII

The group tries to get each member through a tire suspended vertically between two support trees. (*Challenge By Choice*, pgs. 44–45.) The last person can receive no aid in getting up and through the tire but can be helped down.

Problem VIII

On a flat section of cleared ground, arrange a series of used auto tires in a challenging stepping stone pattern between a start and finish line. Use enough tires so that more than one route across is possible.

may run across unaided (feet within the tires).

Any touch outside or on top of the tires requires another trip by that person and his/her rider. As you set up the tires for this event, compassionately consider that each carrier is well loaded and will not be able to take large strides. Think — lots of tires close together.

The object is to get the entire group across the outlined area without stepping on the tires or touching the ground outside the tires. To reach the safe side, a participant must be carried. The carrier must also make the return trip stepping inside the tires. The last person

Problem IX

If you have access to a large spool (as used above between two trees), reeve a 3"x20' pipe through the spool and ask the group, as a final challenge, to push and maneuver this "vehicle" through a short obstacle course. The amount of cooperation necessary to turn this cumbersome wheel from left to right, etc., reveals what can become a nightmarish task.

Try inserting roundish rocks into the cavity of the spool, (take out the pipe first). Fill to about 1/3 full and reinsert the pipe.

The stones provide a "rock concert" accompaniment to this rotational Challenge.

Pushing and navigating a huge noisy wheel up a winding dirt road provides a quadriceps quivering finale to this physical series of events.

Take the time to debrief with a group after they have experienced this series of events. Many things happened during the attempts; some obvious and some that will only be revealed by personal comments from the students about how they observed and physically experienced the events. Set aside the time and attempt to provide the facilitation to allow these valuable student insights to emerge.

Chapter 5
Ropes Course Elements

The time spent at the beginning of a semester, "on the field" with the students, working toward feelings of trust, physicalness, and a willingness to accept the unexpected, is essential in eventually gleaning the most from the somewhat spectacular apparatus of the ropes course. After two or three weeks of classes, as the students first attempt the various elements of the course together, they are physically and emotionally "psyched" for what the experience can be. Thus, the ropes course does not simply become a series of cheap thrills and combat-oriented obstacles that they perform as individuals. Instead, the group plays both an active and supportive role as individuals attempt the various elements on the ropes course.

Note:

It is not the purpose of this book to offer construction help in physically setting up these elements, but rather to offer detailed presentation instructions. (See *Challenge By Choice*, a manual for the construction of Low Elements on a Challenge Ropes Course, available from Project Adventure.) A conscientious attempt has been made to depict many of the elements of the ropes course as clearly as possible. If extensive construction is anticipated, it would be wise to contact an experienced individual or organization to circumvent the problems that will arise from using the trial and error method. A good deal of money can also be saved by getting accurate information about the tools and materials needed. It takes an experienced (or intuitive)

eye to assemble these elements in a logical, safe, and imaginative order. Without this experience you may be building a highly complicated, ineffective, potentially dangerous apparatus. Make use of available experience.

The elements of the ropes course are somewhat standardized in design and can be assembled and used in almost any sequence.

Motivation

The student's arms are limp at his/her side; head tilted upward and moving slowly from side to side; jaw slightly slack but also moving.... "No Way! No way you're getting me to do ***that***!" "You guys aren't getting me up there!" The student looks around at the other transfixed students, smiles, and laughs nervously.

That often-used phrase, "No way," is a preliminary release of nervousness, and rather than indicating a purely negative reaction, the words reveal, "Wow, does that look scary! I wonder if I'll be able to do it!"

The awed student may not be the first to volunteer, but these words are no indication that he won't eventually try. The student who says nothing, begins glancing nervously about, and begins taking backwards steps, is the individual who will need the most support.

Some of the following Initiative problems and ropes course elements were included in *Cowstails and Cobras*. The PA staff chose these oldies as favorites and so, sporting a fresh write-up, here they are again to tax and entertain your players.

Nicki Hall photo

The Low Elements

Commando Crawl
Kitten Crawl

Both of these easy-to-install events require a level of commitment that is based on their height above ground and the degree of physical discomfort involved in continuing any

distance beyond the start. What you wear for clothing and how you position your body mitigates the inevitable rope + body + friction = pain formula. (The students in these photos demonstrate proper position, *not clothing*!)

Objective:

With the body situated in a prone, balanced position, to pull and slide across the top of a horizontally or diagonally suspended rope.

Procedure:

The Challenge of the *Commando Crawl* is to either cross the horizontally strung rope on top in a designated (see top left photo) crawl position or to attempt an underneath crossing by using hands and feet in a sloth-like movement (bottom left photo). A more demanding hand-over-hand technique is possible for the stronger, more adept student. Good spotting is necessary for all crossing methods, but particular care should be exercised when spotting the sloth method.

The *Kitten Crawl* is essentially the same as above, except two parallel ropes are utilized for the crossing, necessitating a different body position (right photo).

Consideration:

Crawling/sliding on these events requires long pants and a long-sleeved shirt, otherwise rope burns might be a problem.

Fidget Ladder

If you have attended many county or state fairs, you probably have seen or tried one of these diabolically tricky ladder devices. If you watch someone who has the "feel" for this event scamper to the top, it's hard to appreciate or anticipate the inherent swiveling difficulty of the climb. Making it look easy is a covert carny "come on" to loosen your grasp from the change burning a hole in your pocket.

If one of your more Tarzanic students is zipping through many of the low ropes course elements with no problem and his/her stifled yawn makes you yearn for a humbling activity, this is it. First demonstrate how it's done (remembering what your 157 previous attempts have taught you) and then ask Mr. Cool to give it a try. As his/her body rotates rapidly from ventral to dorsal, you can smile understandingly and say, "Would you like to give it another try?"

Objective:

To move from the ground onto the *Fidget Ladder* and then, using feet and hands only for support, traverse the length of the ladder in order to touch the far support tree.

Rules:

There are different ways and levels of difficulty available for reaching the top of the ladder (most of them not allowed by the carny folks).

- Hardest — ladder contact with only hands and feet, as in the photo.
- Somewhat easier — allow knee contact.

Nicki Hall photo

- Easier yet — allowing occasional full-body contact for resting.
- The slug technique — for those who need some success — constant and full-body contact all the way up the ladder.
- You gotta be kidding — holding the ladder while the student slugs (slimes) his/her way to the top.

As a finishing touch, remember that making final contact with the support tree using your forehead is much harder than using a hand.

Considerations:

You will find that it makes little difference to the students whether **you** can actually climb the *Fidget Ladder*, as long as you are not reluctant to occasionally "have another go." Most people are eventually more impressed by tenacity than by ease of completion. However, if you find yourself constantly spinning around on the ladder and want to at least move up a couple of rungs, try this:

- Keep your center of gravity low; i.e., keep your derrière down.
- Oppose hand and foot movements; when you press with your right hand, simultaneously apply pressure with your left foot, etc.
- Grasp the ladder rope with your hands rather than holding onto the rungs.
- Don't try going up the center of the ladder.
- Practice — adeptness on this activity does not come easily, but once you get the feel, you too can scamper to the top.

Spotting:

The kinetic nature of this activity presents spotting difficulties and should only be spotted by those who have had training in those techniques. If you provide mats, or some equally softened landing area, you can use the element by simply asking a couple of students to hold the ladder stationary until the climber has his/her balance, and step quickly away.

Two spotters *are* needed to stand by the tree that holds the high anchor eye bolt to prevent

participants who have almost made it to the end from falling and spinning into the trunk.

Hickory Jump

Present this event as an extension of the *Trust Dive* exercise, pointing out that catching a person who misses the bar is essentially the same as catching a diver aiming for the sky. The *Hickory Jump* is a task-oriented *Trust Dive*.

Objective:

To attempt to grab a hanging trapeze by diving from on top of one of a series of 5–7 sequentially placed stumps that are graduated incrementally both in height and distance from the trapeze.

Rules and Procedures:

Indicate that the jumpers can choose any stump to start from and that each time they complete a dive (grabbing the bar), they are to move back to the next higher stump for another try. Emphasize that this is a trust exercise and that each participant should push himself/herself to a maximum effort (an eventual miss).

Before the event begins, give each stump a vigorous lateral kick to establish its solidity. If a stump were to break as the result of a dive, ribs and sternum would suffer. Kicking the stumps in some cases (creosoted poles or stumps newly placed) is superfluous, but your obvious and kinetic caring is noticed and appreciated by nervous novice jumpers.

Set up spotters so that 8–10 committed

so be prepared, but put some of the safety concerns ostensibly on the students' shoulders. Emphasizing some type of verbal exchange to establish readiness is a good idea.

people stand in two face-to-face flanking lines under and in front of the trapeze with each spotter turned at about a 45° angle facing the jumper. Ask the spotters to remove any wrist watches or bracelets. Ask the diver to set aside pencils, pens, large buckles, etc., to protect the spotters' arms. A diver should have the choice to either wear or remove his/her glasses as this event is disconcerting enough without having to deal with a fuzzy trapeze.

Mention that each jumper has the responsibility to make sure the spotters are prepared for the dive. It's actually *your* responsibility,

Nothing fancy — for example, jumper asks, "Are you ready?" "Yes, we're ready, (insert jumper's name)."

After a number of jumps have been made, it may become necessary to step in to emphasize attention to detail and spotting function. After some success and repetition, that initial feeling of anticipation and readiness is less keen. Don't let the spotting become lax. Ask the spotters to change positions in the line occasionally, both to experience a different catching position, and to relieve a repeatedly hit appendage.

If a particularly adept jumper makes it to the last couple stumps, assign two spotters to stand next to the first two stumps to protect the diver's feet. It's ordinarily not a problem (if a diver progresses sequentially to the back stump, he or she is obviously capable of a substantial leap), but a nervous diver may doubt his/her ability and jump only half-heartedly from the last stump. If your two assigned spotters watch only the diver's feet, they will be able to protect toes and shins from contact with the forward stumps.

Ask one of the taller spotters to stop the swinging action of the bar for the next diver. However, if a diver has made two or three attempts from a particular stump to no avail, offer a little help by swinging the bar toward the diver. This pendulum action offers an easier jump 50% of the time.

Considerations:

If you have an experienced group you might want to consider an advanced variation.

After those choosing to do so have made an attempt or two, ask if anyone wants to further challenge him/herself with a blindfolded dive from the stump just in front of the last stump completed. This query is usually met with the typical comments, "You gotta be kidding." Or, more succinctly, "No way!" But there always seems to be one or two in a group who are up for something different.

If you decide to try blindfolded trapeze diving, take some plastic electrician's tape and copiously cover the cable bights and rapid link openings of the trapeze connectors to prevent accidental finger insertion during a dive.

Offer the volunteer a blindfold (bandana). Tie it on securely and escort him/her to the designated stump. Help the diver ascend and assign spotters to assure a balanced posture. Place yourself in back of the trapeze and in line with the diver. Ask the diver to face toward your voice (all other comments must end) and to extend his/her hands (held to-gether) in a dive position. Verbally orient the diver so that his/her hands are lined up directly toward the center of the trapeze. Such orientation is necessary to prevent errant dives toward support trees or away from spotters. Spotters then offer their verbal readiness and the dive takes place.

I think you will be surprised at how many initially reluctant divers will eventually queue up for a blindfolded attempt. Diving for the trapeze blindfolded is not a macho stunt, but rather an extension of the trust and Challenge experienced up to this point. Offer the Challenge, offer support, be encouraging — don't coerce.

Mohawk Walk

This is an excellent low ropes course element to instill participant excitement and encourage working together to achieve a goal. I indicate to a starting group that they are to attempt the cable traverses en masse and count individually the number of times that each person touches the ground; i.e., slips off the

cable. At the end of the traverse, each participant states his/her number of falls, a total is taken, and another attempt is initiated to try and better that mark. This somewhat laid-back approach gets away from the tedium of "...if anyone touches the ground, everyone has to return to the start and..."

Objective:

To move a group from start to finish on top of and along a series of five to seven tautly strung cables between support trees. The cables measure no more than 18" off the ground.

Considerations:

Spotting is dependent on the group's competency and ability to balance. Have members spot each other if you assess that need among participants. Spotting is necessary on the final cable for those people doing it as a solo tension traverse.

Use caution if you time this event because hurrying will cause slipping on the cable and has the potential for diminishing the feeling of working together.

As a further Challenge (for another time when the participants are more comfortable balancing on cable), ask individuals if they can solo navigate the entire *Mohawk Walk.* Again, count the number of falls and ask the cable walker to better that number on the next try. Spotting on both sides of the cable is advised during these solo attempts.

Leadership Issues — *Bob Ryan*

The Mohawk Walk at our training site in Hamilton has quite a few sections and is fairly long and difficult. Partly for that reason I usually think of using this activity when a group is ready for a substantial Challenge. For a typical group that is working together fairly well I like this version of the rules: if anyone falls off (i.e., steps down) or receives support from a spotter, he (alone) must return to the beginning. If a participant falls off and inadvertently pulls off another person, then those two must return to the beginning. One of the reasons that I like this version of the rules is that those individuals who start out in the metaphoric "lead" usually fall off and go to the rear of the line. Participants who were safely located in the middle of the pack suddenly find themselves in the front of the line. The effect of this is usually beneficial in encouraging some risk taking and allowing the group to discover some of the hidden talents of its group members.

When additional spotters are needed, I allow participants to step down at a particular tree, spot for a while, and then return to the spot where they stepped down. This also helps give a rest to those participants who are getting sore feet from standing on the cables. Be aware that enthusiastic participants will sometimes execute a dive-like maneuver as they approach a tree. Safety dictates that you anticipate and prohibit this technique. Although I have seen some creative problem solving involving the use of clothes as aids, I don't allow their use here. Belts all connected together have a bad habit of breaking, connecting them often takes a lot of time, and they're not approved by the U.I.A.A.

I don't think it is necessary to orchestrate the precise outcome of this or any Initiative. Nevertheless, we know that if the problem is too easy or too hard, the opportunity for learning will be less. If time or skill level is limited don't hesitate to change the rules to achieve the desired degree of Challenge. Try counting "falls" as mentioned above or use the same rules and shorten the distance: "See if you can get the entire group to tree #4," in the allotted time. A short (3 ft.) removable section of rope can be added to a support tree or to an overhead cable as another means of changing the level of difficulty. Whatever rules you adopt or adapt, try to be clear and reasonably consistent in following them so that the group's sense of success is not diminished.

Hole In One

This is a fine event for demonstrating to a group that they can improve their efficiency performance by discussing previous attempts and by working together as a team. Decrease in performance time can be dramatic.

Objective:

To move an entire group through a suspended truck/tractor tire as quickly and efficiently as possible — a timed event.

Rules:

- I'd suggest not allowing females to enter the tire feet-first, particularly if the tire opening is small and the group is co-ed. Shirts and blouses will be frictioned above anatomical areas best left covered.
- Encourage a group to try this timed event at least twice so that they can experience the benefits of cooperation (group effort), as evidenced by a faster time.
- Spot the first couple of participants through the tire or until there are enough spotters to take your place. Alert and constant spotting is necessary during timed events.

Maze

If your administrator is concerned about budget matters and/or cutbacks, and asks, "What can we get that's useful for the least amount of money?", *The Maze* is it. I am consistently amazed at the positive response to this very basic Initiative situation.

When presenting this event, and other Initiative problems that require loss of sight, I simply ask the participants to keep their eyes closed rather than hand out blindfolds. The benefits are:

- Hygienic concerns are eliminated (there are never enough blindfolds anyway).
- Being blindfolded (loss of sight) is a double trust situation. The participants trust that the instructor will not make fun of them: the instructor trusts the participants to keep their eyes closed.

This is a Challenge by Choice situation, because if participants are uncomfortable with their eyes closed, they can take an occasional peek to make sure that everything is okay. The level of Challenge is up to the individual.

Objective:

For an individual (or an individual working as part of a group) to make his/her way blindfolded out of a maze fabricated from small diameter rope.

Rules:

- Each person must maintain contact with a rope at all times.
- Maneuvering under a rope is not allowed, unless the rope is overhead.
- Each participant must move slowly and not lead with his/her head.
- As participants find the exit, the instructor taps them on the shoulder, tells them to remove the blindfold (or open their eyes), and quietly watch the remainder of the group try to make their way out of the amazing *Maze*.
- Make up your own rules about helping one another or re-entering the *Maze* after having discovered the exit. Re-finding the exit is not as easy as it sounds.

Younger children seem to appreciate a more fanciful approach — a preliminary story that tells why they are in the maze and why they want to get out. Make lots of jungle sounds and splash around some water to supplement your true-to-life adventure tale.

Nitro Crossing
Prouty's Landing
Disc Jockeys

There's a lot of program to be had from a single swing rope, and these three swinging Initiative elements are excellent examples. A swing rope is highly usable for most groups, providing exciting body movement (swing), and immediate success/failure. The elements often combine group or individual Challenge, are applicable for a fantasy approach, and can be used indoors or outdoors with equally positive results.

Objectives:

- **Nitro Crossing**. To move a group of people and a container of "nitro" from one safe area to another over a measured expanse of taboo turf by means of a swing rope.

- **Prouty's Landing.** To swing the same group from a safe area over a measured expanse of taboo turf and onto a 3'3"x3'3" Prouty's Landing platform, where **all** swingers must remain balanced for a five-second span.
- **Disc Jockeys.** For each individual in the group to swing over a trip wire onto a series of pyramidally arranged 2' diameter wooden discs (hula-hoops, bicycle tires), so that eventually one person occupies each disc.

Rules:

Nitro Crossing

- If a person falls into or touches the taboo turf, only he/she must return and begin again.
- If someone knocks off either of the trip-wires, the entire group must begin again.
- Do not allow *uncontrolled* stepping or jumping on people's backs.

- Use water in a #10 tin can for the "nitro" in an outdoor setting. Use confetti or ping-pong balls in a shallow container when swinging indoors on sacrosanct or warpable gym floors.

Prouty's Landing

- The entire group must swing over an initial trip-wire as in *Nitro Crossing*.

- The ground between the trip-wire and the platform is taboo turf and anyone who inadvertently touches the turf (ground) must begin again.
- Each person must try to land on the platform and stay there until the entire group is on the platform together and remains balanced there for a minimum of five seconds. Stepping or slipping off the platform results in a trip back to the start for the offender.

- If anyone knocks off the trip wire, everyone on the platform must return to the start and begin again.

Disc Jockeys

- Make available wooden discs or used bicycle tires equal to the number of participants.
- Arrange the discs or tires in a pyramidal fashion with the pyramid base located about

8' from the swing rope. Discs or tires are set about 14" apart. A solution requires one participant standing on or within each disc.
- Two feet on a disc is the limit. If three feet end up on a disc, both participants must return to the start.
- A participant can step to only one more disc beyond the one they initially make contact with, IF only one foot makes contact with the first disc. As soon as both feet are located on a disc, that is where the participant must stay.
- A participant may be physically passed onto any disc within the pyramid, if he/she is initially caught.
- If the ground is touched at any time, the erring participant must return to the start.
- If the trip-wire is knocked off its supports at any time, all participants must return to the start.

Spider's Web

A put-up/take-down, customized, fabricated "web" which incorporates the latest in high tech spider design and spinning.

Objective:

• The group must try to get through the web without touching any of the web material (or the spider gets you — you knew that). After a web opening is used by an individual, it is "closed" to further passage by anyone else until all group members are safely through.

Rules:

• If a participant touches a section of web during passage, only that person must return and start again. There is no electricity in the web.

• If a helping person touches the web for any reason, that individual also must return and start again: the spider has eclectic tastes.

• Once a web opening is used, it cannot be used again.

Leadership Issues — *Mark Murray*

One of the most (if not the most) popular low elements on a ropes course is the *Spider's Web*. It has strong visual appeal and tends to generate both excitement and curiosity. When approaching it, the nature of the problem immediately becomes apparent to the group. A sense of Challenge piques the group's interest, and their energy level is elevated. Preliminary comments from the group indicate that not only do they see the element as achievable, but also sense that each of them will have an important role in solving the Initiative.

Spider's Web has the potential for being an extremely powerful Initiative. But it depends on the leader's understanding of two important leadership issues: framing the experience, and

Nicki Hall photo

observing behaviors which exemplify the themes this activity develops.

The initial framing of the experience is critical. Based on your presentation of the rules, the *Web* becomes either a fairly simple activity or an exasperatingly difficult one. The key is in the following two statements; 1.) Once an individual successfully (nobody touches the web) gets through the hole, that hole is closed and can or cannot be re-opened (your choice). 2.) Once a hole is *chosen* by an individual, it cannot be used by anyone else. The can or cannot part of the first statement depends upon the range of consequences established for touching the web. Touches can result in the following; only the person touching returns, all people in contact with the person touching return, any touch means all people return. Deciding on these consequences is determined by assessing your group and your web. Just as no two webs are identical in the number and size of holes, no two groups are identical in the number and size of people. Likewise, the goals of your group, and its stage of developmental readiness, will help you decide on the appropriate consequences.

As a leader, what attracts me to this element are the number of themes that emerge for discussion: organization and planning, group needs vs. individual needs, reinforcement of stereotypes regarding physical strength and gender. At the start of the *Web*, groups often realize that to be successful, some planning and organization is necessary. The difficulty occurs when plans need to be adjusted due to circumstances resulting from an attempted solution. They simply forget to re-group and modify their original plan. Also, in their planning I usually observe that group needs preempt those of the individual: "Denise here is your hole. Justin you go through this one. Eric you should either go first or last because you are the biggest and strongest and we need you to help lift." The concept of individual

choice is lost until the group has a chance to reflect on their behavior. And why is it always the Erics in the group who have to go first or last? Why not Denise or Justin? Gender stereotyping, based on physical size and strength, is overtly reinforced in this Initiative. Infrequently, however, there is that one risk-taker who identifies the issue and verbalizes what many other group members are thinking and feeling. This observation is often met with denial or rationalization, and only after the experience will the group be willing to consider it.

In my experience, the *Web* is often the one element that begins to generate some conflict in the group, even if the group has been successful in its completion. Members start identifying behaviors that focus on task completion without regard for needs or feelings of group members. These observations open the door for discussions as to which is most important in their group: a focus on the task or a focus on the members. I will often return to this activity and repeat it, adding difficulty of another degree or type, such as more stringent consequences for a touch, or imposing some type of handicap on one, some, or all group members. This allows the group to assess by comparison progress made on any of the previously identified issues. Often, they don't complete the web successfully on this second attempt, but they report feeling much better about their work.

Because of the struggles which evolve from this activity, I find that the *Web* becomes a metaphor for the entire Adventure experience. To really understand it, you cannot go over it, under it, or around it. You must go through it.

Swinging Log

The name describes this event. The 25'–30' log is suspended 8"–10" above the ground by support cables connected to the ends of the log.

Objectives:

- From a balanced position at one end of the log (holding onto the cable at the start), try to walk unaided from one end of the log to the other. If a participant falls off, that attempt is over. Spotters can walk on either side of the log walker, if necessary, but this is not a critical spotting situation. If you choose to use spotters, alert them to the danger of a moving log.
- Scratch a line in the dirt parallel to the log and about 3' away. Standing and starting behind this line, try to step up on the log and maintain a balanced position for five seconds. Time starts when the log is first touched. This simple activity is infectiously

fun and more difficult than just reading would indicate.

- Two participants try to unbalance one another and become temporary King/Queen-of-the-Log. Starting position is at each end of the log (holding onto the cable for balance). Players are allowed to walk toward one another in an attempt to dislodge the other person, but there is no physical contact allowed. Contests rarely last more than 30 seconds, and not many log-riders reign as champion for more than a couple of attempts.

- Ask teams of three to try and balance simultaneously on the log and maintain their balance for five seconds. All three must step up on the log together. Do not allow large groups to try a group-mount or the log will sooner or later break: usually sooner than later.
- *Ride the Wild Log* — To swing onto the log from a specified starting point using a knotted swing rope. A participant pushes off strongly in a wide arcing swing; i.e., not toward the support tree, and approaches the swing log at almost a right angle. The object is to land softly on the log (legs acting as shock absorbers) and stay on for five seconds after first contact — a Challenge that becomes more apparent when you are the swinger.
- Wearing a hat on this swinging event (*Ride the Wild Log*) adds some role-playing pizzaz to an already exciting experience. When a rider lands on the log, he/she must release the rope with *one* hand, and in one fluid motion snatch off his/her hat with the free hand — at the same time yelling some appropriate Western yahoo type of exclamation.

Tension Traverse

The triangularly arranged *Tension Traverse* event is a ropes course classic. If you can only afford installing a few elements, make sure this is one of them. Spotting, balance, determination, trust, heavy breathing...it's all here.

Objective:
- To traverse around a low triangular arrangement of taut cables using only a rope attached to one of the trees for balance support.
- A tension cable strung over water or mud provides additional Challenge and consequences that need no spotters or further explanation.

Consideration:

Spotting for the *Tension Traverse* is particularly important because falls are common; spotting positions are critical. The spotters must stand in a position that puts them behind the participant; i.e., between the participant and the anchor point. No matter how many times you tell a wobbling walker to step off the cable and let go of the rope when he/she loses control, the rope remains as the last vestige of control, and it is gripped fiercely while the walker pendulums into the ground (or, more becomingly, into the arms of a properly positioned spotter).

Wild Woosey

Who knows where these crazy names come from. I've named a few, but this one is from the whimsical imagination of a forgotten instigator. *Wild Woosey* doesn't say a thing about the event (I'm not even sure how to pronounce it), but it seems to fit. Know what I mean?

Objective:

- Two individuals creatively and physically support one another as they attempt to traverse the lengths of two diverging cables that are tautly strung between supports about 2' above the ground.

Considerations:

- In keeping with the time-honored technique of not offering instructions amidst the stumbling and fumbling (physical and intellectual) of participants, let a group spend some time trying to figure out the body gymnastics necessary to solve the problem.

- If a hint is eventually necessary, use the architectural example of why some buildings' superstructures are stronger than others. More specifically, ask why gymnasium roofs characteristically leak. The answer to this query, and the problem itself, is that a flat gym roof (like a flat configura-

Paul Radcliffe photo

tion of hands and arms) provides a weaker structure than a peaked roof (hands and arms held high, pelvis in). If your two participants make like an A-frame, it works. Try it!

- Two spotters should be used at the start, standing on the outside of the cables. The spotters then move under the participants after they move away from the start tree. Spotting for this event is best accomplished with the spotters supporting themselves by putting their hands on their knees.

So, why *Wild Woosey*? I have no idea what the name of this event means. I suppose it would be easier and more categorical to use numbers or letters to designate games and ropes course elements: but how abysmally boring. "Today's activities were useful — I particularly liked Game #7, and was pleased at how it prepared us for Event #14 on the ropes course."

Leadership Issues *— Jim Schoel*

Two cables diverging in the woods stretch the body as well as the imagination as participants edge their way out from upright safety toward horizontal vulnerability. Add elements of difference; height, weight, sex, likes and dislikes, and you have a true balancing act. The task should be framed in terms of balance because the participants cannot stand alone. They have to lean against the other person if they expect to be in any way successful. They also need to learn the meaning of the word compensation. If there is a variance in strength, size, and ability, success must come as a result of being aware of what the other person is going through, and acting accordingly. In other words, it won't work for one person to bull through the event. It is similar to when I've taught rowing to crews of four, with one oar per rower. You can pull as hard as you want, but if you're not thinking of the

rower opposite you, the boat will go around in circles.

I like to stress the issues of effort and vulnerability. The amount of effort required surprises everyone who tries the event, for the further out on the wires the participants go, the more exhausting the effort becomes. The element evolves into a mutual struggle of two people who are literally fighting to get to the end. The struggle involves vulnerability because they are laid out with their head, chest, and groin areas exposed. They're safe, but totally dependent upon each other and on the spotters edging along below them. The result is exhilarating, for the mixture of effort and vulnerability creates an opening-up in an intensely physical way.

This is the closest we can get in the low elements to the mutual experience of the *Dangle Duo*. As I sometimes put people on the *Dangle Duo* who either don't know each other or who don't like each other (or both), I'll make a similar match with *Wild Woosey* pairs. This has to be done carefully, of course, and one must be ready to deal with any emergent issues. However, it's a nice way to learn about someone through inter-dependence and to work through problems. And since the group is so necessary for spotting the activity, a large number can become involved in the experience. Beau Bassett, a PA trainer, provides an additional twist by having the participants talk about their goals while doing the traverse. This can take away from the concentration required to complete the objective, but, on the other hand, it provides a mixture of modalities, in that the cognitive and the physical are being forced to operate hand in hand. A level of honesty can be reached in this way. A participant once stated in a debrief that he never would have gotten to his true feelings about his goals if he hadn't had the vigor of this activity to spur him on.

TP Shuffle

Truly an Initiative event that anyone can build. Take a look at the illustration. Could you build that? I guess so! Better build one then — somebody might ask why you didn't.

Objective:

- For a group of ten to twenty students, standing balanced on a horizontal telephone pole, to change ends on the pole without touching the ground.

Bob Nilson

Rules:

- Starting position for a group of twenty is to have two groups of ten facing each other while balanced on the log.
- Time the group effort in order to establish a record that the same group can attempt to best during a second or even third try. Assign a 15-second penalty each time someone touches the ground and add this penalty total to the final clock time.
- The second and third attempts usually result in considerable improvement because of increased cooperation and experience. Don't forget to point out that fact; this isn't all for fun you know...

The Beam

You can think of the *Beam* as an existential *Wall*. Or, you can think of it as a log suspended eight feet off the ground between two support trees. A right or left brain decision, I suppose.

Objective I:

To physically move a group up and over a horizontally suspended beam, the bottom of which measures 8' to the ground. This 8' measurement can vary, of course, depending upon what age level will be using the *Beam*.

Rules:

- Everyone in the group must make it up and over the beam in order to achieve the goal.
- No more than two participants on top at a time, with one additional person in the process of going over.
- Everyone not physically involved in the actual attempt must be in a spotting position.
- Once participants have gone over the beam they cannot return to the beginning and physically help a climber. Spotting, however, is always encouraged.
- Climbers should not be thrown over the log.
- Head-first rolls over the beam are allowed with multiple spotters in position.

Objective II:

To see how many participants can get over the beam within a 2 minute time limit. Discuss spotting roles and positioning before attempting these fatiguing efforts.

Rules:

- Same rules as above except that every person in the group must go over the beam; no repeats.

Objective III:

From a two-arm hang position beneath the beam, to see if an individual can get over the beam by his/her lonesome.

Rules:
- The participant can be helpcd from beneath to get a firm grip on the log.
- Two spotters must stand under the participant when he/she achieves a dorsal-down position under the beam.

The Wall

"If you don't have a *Wall*, you don't have a ropes course." I'm sure there some ex-Outward Bound folks who still adhere to this opinion — I think I used to, and for good reason. The *Wall* provides that initially impossible Challenge that's both visual and physically imposing. You know, standing at the base of a twelve-foot wall, that you alone are not going to be able to scale this formidable obstacle by yourself, but ten to fifteen minutes later, your group pats itself on the back for having achieved the impossible. On reflection, you realize that the word impossible is too often and casually used, and more significantly, that you are capable of more than you dreamed possible. A *Wall* is comparatively expensive...but it's worth it.

Objective:

To physically move a group over an 8'–14' wall in an efficient and safe manner.

The 8'–14' range of height is best considered because of the wide range of student types and ages that will be attempting this Challenge; 8' at the 4–6 grade level and 14' for some adept college groups.

Rules:
- No more than 4 people are allowed on the wall at a time, including the person in transit.

- The sides of the wall may not be used in any way.
- The vertical support trees or poles cannot be touched.
- Cracks and knotholes cannot be utilized for ascending.
- After a person has ascended the front of the wall and descended the back, he cannot come back to the front of the wall and offer physical aid. He may return to help spot, however, and should be encouraged to do so.

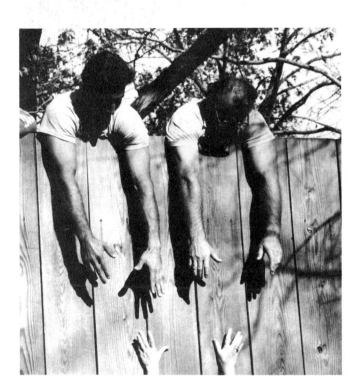

- Anyone not physically involved in helping people over the wall should be in a spotting position, front or back.
- When climbing down, students should have the descending rope in both hands and should touch each 4"x4" with their feet.
- If a person leans over the wall in an attempt to get the last student over, that person must be supported by two other participants, both of whom have their feet on the standing platform.

- Articles of clothing cannot be removed to aid a climber.

Consideration:

The most common fall experienced while ascending the wall results from unintentional lateral movement along the face of the wall before the climber makes hand contact with a person on top. Place spotters laterally on each side of the climbing action in addition to the underneath position.

Leadership Issues *— Jim Schoel*

The most naked and physical item in our "bag" is the 12' *Wall*, leering at us out there in the woods as part of our obstacle course. Instead of touching being a no-no, it is imperative that participants get fully involved in grasping at anything that will get them up, over, and down, safely.

When leading the activity, I go through the usual group questioning of potential safety issues. I fill in what the group left out, stressing the fact that *anyone* who is off the ground must be watched like a hawk by all participants, with the attendant swooping ability of good spotters. Leaders need to stay involved because even highly functioning groups can get carried away with the task at hand and lose sight of each other. More than once I've had to swoop in to catch someone. Also, be aware that no two participants climb the same way. Climbers may be put in compromising, stretched and pulled positions and might need your intervention if unable to express themselves, or if the group isn't listening. Grasped clothing can be embarrassing. If a participant's shirt is pulled off, or pants are pulled down, a wonderful group experience can turn into a solid embarrassment for that person, putting a damper on everyone's experience. Talking about this in the beginning provides the group an opportunity to develop some strategies.

The Wall, as an obstacle, can be seen as that which separates us from what we want to do, from our group goals. It is a group goal that cannot be accomplished without full participation. If framed in terms of issues facing the group, such as communication, *The Wall* then represents a solid lack of it. The goal becomes the defeat of non-communication. Once the group is over, they will be in a "nirvana" where everyone adheres to the Full-Value

Contract. Too bad it's impossible to achieve such a state, but it doesn't hurt to try! It's the fun and extreme energy required from everyone that relieves tension and puts the group on an elevated level. They feel capable of anything, even if only for a little while.

Another way to frame *The Wall* is to get the group to think in terms of personal walls. "What obstacles stand in your way, that keep you all tangled up?" "Are there walls in your life between your friends, or members of your family?" When everyone is over, get them to think about breaking down or conquering those personal walls. It sure helps having other people give you a hand to get over.

King's Finger

This used to be called "The Vertical Pole and Tire," but someone commented, "There must be a better name than THAT." So now we call it *King's Finger*, and WHO KNOWS what that means. See the following scenario fabrication to further confuse the issue.

Objective:
To take the tire off the vertical pole, touch the ground with it, and put the tire back on the pole as quickly and efficiently as possible.

Scenario I:
To take the "ring" off the *King's Finger* in order to save the Prince's life, because the ring was enchanted and was part of the betrothal package that the King's mother surreptitiously lifted from her son's ex-wife's jewelry box. She was, of course, really ticked off and vowed revenge (or worse!) against the poor Prince who wasn't even aware that his Dad's ex was the "girl" he planned to marry. Well, you can imagine...

Scenario II:
To put the "ring" on the *King's Finger* because...Your turn to dream up an applicable fantasy.

Considerations:
- Acting as the safety factor, watch the people who are being used as stepladders and stop the process if they are in obvious pain.
- Keep people aware of not letting the tire fall in an uncontrolled fashion.
- Do not allow participants to sit or stand on top of the pole.

Tire Traverse a.k.a. Swinging Tires

Rules and Procedures:
The Challenge of crossing the tires can be experienced either as an individual or as a group (perhaps including some fantasy about having to carry a heavy object during the traverse or having to escape a herd of rabid gerbils that are to arrive in 27 minutes, ± a few seconds).

Timing individual and group attempts across the tires also has merit if win/lose competition is downplayed. Including a 4"x4"x12' extraneous board (that can't touch the ground) tempts a group to try things that may not be necessary.

Stretch short sections of 1/2" polypropalene rope (brightly colored and cheap) perpendicular to the desired swinging direction of the tires, to act as starting and ending lines. How else will you know where the poisoned peanut butter starts and ends?

If your geographical locale has the advantage of various wet or muddy spots, I'd suggest stringing a few tires over such an obvious area of viscous Challenge. (See photo above.)

Objective I:

To move the entire group across a don't-touch-the-ground-because-the-instructor-said-so area using only the swinging tires as transport.

Rules:

- If an individual touches the ground (taboo area?) between the start and finish lines, that person must return to the start.

- If a "bomb" is one of the props available and the bomb touches the turf (BOOM!), everyone who has made it across must return.
- If a 4"x4"x10' board is one of the props and it touches the turf, everyone must return to the start and use of the board is terminated for the remainder of the problem.
- If a rope length is available as a prop and it touches the turf, use of the rope ends at that point.

Considerations:

Spotting is optional on this event because the tires swing in erratic arcs with the resulting difficulty of staying near the participant while at the same time trying to keep from being hit by a tire. Some participants will require spotting because of a lack arm strength, and group members can help by spotting these participants. Make sure the potential fall area under the tires is "softened" earth, completely rid of obstacles.

It is a good idea to spot at the far end of a traverse as the fatigued participant attempts to swing over the end line.

Objective II:

To individually cross the suspended tires (Start to Finish) as fast as possible.

Rules:

- Go for it and don't touch the ground.

Consideration:

Do not try to spot these speed attempts.

Nicki Hall photo

The High Elements

"Yet lofty ropes may offer respite from the murky gambit of tedious days" — *Adonious Clavidicus, 337–369 AD*

High ropes! Dry mouth, sweaty palms, trembling knees — the whole negative anticipation scenario; and it's a bad rap. Now, I'll admit that Project Adventure uses fear as a tool toward achieving greater self-awareness and as an obstacle to overcome (unseen but keenly felt), but using fear as a prod or an evaluation ploy should not be part of the programmed Adventure scene.

The use of high ropes course elements makes up a comparatively small part of the Adventure curriculum as a whole; maybe 15–20%. There is a lot of semester space filled with games, Initiative problems, and trust activities (many of which involve low ropes elements) used in a preliminary way to promote recognition of each other as capable humans that are rather likeable, and to cause comfortable communication to happen (talking) as the result of taking part in the activities. The high ropes elements offer a sense of pizzaz and closure to the low activities. The "psych" value of leading up to high ropes participation guarantees (with most students) active and enthusiastic participation, notwithstanding the innate fear of heights, because of the weeks spent communicating, cooperating, and building trust. To bring a group out on a one-day basis is not necessarily bad, but a no-preliminary approach hints of cheap thrills (performing for the rush rather than the accomplishment), and does not begin to utilize the affective benefits of high ropes participation.

Schools and various groups do contract with Project Adventure to come to our ropes course site and use the course on a per day basis. Such brief participation is a scheduling and administrative fact of life. However, I want you to be aware that the semester or even full year approach to the PA model provides by far the best and most effective utilization of instructional time and facilities.

Let's take a look at some high elements.

Two Line Bridge

The *Two Line Bridge* is actually a three line bridge (including the belay cable). The two parallel cables that provide support for hands and feet are about 42 inches apart and can be located as high off the ground as the support trees (or poles) allow. *Two Line Bridges* in excess of 100 feet long have been installed, but remember in your planning that the longer the cables, the less stability will be available toward the center of the crossing.

The *Two Line Bridge* is a good choice for a FIRST high element. Navigating the crossing is relatively easy and stability of the student can be unobtrusively controlled by the belayer.

In over twenty years of working on and with ropes courses, I have never seen anyone spontaneously fall off a *Two Line Bridge*. I'm sure that observation has some significance, and if it does, you're welcome.

Leadership Issues — *Dick Prouty*

One of the leadership issues present in all high elements is introducing the element in such a way that the Challenge relates to group goals. An alternate name for the *Two Line Bridge* is the Postman's Walk. Square rigged vessels in the era of sail had a rope line running under the cross beams, or posts, that held the sails. Sailors set the sails by walking out on these lines, often at heights considerably higher than forty feet, and often with a moving deck below them. Using this name for the element points to the similarity of the move-

ments and Challenge between the two activities. When introducing this activity to young adolescents, I often call it the Postman's Walk and describe the parallels. By discussing the age of the sailors who set sails aloft (often 14–17 years old, many schooner captains were under the age of twenty), students are more readily able to relate to the activity. By discussing the differences in life responsibilities between adolescents in the age of sail and today, students begin to make a connection between the Challenge of the *Two Line Bridge/* Postman's Walk and the Challenges of taking on more responsibility in their own lives. The five to ten minutes spent framing the activity within this context (or another more relevant to the goals of your group), can make a big difference in how participants approach the activity.

Using a low *Two Line Bridge* as a first belayed activity has several advantages; the height is less intimidating than other high elements, the activity itself is usually not that physically challenging, and the belay down is a nice, modestly challenging activity that gives the instructor a chance to discuss the meaning of appropriate support from the group. The use of the Challenge by Choice philosophy in framing the Challenge, lets each individual know that they are in control of their choice, and keeps possible panicky fear reactions to a minimum. It is appropriate, when debriefing the first student's descent, to model positive support, and if necessary, actually show students what this support is.

Dangle Do (Duo)

This physically demanding ropes course element is a real fooler. As you stand at the bottom looking up at each ascending rung, the difficulty of moving your bod from rung to rung is apparent. The hidden Challenge, obscured by the perspective of your bottom-looking-up location, is that each rung is 2–3 inches farther apart than the previous pair. This sneaky construction positioning is, of course, purposeful in order to provide a subtle Challenge. Being occupationally involved in Challenging people, I have found, with few exceptions, that if you present a series of tasks where uncertainty of outcome and a reasonable amount of risk and/or fear is involved, people will select the easier Challenges. Sometimes, therefore, the situation invites a bit of clandestine Challenge.

Leadership Issues — *Bob Ryan*

This has become one of the most popular and effective of the high elements. There are a couple of things that make this element special. While most high elements feature the participant coping with a more or less individual Challenge, *Dangle Duo* is a two-person Challenge where team work and strategy are more important than height or athletic ability. And where some elements may turn out to be easier than they look, that's not the case here. Two classic observations are made by climbers; "It moves," and, "Say, are these rungs getting farther apart?" This is usually observed by the first pair of volunteers as they sit on rung #3. Since the side support cables are off limits, proper spacing of the rungs is very important for achieving the right degree of Challenge. Typically, this means that after the first several rungs, climbers can no longer reach the next rung from a sitting position. The commitment required to continue after this point is part of the power of the element. Participants seldom forget with whom they attempted the *Dangle Duo*.

Some practical considerations for running this element: Participants should be carefully spotted from the ground until the belays become effective. Usually this means when the climbers are standing on rung #1. Spotters should take care not to be injured by the swinging bottom rung. Belayers should be

Nicki Hall photo

particularly alert to falls off one rung and onto the rung below. A very loose belay is not usually appropriate. Watch for wrapped belay ropes that occur when the climber ascends the "wrong" side of the rung. And when lowering the climbers down, have other participants pull the bottom of the ladder away from the climber's line of descent.

Zip Wire *a.k.a.* **Flying Fox**

This exhilarating event is pure experiential gravy: literally all thrill, no skill. *The Zip Wire, Flying Fox, Slide-for-Life*, is the classic and most exciting way to descend from a high ropes course. From thirty to one hundred feet up, looking down at a lot of space below your feet, and experiencing the anxious anticipation of sliding into that void, provides a poignant moment of decision. The ride down, although admittedly fun, doesn't have much programmatic function. The value remains in the decision-making process (getting your butt off the platform) that must take place in order to begin the ride: the reaction to trust, or "letting go."

Most *Zip Wire* set-ups exhibit one of two stopping or braking systems; the TRUST brake and the GRAVITY brake. A gravity brake is the most predictable of the pair. Using gravity as the impetus, a rider zips to the bottom of the cable's arc (the belly) and then begins the slowing process as he/she continues rolling up the sloping cable until gravity and friction exert enough drag to slow the rider to a stop. Of course, there will be considerable retromovement back down the cable from the ending point, but that return to the bottom facilitates detaching from the cable.

The trust system necessitates having someone or something responsible for humanely stopping the speeding rider. Such braking systems can be quite efficient and safe or dangerously poor. The good systems utilize a shock cord and brake block arrangement to compassionately stop the rider. The less efficient system involves asking the assigned "brakers" to hold onto a section of rope or webbing between themselves, and aim for the rider's midsection: exciting but often painful.

Project Adventure's well designed and massively strong two-wheel snatch block pulley is a state-of-the-art-riding system. Riders are attached to the pulley via a rope/

yourself in professionalism, and once again verify in your own mind that you DO have a function on the platform other than just switching belays and smiling a lot.

Focus on trust, decision-making, letting go. Verbalize the only two alternatives; zipping down the cable or climbing back down the tree. Step back (not too far) and support whatever happens. Try not to say, "Go For It." Fade to a successful decision.

Pamper Pole or Plank

Pole or *Plank*, if you are looking for the ultimate head-trip on a ropes course, this one will do it to you.

A useful debriefing session, after an attempt, can be centered around what constitutes success on a ropes course element. Do participants need to feel the trapeze in their hands to

carabiner attachment so that there is no chance for a person to disengage him/herself from the pulley.

High Ropes Course Scenario:

Having sent umpteen people down the *Zip Wire* this day, you stand closely juxtaposed to a hesitating clipped-in student on the platform, who anxiously contemplates the next step (big one). Having heard the same "Boy-am-I-scared" type of comments over and over, you are surprised to hear this student softly ask, "Would you give me a little push?" Confounded by the request, and in a fit of pedagogic compassion, you slowly draw back your foot, and place it immediately behind the rider's seated posterior. "No, I'm sorry, I can't do that," you say. "The decision to go must be yours." The temptation passes as you wrap

agree that the *Pole* grabs you like no other element. The intensity of the experience seems to result from not having anything to hold onto while precariously attempting to stand on top of a ridiculously small platform affixed to a quivering pole of some length. From there, it's just your balance and the will to remain erect that keep you from teetering off the top. Certainly a series of moments to remember and savor.

Why the Pamper inference? Available as a commercial product, Pampers provide a temporary and comparatively inexpensive absorption item for spontaneously released body fluids. The *Pole* climbing and standing scenario mentioned above has, on occasion, caused the loosening of sphincter muscles controlling the release of those fluids. **PAMPER** — absorption system. **POLE** — micturating stimulus. Get it? Good.

Multivine Traverse

Take a look at the photo on page 124. Can you appreciate why people say this event has more consecutive Challenge than any other? Not only do you have to GO FOR IT to grasp the first dangling rope, but each sequenced hanging rope is so distanced from the others that each additional grasp requires GOING FOR IT again.

The amount of tension that the belayer applies from below has a lot to do with how successful a wire-walker will be. This unsolicited aid can be applied without participants being aware, as their attention is fairly riveted on the next rope in succession and subliminally on their own survival.

Leadership Issues — *Mark Murray*

What strikes me most about this element is the range of Challenge offered both from its construction, and in briefing participants on how the event can be done. The *Multivine* consists of a single foot cable stretched between two trees, and a parallel cable overhead

experience that flush of recognized success, or will a few halting moves up the pole suffice? This is experiential education at its poignant best.

This element is definitely more mental than physical.

It's simple. See, all you have to do is climb to the top of that pole (25'–50'+), stand up on top of the generously sized 12"x12" platform, and dive to catch the trapeze, or perhaps slip while trying to maneuver vertically onto the platform. There is a wonderfully strong and resilient rope attached to you (a belay) that prevents rapid trips to the turf.

In terms of thrill, commitment, and nitty gritty decision-making, the *Pamper Pole* offers the "sine qua non" of ropes course personal experience. Sky divers, rock climbers, hell-for-leather skiers, and other adrenaline junkies, all from which lengths of multiline rope are suspended at varying intervals. A third cable is placed above this as the belay cable. In building this element, the degree of difficulty can be determined by varying the length of the multilines, the distance between each line, and the distance from the anchor tree to the first dangling vine. When briefing this event, inform participants that the *recommended* method of crossing is with a loose belay and to avoid using the belay rope as a means of support. What follows is often the exact opposite. Participants implore their belayer for more tension, and usually hold their belay rope with one hand while reaching for the vine with the other. Using this approach makes a successful traverse almost a certainty. If you, as the leader, are belaying this element, it's necessary to comply with these requests for tension because of the trusting relationship

which is so vital between belayer and climber. You will have time later to explore the issues behind the request.

By the time most participants are ready to do the *Multivine*, they have had the opportunity to experience a fall while on belay, and at some level have trust in the belay system. What emerges when discussing this activity, is the concept that fear of falling is often related to fear of failing. The nature of the element is such that a fall should be the norm rather than the exception. I ask, "Why then is it so necessary that the crossing be made in such a state of security? Is it that we are focused on the end goal rather than the Challenges along the way?" It seems that success is measured by gaining that last tree and not by the intensity of the effort. The excitement of the vibrating cable (along with your feet), the vine that is jiggling just out of reach, and that moment of

Paul Radcliffe photo

Paul Radcliffe photo

commitment where you abandon one vine and go for the next, are lost when all that's important is reaching the end.

An experience I had that exemplifies the above issue was with a group that would be leaders on their own ropes courses. I started by briefing the activity (as I described earlier) and, as could have been predicted, each participant went through the element demanding a tight belay, holding onto the belay rope, and without a fall. The established norm was that everyone would make it. The debrief centered not so much on the Challenge of trying, but on the pressure to succeed. Each of them recalled feeling more concerned about comparisons to their peers than with personal safety. No one wanted to be the only one not to make it all the way. There was also concern about how they would be perceived by their own students when asked if they had done the *Multivine*. They might have to answer,"I tried and failed." I suggested that they reframe the thought and state, "I tried and fell."

If we, as the leaders of Adventure activities, are unwilling to give ourselves permission to be imperfect, then those whom we are leading will have difficulty being comfortable with their own imperfections. Personal growth and change is difficult in this atmosphere.

Centipede

Climbing these disjointed boards is much easier than the visually difficult picture the activity presents. The *Centipede* is used either as a vehicle for access to high events, (taking the place of a rope ladder) or simply as a challenging climb to a predetermined height.

If you decide to build one of these bizarre "ladders," pre-drill the holes for 1/2 inch staple placement, otherwise the boards will crack. Alternate placement patterns of the staples from board to board so that a climbing sequence or routine is not established. Think Challenge, because the climb itself is not difficult.

Burma Bridge

A *Burma Bridge* is essentially an expensive *Two Line Bridge*. The *Burma Bridges* requires more material and time to construct and therefore costs more than other similar high ropes course elements.

The cosmetic and characteristic herring-bone-cross ropes, connecting the three parallel *Burma Bridge* cables together, are highly visible and desired by people who like that Raiders-of-the-Lost-Ark look. These cross ropes are practically non-functional and cause time-consuming belay hassles if someone falls or decides to be belayed down in the middle of the event. Is my bias showing?

Leadership Issues — *Ann Smolowe*

The *Burma Bridge* is an excellent first high event. And while it's viewed by some participants as one of the easiest high elements, others can be greatly intimidated by this "bummer" of a bridge!

With support constantly available for both hands and feet, less-than-confident participants are often able to build their confidence with a satisfying, albeit shaky, traverse. However, like so many elements, this activity can either be fairly simple or surprisingly difficult. It depends on the individual.

Engaging participants in a discussion concerning definitions of success and failure, is invaluable to briefing this activity (or any

other high activity). It's important that each and every individual set realistic and attainable goals, and not get caught up comparing their successes to the successes of others in the group.

I find the *Burma Bridge* to be a great element for more relaxed, self-assured, and confident individuals to explore more deeply their level of risk-taking. One way to increase the level of Challenge is for the participant to close his/her eyes, or use a blindfold while traversing the bridge. While this variation and degree of risk-taking often demands a higher level of trust and commitment, I find it to be far less paralyzing or terrifying on the *Burma Bridge* than on other high elements. Despite the loss of visual sense, such a handicap on this activity leads to a *gradually* increased Challenge, versus a quantum leap, since the individual can still hold onto the hand cables and feel somewhat secure. For those who find the blindfolded variation too easily accomplished, the level of Challenge can be increased yet again by traversing the bridge backwards.

If we take the other extreme, like an acrophobic individual, the climb *up* to the bridge can be a terrifying activity in itself. Climbing a few steps on a ladder, gnarls on a tree, or a couple of staples, can be an extremely powerful and rewarding experience for a participant petrified of heights.

In these situations, one individual may need absolute silence in order to concentrate on his/her every step, while others prefer a cheerleading squad. Some individuals are receptive to suggestions concerning control of their breathing, or how to steady their spaghetti legs through isometric techniques. Others simply are unable to receive any information at all. Experienced facilitators, belayers, and group members, can usually sense what words of encouragement, suggested techniques, helpful recommendations, or levels of dialogue are appropriate to help along the more anxious participant.

I often facilitate groups comprised of individuals from both extremes — and everyone in between. In the final debrief, I invariably hear the most physically adept participants describe their most satisfying moments as watching, sharing, or participating in the accomplishment of another less adept participant. Sharing in the success of others often becomes the greatest takeaway.

Vertical Playpen

Each *Playpen* that our builders fabricate seems to be different from the last. The basic series of vertical Challenges is adhered to, but the format lends itself to creativity. Tires, boards, poles, ladders, and ropes, all have their place and various orientations in each *Vertical Playpen* installation scheme.

A typical climbing pattern might be the following: Suspended horizontal beam (to get

off the ground) to…a three- to four-foot rope ladder connected to…a vertically suspended truck tire. Standing on top of this tire, you gain the top of a horizontally strung section of large diameter rope. Reaching up from this rope you continue onto a horizontal pole. From here it's a simple mantle up to a horizontally suspended tire. Up and through the hole and you're finished — literally.

Tired Two Line

Have you ever crossed the *Cat Walk* (see pg. 131) and seen only an eight inch or so diameter log to walk on? The *Tired Two Line* is like that, except when you look down, there are only two 3/8 inch diameter cables to shuffle across on — no support for the hands, of course. Controlling your feet isn't too hard. Controlling your head is another matter.

Substantial balance aid can be overtly or covertly applied by the belayer.

Leadership Issues — *Dick Prouty*

This is another ideal element to use early on in a typical high element sequence. It can be constructed with the cables at 18–20 feet, and as such seems a fairly easy Challenge, from the ground anyway. However, the Challenge of doing a no-hands traverse (especially when the previous elements have included a *Two Line Bridge*, as they usually do), makes this element a frequent "surprise Challenger."

I once had an adult participant on this event who had been a frequent participant on ropes courses at other sites. He'd also done a fair amount of rock climbing. This was his first encounter with the *Tired Two Line* and, being eager to try, he became the first participant to have a go. But the looseness of the cables and the hands-free aspect were a real shock to him. He developed a great case of "sewing machine-itis" in his legs before going more than six feet. He struggled for about 10 minutes before falling off the element, on belay, and coming quickly to the ground. In debriefing the experi-

ence, he came to the conclusion that part of his shakiness was his anxiety in front of the workshop group, who, until this element, saw him as a "super-performer." It was a good experience for the whole group to see him work through an understanding of the sources of his fear and get a better handle on them.

Because this element contains a surprise anxiety aspect, I find it a good place to have participants begin practicing the breath control method for dealing with anxiety. Taking stock of your breathing, when you are uptight, often reveals that your breath has become restricted and shallow. By exhaling, and breathing slowly and deeply, you can often bring a bad case of sewing machine legs under control. "The body follows the breath," is an old Yoga maxim. This element gives you an early and dramatic opening to have participants experience this in a concrete way.

For many participants, holding on to the belay rope as an aide, makes the crossing much easier. Depending on your assessment of the group's ability and goal setting process, you can get them to try this element with or without this balance aide. For many participants, letting go of the rope with their hands on the way back from the first tree, or on a second try, can be a significant breakthrough experience.

Don't forget that every event is different for every participant. I had another participant who became so relaxed on the *Tired Two Line,* even though he'd been very apprehensive, that he started doing a rock and roll dance move and humming. He was obviously pleased with his performance and gave everyone else a big lift with his antics.

Flying Squirrel

(See primate participation photo on back cover.)

Flying Squirrel — To allow an individual who is handicapped, or thinks so, (physically/emotionally), to be hoisted up on a rope/pulley system (to a jointly determined height) by the remainder of the group.

The above rationale provides programmatic incentive to build this element and have some fun with it yourself.

The vertical ride up, provided by your buddies, is just plain exhilarating and can't be appreciated from ground level. This is truly one of those times when "you had to be there."

Heebie-Jeebie

When you think about it, most everything on a ropes course requires some kind of connector event between supports (trees). Here's another one with a twist.

If you want to really increase the Challenge, remove one of the diagonal hand ropes so that either the first third or the last third of the cable crossing must be made without hand support. More GO FOR IT stuff. Remember to change the name of the event if you decide to adjust the Challenge. It will be either a Heebie or a Jeebie, depending upon which rope you remove. You think I'm kidding? Try it.

Leadership Issues — *Jim Schoel*

This wonderful element is a good next step for progressing from *Two Line Bridge, Inclined Log,* and *Tired Two Line.* The looseness of the ropes, the fact that the starting rope triangulates down to nothing, and the far side's rope begins about ten feet before the start rope runs into the cable (maybe you should check the photo), make for some tenuous climbing

situations. Of course, most of the tenuousness is a result of how tight you make the prusik knots on the multiline hand ropes, as well as how tight you hold the belay rope. "Butt out!" "Hands forward!" "Balance!" "Push!" "Traverse!" "Keep going!" "Reach around!" "Keep the pressure away from you!" (Exciting, ain't it?) "Make that move!" "Go for the rope!" — are helpful suggestions you can offer from the ground. Then, after you and the group offer all this sage advice, your climber swings out and around, ending up under the element. What now? Pull them up? Let them hang? Lower them to the ground? Or something in between? These are choices you must make according to abilities and goals.

If you read that the person is fairly confident in their early climbing but he or she still requests that the belay rope be kept tight, suggest that on this element you would like to loosen it up — just a bit — so they have a chance to be more independent. This sugges-

tion may be rejected immediately, or they may give it a try. Or they may want to have the rope tight the whole way across and on the return voyage try a loose or looser belay. Reading the participant's eyes and body language for the terror factor (for example, how quick hands come up to grab onto the belay rope), helps you develop a good rapport regarding the belay dynamic.

Of course you may decide to push someone in order to get his/her attention (in fact that's one of the *only* real reasons to push). The participant may be clearly able but is devaluing the activity and others. "This stuff is stupid." "I can do it with one hand." "I can climb this thing a lot better than so and so." You may have a participant who doesn't understand the activity, isn't particularly interested in learning about it, and is just going through the motions. If you give them too easy a ride, they might miss out on the power of the experience. On more than one occasion the participant and his/her blasé attitude has ended up under the cable in an awkward and somewhat embarrassing position. Now what! You can rush to save them, or, if they are strong enough to remount and need/want the Challenge, let 'em suffer. The element can be remounted and the climber can continue on and complete it, though not without a great deal of grunting and scrambling. But what pride the completion bestows upon them!

"Loose" and "looser" also apply to the tightness of the prusiks. Tight prusik knots make the element infinitely more easy than loose ones. Making the adjustment for different individuals is difficult: you'd have to climb the tree on a self-belay to accomplish it. You could ask more daring participants if they would like to loosen the prusik themselves for the sake of the Challenge. Of course they would not be able to loosen the other side until they got there, but the return trip would be quite an adventure. Adjustments can also be accomplished during the second or third times the participant tries the element. Blindfolds, going backwards, using just one hand, using the tension traverse rope, and ignoring the Heebie ropes, are some of the endless complications wrung out of this fascinating element.

Cat Walk a.k.a. Balance Beam

If you took this same suspended log and set it on the ground I doubt if anyone would have trouble balancing along its length. Suspend the same log so that the sky walker sees a substantial expanse of air beneath his or her feet, and the Challenge manifests itself by a series of physical and emotional reactions that are both revealing and eventually useful to the participant.

Make sure that you suggest to the beam walker that they try more than one crossing, so that they get the chance to experience an increase in their own efficiency and confidence. Once across is a stunt; three times across is an accomplishment; ten times across is showing off.

Leadership Issues — Mark Murray

Gazing at the *Cat Walk* evokes childhood memories of fallen logs across streams which absolutely had to be crossed. "What method should I use: crawl, straddle, or walk? What's the worst that can happen, wet clothes and a bruised ego? Once I make the commitment to go, will I be able to return to the safety of the shore? Why does this log feel so shaky and seem so high?" These are some of the questions I asked myself before embarking on this adventure. Our man-made fallen logs are secured between two anchor trees but I see some parallels with nature. The length of the log, height from the ground, slope between trees, and shape, all provide for a nice variety in creating a challenging *Cat Walk*.

While working with individuals on the *Cat Walk*, I also discover that many of the same

questions arise. The issues of success and risk-taking stimulate inner conflict. If participants views success as traversing the log without a fall, then their willingness to increase the risk factor is diminished. Often, participants are more likely to request that their belay be hooked in the front, thus reducing the feeling of exposure. The request made of the belayers is that they provide a good deal of tension, minimizing the overall feeling of unsteadiness. After the climb, time spent at the anchor tree before crossing is usually filled with thoughts of falling and failure. This only fuels the anxiety already present.

I find that preparation on the ground enhances the willingness of participants to

increase their level of risk taking. It also helps develop strategies to manage anxiety. Discussing with participants the significance of falling off the log prior to the end, stimulates conversation relative to the theme of success versus failure. Also, encouraging group members to recall times when they placed themselves in higher risk situations allows them to choose more exposure by using a rear belay, and more steadiness by requesting a loose belay. Discussing concepts of controlled breathing, along with visualizing a smooth and deliberate journey across the log, assist in helping the participant make those commitment steps out onto the log, thereby shedding the safety of the anchor tree.

At times, ground preparation does not result in participants being more willing to Challenge themselves. Only after experiencing the element at their chosen risk level are they willing to accept another level of Challenge. One incident comes to mind which exemplifies this situation. A group with whom I was working came to the *Cat Walk* after trying a few other high elements. I gave them my ground briefing and each participant asked for a front belay. When they were finally on the *Cat Walk*, each participant demanded extreme tension while holding onto the belay rope. Needless to say, each group member completed the traverse without a fall. In our debrief, the question was asked if we had any elements that could be more challenging. I asked if they believed that they had exhausted the Challenge available in this element. Upon reflection, each individual chose to repeat the *Cat Walk* and all increased their level of risk. As a leader in this situation, I realized that the issues of trust, commitment, and success are such integral parts of the *Cat Walk* that it was imperative I listen and comply with their requests. If I were to have decided the level of Challenge for them, they may have learned that their choices had little value in my eyes.

Inclined Log

Walking up the *Inclined Log* on belay provides a challenging means of access to higher elements on the ropes course. This angled log also provides access to anyone who wants to fall off it after hours. So, you have to decide if this event is reasonable to install in your geographical area.

Have you ever walked the length of a log? Have you ever seen a downed tree that didn't finish its fall to the forest floor? Ever wonder what it would be like to walk up that inclined log? Well, here's your chance, because that's exactly what the *Inclined Log* is all about.

Referring back to my original question about walking on a log, your answer was probably yes, because it's kind of fun and not very threatening. But, begin to increase the log's angle of incidence and the joy shifts toward anxiety, and rightly so, because your Mom always told you to "Be careful," and "Don't get hurt." But it's OK now, Mom, because we're using a belay. So get psyched, get challenged, and get ready for the attempt.

You are looking at a thirty foot plus log that leans against its support at about a thirty degree angle. Remember, it's the same log that you had no problems with at ground level. The only thing that has changed is your perception of the Challenge ("I might fall, I might get hurt, my Mom might get mad," etc.). If you attempt to walk up the log in a bent over position (your body WANTS to be near something solid), your weight tends to push your feet down the log's incline (a slip). If you move up the log so that your body remains erect (perpendicular to the ground) your weight will be directly over your feet, achieving maximum friction and control.

"So what's the big deal? I am not going to make a living walking up inclined logs or inclined anythings. Are you trying to scare me, or make me look foolish?" Not at all, I'm just asking you to try something that might give you a better look at yourself in a stressful situation. If you can overcome your body's (mind's) natural reluctance to try an intimidating event, the carry-over to "real life" may allow you to try something that intimidates you on a day-to-day level: applying for a new job, asking someone out for a date, trying a new sport.

You are supported on the log by a belay rope in case you fall. In school, or at home, the support of your friends and family allows you to "fall" and realize that you are not going to get hurt. You just get up and try again.

The *Inclined Log*, like so many of the high ropes course events, is a metaphor for those sometimes intangible problems of life that we encounter everyday.

Paul Radcliffe photo

Curriculum Models

There is a wide variety of Project Adventure programs in schools, colleges, camps, and recreational facilities. The programs range from a one-week unit of games and Initiative problems in a 7th grade physical education class, to a K–12 system-wide approach that infuses PA curricula of increasing complexity at each grade level. The following curricula were chosen because they offer a well-developed example of a PA curriculum in each of the areas covered. Each makes use of many different PA activities; from warm-ups through the high elements. As complete as some of these curricula are, it is not our intent for them to be copied directly by those wishing to start or enlarge a PA program. These curricula are intended to serve as guides to putting together a curriculum that makes most sense for your program needs and abilities. Obviously, many people adopting a PA program will start with something smaller than those represented here, but that is in keeping with the tried and true PA implementation strategy of starting small and working from strengths. Most of the people who started these programs started much smaller than the curricula represented in this chapter. For the instructor, part of the fun of running a PA program is expanding your Adventure base and watching your program grow.

In thinking about starting a PA program, many people have heard of other PA models such as Adventure Based Counseling in therapeutic programs, or the use of PA team learning strategies in academic programs. To clarify questions that often arise about the differences between these approaches, the following diagram is something we have found helpful:

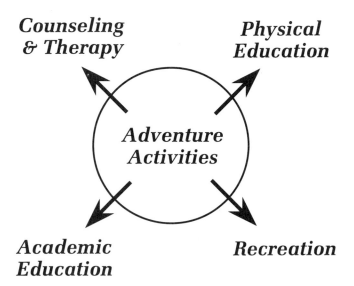

The inner circle is all the possible Adventure activities such as A*dd-on Tag, Nitro Crossing, Tension Traverse*, or a high *Multivine*. Each discipline makes use of the same activities from the inner circle, but each discipline frames the activities differently using its own goals and objectives. The following definitions highlight these differences:

Physical Education is used to accomplish the physical education goals of endurance, balance, and physical fitness, as well as address the more general school or program goals of improved self-confidence, problem solving skills, and acceptance of differences.

Counseling and Therapy focuses on the need for participants to consider their behavior and to change or modify that behavior. Initial goal setting and debriefing sessions are used extensively to provide a place within the activity where behavior change can be focused on to better advantage.

Recreation can be one short session of experiences, and/or skills instruction with the simple goal of just having fun, to longer programs where personal and interpersonal growth are emphasized. (Fun, by the way, is enjoying a bit of a renaissance. There is increasing evidence that it is therapeutic not to spoil the fun.)

Academic Education utilizes the process of Adventure groups to promote a more active and involving academic curriculum for educational programs. Cooperative learning strategies, acquired in Adventure training, can then be used in the classroom to learn basic skills or produce real world products with more efficiency, and with more team skills available for future transfer to the workplace.

All of these categories overlap and are interactive in the real world. Some of the best programs are often interdisciplinary in a planned way and intentionally fuse two or more of the outside circles. Physical education, recreation, and counseling goals, are all a conscious part of the American Youth Foundation camp curriculum that follows. Physical educators also accomplish counseling goals, and not just in PA classes. However, the PA approach to Physical Education allows the instructor to address attitude and behavior change in a more natural and effective format than do most other Physical Education options available to the instructor. Increasingly, physical educators are attending PA counseling (ABC) workshops to learn more effective briefing and debriefing skills, or to learn how to deal with the difficult student. The emphasis on mainstreaming special needs students has made it necessary for school PA program leaders to be able to deal with a greater variety of students. Being comfortable with debriefing strategies makes this task much easier.

The Implementation Process

In order to understand the following curricula as guides, and not as exact prescriptions to follow, it is helpful to look at the process by which a school, camp, or recreation facility

adopts a PA program and makes it their own. In the beginning, it could be that a superintendent or principal has become convinced of the desirability of using the PA Challenge by Choice approach to address some pressing student issues; or perhaps a department head wants to improve student morale in the department; or, most likely, it could be that a teacher or camp director has become aware of the PA approach in some way (friend, neighboring district, professional conference), and has become excited about adopting the program.

At this point, the best course is for a planning team of interested staff members to be put together (formally or informally), and proceed to get training as a group. In some other kinds of curricula you might be tempted to plan a curriculum from a book, such as this, before training was attempted. However, because of the innovative and personal nature of the PA

approach, it is recommended that training come before a formal plan is established. A preliminary proposal outlining goals, grade levels, numbers of students, staffing plan, and general budget figure, is often necessary for program approval. After training, planning team members will have a common understanding of the PA approach and a base from which to begin to design the program curricula, with specific activities and elements appropriate to both their student's needs, the budget, and members' own interests and abilities.

Drawing up the plan can be a rather intimidating process for some. The curricula examples are intended to help in that regard by showing different formats for a plan. Once the decision to go ahead has been made, however, we do strongly advocate that some sort of written plan be drawn up. Often, a plan is necessary for obtaining either outside funding through a grant or inside funding from a policy or funding board. Even when it is not officially required, a plan is still a good idea for the clarity it requires and forces upon all concerned. A plan can always be modified, but until you have one, you don't really know where you will end up. Although this winging-it attitude may be more engaging and fun in some Adventure activities, where student achievement is the goal, planning usually makes for better results.

Each of the institutions represented by the curricula to follow went through the same process; getting staff training in Adventure skills, drawing up a plan that makes sense to the site's needs and themselves, and then beginning to implement in a way that the budget would allow. In most cases, curricula such as these did not spring full-blown into being. David Marsh's history of his program at Ridgewood High School is a good example of starting small and building each year. Bill Bates of Cambridge began as an elementary school teacher who started a small unit as a result of attending a PA workshop in 1978. Two years later, Bill wrote and was awarded funding for a major three-year developmental grant which allowed the UMPA program to be formed. The grant process is one way many programs have been able to grow from smaller beginnings. But as you read these curricula, please remember that while a grant or a large start-up budget is perhaps optimum, it is not necessary. Attendance at a training workshop, and a beginning unit of games and Initiatives, can enliven any program and be framed to address the needs of the students. Many programs then grow incrementally out of annual budgets.

One hurdle to many teachers, and others implementing a program at their site, is their own preconceived barriers that this type of program is beyond them. Our experience at PA, over the last nineteen years of helping many kinds of programs and persons get started in this field, is that most people can learn the skills necessary to teach in a PA program. It is a somewhat different type of program than many are used to, but once they have experienced the Challenge by Choice philosophy in a training setting, they almost invariably want to work with students in this way. One need not be a certified wilderness expert, whatever that might be, in order to be a great PA instructor. Enthusiasm, and a desire to keep renewing one's self in one's work — these help, and are in turn helped by the work itself.

Dick Prouty

Chapter 6
Elementary/Middle Schools

Nicki Hall photo

Cambridge UMPA

The Urban Modification of Project Adventure (UMPA) initiative started in 1978 in Cambridge, Massachusetts public schools. The purpose was to adapt Adventure ideas, which had been field tested primarily in suburban schools, to an urban school system. What the Cambridge schools produced is one of the most, if not most, comprehensive adaptations. Every school in the system has some sort of ropes course, leading up to the famed "Lover's Leap" high trapeze jump in the gym of Cambridge Rindge and Latin High School. The curriculum goes from kindergarten to twelfth grade. While building this successful curriculum, they have dispelled two myths, among others: one, that the urban physical education class is too large and the space provided is too small to implement Adventure; and two, that Adventure curriculum must be primarily an outdoors curriculum.

The enthusiastic response reported by the Cambridge teachers over the years has laid the foundation for our urban Project Adventure work. When we speak of the present eight adoptions in New York City, and the close to 20 programs operating in the Pittsburgh Public Schools, we say that all roads lead from Cambridge.

Introduction

This project has grown from an idea in the minds of a few Cambridge Physical Education teachers early in 1978, to a pilot program at the Longfellow and CAPS schools, to a Title IV C project, and finally to its present state — a city-wide non-traditional approach to Physical Education in the Cambridge Public Schools.

The overwhelming personal and organizational support that the UMPA staff has received at all stages of project development has been a major factor in the success of the UMPA project. The UMPA Staff and Curriculum Committee would like to say "thank you" to all the people and organizations who have helped make our ideas become realities for the children of Cambridge — possibly for urban youth everywhere.

The UMPA curriculum is built on a particular unit plan or progression. UMPA is being developed over the long range as a K–12 curriculum. In order to keep activities challenging and non-repetitive, a specific sequence of activities is essential.

The 5th, 6th, 7th, and 8th grade program (the upper elementary components) consists of twelve to sixteen lessons to be implemented in a six- to eight-week intervention period. Students meet for 90 minutes per week. By the end of the 8th grade, a student will have been exposed to an equivalent of not less than 14 and not more then 32 weeks of UMPA activities. These students acquire the skills and knowledge to participate in eight-week UMPA Indoor and Outdoor Electives at the high school level if they so choose. These "electives" include indoor Adventure and ropes course activities, as well as a series of outdoor Adventure courses; e.g., backpacking, camping, orienteering, bicycle touring, canoeing, down-hill skiing, cross-country skiing, rock climbing, and sailing. Three levels are being developed in the high school program — introductory, advanced, and leadership. (Another supplement to UMPA will be a Primary Cooperative Play and "Creative Adventure Playgrounds" curriculum for physical educators and classroom teachers of K–4th grade children.)

All activities in this curriculum are listed by grade level. UMPA teachers are asked to refer to these lists when planning their lessons. The unit plans given are to be used as a guide. Any variation to these units should be made using activities from the appropriate grade level lists.

Teachers need a good grasp of all activities — not just a few "great ones." By adhering to the sequence we insure that all students involved in Cambridge's UMPA program will always be receiving fresh, exciting challenges.

Philosophy

The UMPA program was founded to bring the benefits of Adventure programming to urban students. In essence, these benefits are; a) significantly enhanced positive self-image; b) significantly increased mutual support.

Just as Project Adventure adapted Outward Bound activities to meet the needs of urban school systems, UMPA is based on the belief that, with imagination, hard work, and organizational support, Adventure activities can be enjoyed by students even in the most limited urban environments.

UMPA was designed to provide urban students with the opportunity to participate in Project Adventure type activities not only because these activities are dramatically new and exciting, but because the student objectives of Project Adventure are particularly relevant to the needs of urban youth.

This need is perhaps best demonstrated by considering the more global goals of public education in our modern society.

Desegregation. In order to effectively bring students together from racially imbalanced schools and ethnically isolated neighborhoods, urban schools must have programs which concentrate on increasing mutual support and respect among students. UMPA can, therefore, play a significant role in desegregation programs in urban systems.

Multicultural Education. Self-concept and self-image is a central theme in multicultural and bilingual education. A foreign student entering a new classroom becomes a "minority." He or she needs as much assistance as possible in developing and keeping a positive self-image. Therefore, UMPA is effective in assisting in the achievement of the central goal of multicultural education.

Special Education. Special educators need programs which help them increase the characteristically low self-image of special needs students. Special needs students can participate profitably in UMPA activities, and UMPA, therefore, can be instrumental in helping special educators achieve one of their primary goals. Because there is a significantly high proportion of special needs in children from lower socio-economic backgrounds, and because a large proportion of disadvantaged families live in urban areas, special education in urban schools is of particular importance.

Although UMPA is being developed as a K–12 curriculum, its origin was in the 6th, 7th, and 8th grades in Cambridge. Sixth, seventh, and eighth grade ages are among the most troublesome and confusing years. Physical education programs, which emphasize competitiveness and performance, can often have an adverse effect on adolescent development. The noncompetitive mutual support, positive self-image, and personal confidence provided by UMPA type activities add an important dimension which has been missing in urban adolescent education.

Project Adventure is unprecedented in its success in providing students with activities which are focused on enhancing self-esteem and mutual support. UMPA offers, for the first time, a means by which urban students can enjoy these activities and their benefits.

Objectives

UMPA's Student Objectives are to provide urban students with the same benefits as those received by students participating in suburban and rural Project Adventure programs via:

- **Increased Mutual Support Within Groups.** Urban students will learn to respect and support each other by working in racially, culturally, sexually, economically, socially, and physically diverse groups to solve problems that are designed so that group members must take advantage of their combined physical and mental capabilities in arriving at a solution.
- **Enhanced Self-Confidence.** Urban students will view themselves with increased self-esteem after attempting a graduated series of challenging activities which motivate them to venture beyond previous set limits.
- **Improved Agility, Coordination, and Physical Fitness.** Urban students will increase their level of physical competence through participation in a variety of innovative and relevant activities, which are introduced with a joyful noncompetitive approach that encourages rather than requires participation.
- **A New Appreciation of Their Environment.** Students will develop a new awareness and appreciation of themselves in relation to their environment through the creative and adventurous use of limited space playgrounds and facilities.

When conducting UMPA activities, particular attention should be given to the first two objectives — mutual support and self-confidence/esteem. As mentioned in the philosophy, the importance of these objectives is what makes UMPA so relevant. If you make these two "psycho-social" objectives primary in conducting each lesson, you cannot help but positively influence your students.

Project Adventure has recently expanded or redefined their learning goals. Some of these expanded goals are mentioned below in order to help the UMPA teacher develop the focus needed:

In redefining their goals, Project Adventure also includes:

- To develop abilities that contribute to group decision making and leadership.
- To foster appreciation and respect for differences existing within the group.
- To develop an appreciation of the interdisciplinary nature of real problem solving.

It is also appropriate at this time to mention a method which UMPA has adopted from Adventure Based Counseling. This method helps teachers and students accomplish the objectives of UMPA. The method is in the form of a rule — one rule. The rule is that there are "No put-downs!" during the UMPA unit. No one does or says anything that will put themselves or anyone else down. Actions which cause embarrassment, create uncomfortable feelings, show disrespect or inconsideration are not accepted. Every participant's sole purpose is to help themselves and their peers attain higher levels of personal and group achievement. If this is to be accomplished, there is no room for "put downs."

Cambridge UMPA Unit Plan — Elementary (Grades 5–8)

Editors note: Specific activities listed reflect only a sample of the many activities available within the Cambridge curriculum.

Week #1 & 2 (classes 1, 2, 3) — New Games

Objective	Activity	Hints/Comments
Students will understand the framework of UMPA and Project Adventure	Overview of program	Emphasize: • Group cooperation • Self-confidence • Success with help from friends **One Rule: "No put-downs!"**

Students will:
• increase flexibility and cardio-vascular fitness
• "get the blood moving"
• be exposed to new warm-up activities
	Warm-ups, (5 minutes each class)
	• Coordination and Cardiovascular Movements
	  Hopping, Heel Clickers, Entrechat, Chorus Line
	• Limberness and Flexibility Movements
	  Cobra, Angel, Duo Stretch, Red Baron Stretch
	• Activities for Covering Distance
	  Forward Jog, Backward Jog, Falling (teach as activity)
	• Small "Apparatus" Warm-Ups
	  Hula Hoops, Jump Ropes, Tubes, Parachute
		Make warm-ups enjoyable.
		Teacher participation can break down inhibitions.
		Improvise and be creative.
		Do not force, push, or intimidate anyone.

Students will learn:
• initial concepts of group cooperation
• the meaning and purpose of non-competitive games and cooperative play
 	
Students will:
• begin to overcome the inhibitions of physical contact (touching)
• continue to improve their cardiovascular fitness
	Games:
	• Grade 5
	  Yells, Python Pentathlon, Moonball, Rope Jousting, Aerobic Tag
	• Grade 6
	  Blindfold Soccer, Aerobic Tag, Soccer Frisbee
	• Grade 7
	  Balance Broom, Moonball, Aerobic Tag, Frisalevio
	• Grade 8
	  Yurt Circle, Impulse, Group Juggling, Ultimate Frisbee
		Explain the purpose of the game.
		Emphasize safety.
		Everybody can play, nobody gets hurt.
		Avoid embarrassment.
		Read glossary of games in order to accomplish stated objectives.
		Leave time for discussion.
		"Did this game meet stated objectives?"
		Important: if using sling ropes to tie "Swiss seats," consider starting instruction at beginning of unit.

Week #2 & 3 (Classes 4, 5, 6) — Initiative Tasks

Objective	Activity	Hints/Comments
Students will build skills for: • listening • leadership activities • assessing the problem and formulating a solution to enhance group responsibility for safety of its members • group cooperation • developing perseverance Students will begin to overcome the inhibition of physical contact (touching). Students will learn: • proper spotting techniques to develop trust in each other • to take risks and overcome fear to support and encourage one another's efforts and mutual support	Initiative Tasks: • Grade 5 *Blind Polygon, All Aboard, Swing Island* • Grade 6 *The Wall, Mohawk Walk, Chariot Pull, Trolley* • Grade 7 *Ten Member Pyramid, Trust Fall, Human Ladder* • Grade 8 *Electric Fence, Nitro Crossing, Up and Over*	"Brief" each class prior to initiative tasks. Make stories (situations) exciting, be creative. Give some group goals. More guidance in group process and interpersonal guidance is necessary at first. Do not help by solving problems, but rather by facilitating group and individual process. Stress safety. Emphasize: • only group success is rewarded • understanding and helping each other • necessity of knowing individual strengths and weaknesses • trust and respect for each other • "chain is only as strong as each link"(e.g., if someone does not take the task seriously, it limits the whole group.) • does the group need a leader or facilitator? "Debrief" after each class. If group is vocal, then guide discussion. If not, you may have to pull it out or make statements yourself. End on a positive note; e.g., "Here is what we did well." "This is what we will work on next time."

Week #4 & 5 (Classes 7, 8, 9) — Low Ropes Course Elements

Objective	Activity	Hints/Comments
Introduction to Lower Elements	Warm-ups, (5 minutes each class)	Encourage 100% participation. Stress safety factors.
Students will: • exhibit mutual support for one another • develop cooperation, trust and support	Low Elements: Grade 5, restricted to: *Tension Traverse, Low Wall Climb, Scooter Swing, Whittle, Climbing Ropes Swing*	Help students feel comfortable with all levels of achievement. All students should demonstrate a high level of mutual support. Emphasize building up to high ropes.
Students will demonstrate: • proper spotting techniques • giving cooperation • trust • mutual support • commitment All students will participate by watching, encouraging and spotting. Students will take sensible risks!	Grades 6–8 *Tension Traverse, Fidget Ladder, Wild Woosey, Inclined Log*	Each student should be demonstrating that they are ready to help each other achieve and overcome fears. *Important: if using sling ropes to tie "Swiss seats," you should definitely be teaching it at this point in the unit.*

Week #6–8 (Classes 10, 11, 12) — High Ropes Course Elements

Objective	Activity	Hints/Comments
Students will: • learn properly about the Swiss seat and all safety knots • demonstrate trust in the ropes course and instructor by climbing and falling on belay • watch and encourage • continue to exhibit group cooperation, trust, and understanding • learn to address their fears • take sensible risks	Warm-ups, (5 minutes each class) High Elements: (These elements are not used with grade 5) Grades 6–8 Progression: 1. Review swiss seats 2. Climb and fall on belay 3. Moderately difficult elements; e.g. ,*Two Line Bridge, High Beam, High Wall, Commando Crawl,* etc. 4. Difficult ("Big Commitment") elements; e.g., *Swinging Beam, Trapeze Dive, Maniac Swing,* etc.	Classes may be divided into groups or may move freely (whatever teacher prefers). Don't threaten or force students to climb higher than they wish. Make sure students climb high enough so the rope will be able to reach its stretching point. Spectators' encouragement is as important as the individual performances. Help students feel comfortable with whatever height they choose. Do not intimidate. Don't allow students to remain too long on platforms.

The Project Adventure Program at the John Read Middle School

May, 1987
Revised — October, 1987
Revised —July, 1988
Revised —January, 1989

Project Adventure Staff

Beth Ault
Laura Beattie
Nancy Bowen
Richard Engel
Michael Svanda
John Hichwa

Principal — Dianne Otteson
Assistant Principal — Dr. Averill Loh
Superintendent — Lawrence Miller

The Project Adventure program at the John Read Middle School is presented to the entire student population as a separate course, taught by trained Project Adventure teachers. It is an integral part of the curriculum, with its goals and objectives specifically aimed at the middle school child.

The following goals are from Project Adventure, Inc.:

- To increase an individual's sense of confidence and self-esteem.
- To increase mutual support within a group.
- To develop abilities that contribute to group decision-making and leadership.
- To increase agility, physical coordination, and joy in one's physical self.
- To foster appreciation and respect for differences existing within the group.
- To develop an increased familiarity and identification with the natural world.
- To develop an appreciation of the interdisciplinary nature of real problem solving.

The Project Adventure program at John Read incorporates all of the above. Emphasis, however, is placed on the areas which promote the following:

- Building student self-esteem through both physical and mental risk-taking activities.
- Involving students in activities which promote self-responsibility and self-initiative.
- Having students recognize their own strengths and limitations and gain a better understanding of their peers.
- Having students become enthusiastic learners.

The components of the program include the following:

- Warm-up activities
- New Games
- Initiatives
- Ropes Course — Indoors and Outdoors
- Orienteering
- Rock Climbing

Every student at the John Read Middle School is involved in participating in the Project Adventure program. The schedule is as follows:

6th Grade — One marking period (1/4 of the year, 22 sessions)

7th Grade — One marking period (1/4 of the year, 22 sessions)

8th Grade — Two marking periods (1/2 of the year, 44 sessions)

All classes meet for forty minutes, every other day. The student/teacher ratio for these classes is one teacher for every eight students. The average class size for a Project Adventure class is 25 students.

The outline of daily activities offered in the 6th, 7th, and 8th grade Project Adventure program is as follows.

6th Grade Project Adventure Activities

Class #1
Intro. — *Anticipation* *
Toss-A-Name Game
Toe Touching
Name Chase
Triangle Tag

Class # 2
Hog Call
Debrief (Students introduce
    partners to class)

Class #3
Everyone It
Aura
Springback
Squat Thrust
The Clock

Class #4
Jump Rope Mimic
Fall Back
Blade in the Grass
Trust Fall

Class #5
Trust Fall (con't)
Texas Big Foot
Lemonade
Logs — *Feelings* *

Class #6
Hickory Jump
Spider's Web
Tire and Pole
TP Shuffle

Class #7
Hickory Jump
Spider's Web
TP Shuffle
Tire and Pole

Class #8
Blob tag
Yurt Circle
Trust Walk
Compass Walk

Class #9
Floppy Frisbees
Ultimate Frisbee

Class #10
Hospital Tag
Prui
Steal the Bacon

Class #11
Wickett
Tractor Tred
Surf's Up
Basic Wink

Class #12
Nitro
Tension Traverse
All Aboard

Class #13
Elbow Tag
Swiss seats
Safety — Rope Care
Knots
Logs — *Anticipation* *

Class #14
Review Swiss seats
Climbing Walls
Logs – My First
Climb

Class #15
Climbing Walls
Cargo Net
Notes to Parents
Student/Parent
    Project Adventure Night

Class #16
Climbing Walls
Cargo Net

Class #17
Climbing Walls
Cargo Net

Class #18
Frantic
Rolling Raft Adventure

Class #19
Star Wars

Class #20
Apples-Bananas-Oranges
AH! SOOOO!
Loose Caboose

Class #21
Capture the Flag

Class #22
Student evaluation (written)
Parachute — Shark and Cat and Mouse
Sit Back

Debriefing Sessions

7th Grade Project Adventure Activities

Class #1
Intro– *Anticipation* *
Blanket Name Game
Pairs Tag
Boffer Blob

Class #2
Everyone it
Wickett
Tattoo
Pick and Choose

Class #3
Frogs and Flies
Rabid Nugget Rescue
Trust Run
Elbow Tag

Class #4
Spring Back
Fall Back
Trust Fall
*Feelings**

Class #5
Trust Fall (con't)
Booop
Fire in the Hole
Swiss Seats

Class #6
Review Swiss Seats
Safety — A+B=C
A=Attitudes,
B=Equipment
C= Perfect Safety Record
Climb Walls

Class #7
Climb Walls
Prusiking
*Year #2 vs. Year #1**

Class #8
Climb Walls
Prusiking
Cargo Net
Trapeze Jump

Class #9
Climb Walls
Prusiking
Cargo Net
Trapeze Jump

Class #10
Nitro
Hickory Jump

Class #11
Tension Traverse
Tire and Pole

Class #12
Data Processing
Lemonade
Glut Walk
Goonies Like

Class #13
Planet Pass
Space Chase
Ball Crawl

Class #14
Boffer Bonkers
Samurai Warrior
*Games**

Class #15
Popsicle Push-up
Bottoms Up
Wink — Mats

Class #16
Wink Berserk
Sock Tag
Balls Galore

Class #17
Moon Ball
Rolling Raft Adventure

Class #18
Spider Web
TP Shuffle
*Cooperation**

Class #19
Indoor Ropes Course
Zip Line

Class #20
Indoor Ropes Course
Zip Line

Class #21
Capture the Flag

Class #22
Evaluation — Written
Star Wars

Debriefing Sessions

8th Grade Project Adventure Activities

Warm-Up Activities	New Games	Initiatives
Triangle Tag	Frogs and Flies	Trust Fall
Sock Tag	Star Wars	Mohawk Walk
Boffer Blob	Wink (Mats)	Whittingham Trolley
Pairs Tag	Wink (Berserk)	Human Ladder
Pairs Pairs Tag	Capture the Flag	Prouty's Landing
Elbow Tag	Boffer Bonkers	Knots
Tattoo	Engle's Frisbee Folly	Hickory Jump
Goober Tag	210 Stomp	Hanging Teeter-Totter
Tug-of-War	Butt off	Pick and Choose
	Octopus	Balls Galore
	Two Ball Soccer	Spring Back
	Siamese Soccer	Scooter Slalom
	Moon Ball	Popsicle Push-up
	Striker	Bottoms Up
		Rolling Raft
		Two-in-a-row
		Turnstile
		It's not what you do...
		Spider Web
		Great American Egg Drop

Additional Activities

Readings (whenever) from Outward Bound book

Student Reactions — Written and oral

Video Taping — Students taping the action and producing Project Adventure Video Tapes

Orienteering — Map and Compass

Rock Climbing — Student Belaying, Rock Climbing, Knot tying, Rappelling

Indoor Ropes Course — Three climbing walls, Trapeze Jump, Zip Line, Prusiking, Cargo Net, Rappelling

Outdoor Ropes Course (high elements) — Two Line Bridge, Dangle Do, Cat Walk, Trapeze Jump, Heebie-Jeebie, Vertical Playpen, Zip line, Rappelling Station

Outdoor Ropes Course (low elements) — Trust Fall, Spider Web, Tire and Pole, Mohawk Walk, Tension Traverse, Nitro Crossing, Prouty's Landing, Hickory Jump, TP Shuffle, Hanging Teeter Totter

Suggested time allotments for each component:

Warm-up Activities, New Games, Initiatives: 16 class sessions

Indoor/Outdoor Ropes Course: 18 class sessions

Orienteering: 6 class sessions

Rock Climbing:
- Teaching belaying/rappelling techniques: 2 class sessions
- Rock Climbing at the site: 1 class session
- Debriefing — written/oral: 1 class session

Some Important Thoughts on Adventure Programming

On Taking a Risk

The Project Adventure Program at the John Read Middle School is designed to provide each student with the opportunity to take a risk — a positive risk. Whether it's volunteering suggestions during an Initiative, asserting oneself in a noncompetitive game, holding hands with a person of the opposite sex, or jumping for the trapeze, each student is consciously making decisions. These decisions are made with the encouragement and support of others. Yet, the final decision whether to *go for it* lies solely with the participant. It is a Challenge by Choice. It is a conscious decision with the student having been exposed to the consequences. It is this awareness and sense of consequence which makes taking such a risk, a positive one. The absence of conscious development could lead to a student taking a risk which could have a negative consequence. Our Project Adventure program encourages students to take positive risks, thus enabling them to increase their level of self-worth and self-confidence.

Physical Education and Project Adventure

In comparing the physical education program with the Project Adventure program, we have similarities of purpose. The differences, however, help us better meet the needs of each student. The Project Adventure philosophy has flowed over into the daily physical education program and the excitement created by the PA program has helped us bridge the gap with the non-traditional physical education student.

Project Adventure Parents Programs

After each 6th grade Project Adventure course, the students and their parents are invited to a Project Adventure Parents' Night. The parents and the students participate in warm-up activities, new games, Initiatives, and climb the walls in the gymnasium. The purpose of the evening is to familiarize the parents with the Project Adventure philosophy through active participation and have them glean a better understanding of the Adventure program.

The 8th grade parents are invited to a one-day workshop in May where new games are played, Initiatives are attempted, and the high rope course elements are made available to them.

Through these two parent activities, we are able to keep the parents informed and involved. We feel that these two activities play an important role in the Adventure program at John Read. They serve as a vehicle of communication to help parents better understand the Adventure programs at John Read.

Note: Parents' nights have been discontinued for the present. Our insurance covers only John Read students and the certified Project Adventure instructors. We do feel, however, that for the five years we did hold the parents' days, they were most beneficial.

Student Reaction Forms

Students are asked to write at different times during their Project Adventure classes. In the 6th grade, each student keeps a log and records feelings, happenings, etc. At the conclusion of their experience, students react to the following questions:

1. Tell us about Project Adventure!
2. How did it affect you?
3. Describe your feelings about the class relationships.
4. Ten years from now, what will you remember the most?

In the 7th grade, students are asked to write at the end of their experience and they react to the following questions:

1. How do you feel about the Adventure program?
2. Have you learned anything about other people in your class?
3. Has Project Adventure helped to increase your sense of personal confidence? If so how?
4. Do you wish to be in the 8th grade Adventure program? Why? Why not?

In the 8th grade, the students are asked to react in the first class session. They are asked to respond to the following questions:

1. Describe — What am I getting myself into?
2. What do I expect to gain as a result of this experience?

After their rock climbing experience, they are asked to write about the following statements:

1. How did you feel about the day — in general terms?
2. Students belayed students. How did you feel when you were being belayed and what was it like to belay someone on the ledge?
3. How far should teachers/students "push" a climber to achieve a goal?
4. Did you feel challenged? If so, how?
5. Did you learn anything about the people in this group as a result of this rock climbing experience?

(At the site, a debriefing session is also held)

At the end of the 8th grade Project Adventure experience, students respond to the following questions:

1. What did you get out of this Project Adventure experience?
2. Ten years from now, when you look back at this Project Adventure experience, what do you feel will be your most memorable experience?
3. How did you feel about the students' behavior toward their fellow classmates? ...their Project Adventure teachers?
4. What would you do to improve the Adventure program at John Read?

These samples of writing are used to evaluate our work. They act as a formative evaluation tool, giving us input at all times. As a result, we constantly update and re-evaluate elements of our program. We also get a sense of the program from the students' point of view.

Diagram of the Physical Education Program at the John Read Middle School

Physical Education

Gymnastics	Volleyball
Dance	Team Handball
Conditioning	Cross Country
Fitness Test	Softball
Basketball	Track and Field
Floor Hockey	Badminton
Soccer	Ultimate Frisbee
Flag Football	Field Hockey

Project Adventure

Warm-up Activities
New Games
Initiatives
Ropes Course Indoors/Outdoors
Orienteering
Rock Climbing

Student

Learning
Experiencing
Being Challenged
Cooperating
Competing
Growing
Sharing

After School Sports Program

Field Hockey
Soccer
Basketball
Floor Hockey
Volleyball
Softball
Track and Field
Project Adventure

Life Education

Self-esteem
Communication
Male/Female Roles
Adolescent Growth & Development
Physical Fitness
Nutrition
Reproductive System
Decision Making
First Aid

Chapter 7
High Schools

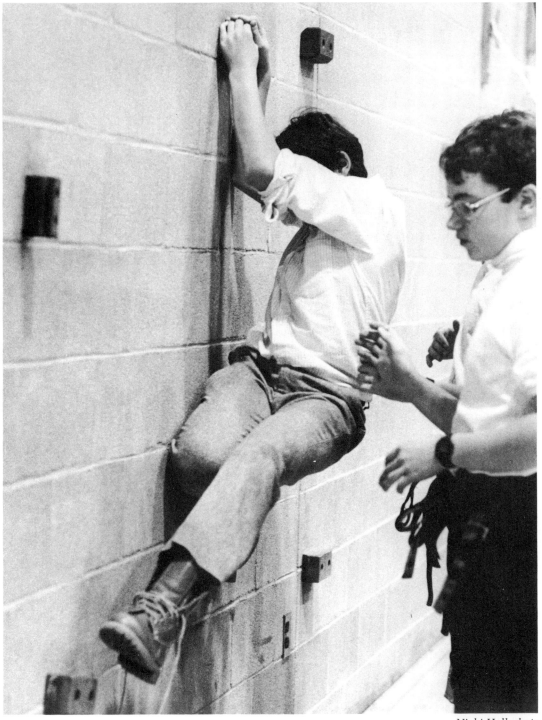

Nicki Hall photo

Project Adventure at Ridgewood Public Schools Ridgewood, NJ

Richard Bennett
Jack Elwood
Jeffrey Yearing
David Marsh

The History of Project Adventure in Ridgewood

There has been a commitment to Adventure based programming in the Ridgewood Schools for many years. Full implementation of all phases of the program, as well as required course offerings, were instituted in 1985 with the reorganization of the school district from a K–6, 7–9, 10–12 district to a K–5, 6–8, 9–12 configuration. Until that time, courses entitled "Outdoor Recreation" were added to the elective course offerings at the junior high school level. These courses dealt with trust-oriented activities, group initiative problems, and ropes techniques in the area of rappelling. Some outdoor survival and first aid techniques, as well as camping skills and cross country skiing, were also included. These 8th grade offerings would culminate with a day trip to Ramapo County Reservation where students engaged in activities in each of the above-mentioned areas.

In 1979, the addition of a large climbing wall at Benjamin Franklin Middle School brought the program into greater prominence and visibility. In the spring of 1981, the first Ridgewood staff members attended a Project Adventure workshop. The curriculum at Benjamin Franklin then called for a course entitled "Ropes" to be taught in the elective program. This course consisted of basic knots, belaying, rappelling, and climbing skills. As a result of staff attendance at Project Adventure workshops, New Games became part of the program at Benjamin Franklin. The program at George Washington continued to be taught under its original general outdoor recreational skills format. These two courses continued to be very popular with students with strong parental support as well.

As more staff members attended Project Adventure workshops and became familiar with those teaching strategies, interest grew in the program. With the reorganization of the school system planned for the fall of 1986, it seemed an appropriate time to examine the total Physical Education curriculum. As a result of this, a committee of professionals and parents came up with a proposal to include Project Adventure as a core program required of all freshmen and sophomores.

In the spring of 1986, a proposal for an indoor, as well as outdoor ropes course, was approved by the Superintendent. This work was completed in August 1986 at the cost of $6,000. The first students to use it were the freshmen and sophomores, who, in that same year, had entered the High School. Their immediate response was overwhelmingly favorable, and the only complaints came from juniors and seniors who felt cheated because they could not participate.

Program promotion that first year included a showcase video presentation of the John Read

Middle School program from West Redding, Connecticut. This tape, on loan from John Hichwa, was used on Back-to-School Night, and at a formal presentation to the Board of Education. In both instances, the response was extremely positive and public support for the program continued to grow. That spring, a Parent's Night was held in which the parents of the participants in the program were invited to an open house to take part.

Throughout the year, newspaper releases were written and numerous visitations were made by reporters and personnel from other school systems. As a result of personal interest and involvement in the program, administrative support was very strong at all levels.

The curriculum for the first year was developed by the instructional staff from materials taken from other similar programs and the publications provided by Project Adventure, Inc. The staff developed a clear cut, day-by-day sequence that gave them general guidance but did not tie them down. Subsequently, a two-year sequentially based program has been developed and field tested by the staff. Course descriptions for these two courses follow.

The demand for an advanced course for upper-classmen has continued. This demand may well result in a peer leadership program being implemented in 1988–89. Parent interest in the program has also resulted in a course being offered by the Ridgewood Community School. This too has proven extremely successful, receiving very high praise from participants. The course has also been inserted into the regional summer school program where it serves students making up lost credits in Physical Education.

Overall, the response of the community has been extremely positive. The concept upon which it is based is a powerful tool for positive self-concept development in young and old alike. Participants demonstrate increased concern about others and greater confidence in their own ability to achieve. It has been well accepted as an integral part of the education process in the Ridgewood Schools.

Project Adventure I

Course Description

This is a required course for all freshmen students that has been modeled after highly successful programs using the Outward Bound philosophy. Through a carefully planned curriculum of group and individual initiatives, the students progress through an experientially based self-discovery program that emphasizes interpersonal relationships and individual growth.

Participation in Project Adventure encourages students to develop greater self-confidence and at the same time acquire a sense of trust and commitment to their classmates. The emphasis in the course is on participation, and students are encouraged to extend their limits both physically and emotionally. Students are required to participate in all group activities but may decline to attempt individual challenges that they feel are beyond their personal limits.

At the conclusion of the course, students will be required to write a self-analysis of their activities during the quarter. Grades will be based upon this paper, as well as their participation in group activities and the completion of safety related tasks which they are assigned. Students must receive a passing grade in this quarterly core program in order to graduate from Ridgewood High School. Students will be expected to dress in appropriate activity clothing unless otherwise advised by teacher.

Course Objectives

Students will:

- Demonstrate improved self-confidence in individual and group challenges.
- Demonstrate the ability to work cooperatively toward the attainment of group goals.
- Demonstrate the ability to spot fellow students in low ropes course activities.
- Demonstrate a working knowledge of the basic knots and equipment necessary to participate safely in high ropes challenges.
- Demonstrate basic trust in classmates in matters pertaining to personal safety.

——————— **Week 1** ———————

Day 1

Activity: *Knots and Tangles* (Gordian Knot)
Goal: Social goals for group initiative
Size of Group: Try to arrange groups of 10–14
Equipment: None
Resources: *Silver Bullets*, pp. 117–118
Setting: Indoors or Outdoors
Time Duration: 10–20 min.

Day 2

Activity: *Circle the Circle* (Pass the Hoop)
Goal: Teamwork rather than winning
Size of Group: 15–30
Equipment: Large hoops (4 of each color)
Resources: *Silver Bullets*, pg. 60
Setting: Indoors or Outdoors
Time Duration: 10–15 min

Activity: *Hoop Relay*
Goal: Social interaction and mild competition
Size of Group: Groups of 6–8
Equipment: 3–4 hoops per group
Resources: *Silver Bullets*, pg. 61
Setting: Indoors or Outdoors
Time Duration: 5–10 min.

Day 3

Activity: *Stand Off*
Goal: Develop balance
Size of Group: Partners
Equipment: None
Resources: *Silver Bullets*, pg. 94
Setting: Indoors or Outdoors
Time Duration: 5 min.

Activity: *Indian Wrestling*
Goal: Develop balance
Size of Group: Partners
Equipment: None
Resources: None
Setting: Indoors or Outdoors
Time Duration: 10 min.

Day 4

Activity: *Two by Four* (Group Jump Rope)
Goal: Group problem solving
Size of Group: 8
Equipment: One long jump rope
Resources: *Silver Bullets*, pg. 123
Setting: Indoors or Outdoors
Time Duration: 15–20 min.

Day 5

Activity: *Traffic Jam* (Group Jump Rope)
Goal: Group problem solving
Size of Group: 8 or more
Equipment: One long jump rope
Resources: *Silver Bullets*, pg. 122
Setting: Indoors or Outdoors
Time Duration: 15–20 min.

Week 2

Day 1,

Activity: *Tension Traverse* (Rolls and Falls)
Goal: Spotting, Balance, Agility
Size of Group: 2 at a time — plus spotters
Equipment: 2 tension traverse ropes
Resources: *Cowstails and Cobras*
Setting: Indoors
Time Duration: 10 min.

Activity: Falling
Goal: Improvement of physical fitness; Improvement of emotional strengths
Size of Group: Unlimited
Equipment: Open space
Resources: *Silver Bullets*, pg. 85
Setting: Indoors or Outdoors
Time Duration: Unlimited

Day 2

Activity: *Rope Swings*
Goal: To improve a coordination commitment activity
Size of Group: All
Equipment: Take-off perch, landing perch, swing rope, chalk
Resources: *Cowstails and Cobras*
Setting: Indoors
Time Duration: 1 period

Day 3

Activity: *Prouty's Landing*
Goal: Improvement of Socialization Skills
Size of Group: As many as possible
Equipment: Swing rope, trip wire, platform (auxiliary platform if large class)
Resources: *Silver Bullets*, pg. 142
Setting: Indoors or Outdoors
Time Duration: All period

Day 4

Activity: *Bottoms Up, Stand Up, Group Stand Up, Lap Game*
Goal: Physical as well as a great social activity
Size of Group: Any number
Equipment: None

Resources: *Silver Bullets, Cowstails and Cobras*
Setting: Indoors or Outdoors
Time Duration: 10 min. each

Day 5

Activity: Tag Games
Goal: Aerobic activity
Size of Group: Any size
Equipment: None
Resources: *Silver Bullets, Cowstails and Cobras*
Setting: Indoors or Outdoors
Time Duration: 7 min. each

Week 3

Day 1

Activity: *Smoke Stack/Quail Shooter's Delight*
Goal: Dealing with failure; group initiative
Size of Group: Any
Equipment: Hula hoops, tennis balls (lots), 7–8 paper cores
Resources: *Silver Bullets*, pp. 20, 63
Setting: Indoors or Outdoors
Time Duration: 1 period

Day 2 & 3

Activity: *The Electric Fence*
Goal: Improvement of socialization skills
Size of Group: Any
Equipment: 8-foot log, rope, rope supports
Resources: *Silver Bullets*, pg. 136
Setting: Indoors or Outdoors
Time Duration: 2 periods

Day 4

Activity: *Hog Call/Diminishing Load*
Goal: This is a social activity to break down inhibitions, and help students become acquainted with one another.
Size of Group: Any size
Equipment: Blindfolds
Resources: *Silver Bullets*, pp. 98 & 138
Setting: Indoors or Outdoors
Time Duration: 2–3 min.

Day 5
Activity: *Blindfold Crossing*
Goal: Establish new leadership; alternating forms of communication
Size of Group: All
Equipment: Swing rope, 2 ropes (start/finish line), several blindfolds
Resources: R. Bennett
Setting: Indoors or Outdoors
Time Duration: 1 period

──────────── **Week 4** ────────────

Day 1
Activity: *Trust Walk* (One-On-One)
Goal: Develop trust
Size of Group: All; in pairs
Equipment: Blindfolds
Resources: *Silver Bullets*, pg.47
Setting: Indoors or Outdoors
Time Duration: All period

Day 2
Activity: Parachute Games
Goal: Cooperation
Size of Group: All
Equipment: Parachute
Resources: *New Games*
Setting: Indoors or Outdoors
Time Duration: All period

Day 3
Activity: *Reach for the Sky*
Goal: Develop spotting
Size of Group: 10–15
Equipment: Chalk or tape, crash pad
Setting: Indoors
Time Duration: All period

Day 4
Activity: *Monster* (The 4 Pointer)
Goal: Communication
Size of Group: 7
Equipment: None
Resources: *Silver Bullets*, pg. 133
Setting: Indoors or Outdoors
Time Duration: 10–12 min.

Activity: *T.P. Shuffle*
Goal: Communication
Size of Group: 20
Equipment: None
Resources: *Silver Bullets*, pg. 110
Setting: Indoors or Outdoors
Time Duration: 10–12 min.

Day 5
Activity: *Spiral Walk*
Goal: To work as a group
Size of Group: All
Equipment: Length of rope
Resources: *Silver Bullets*, pg. 101
Setting: Indoors or Outdoors
Time Duration: All period

──────────── **Week 5** ────────────

Day 1
Activity: *Shipwreck*
Goal: Group cooperation
Size of Group: 8–10 per team
Equipment: Plywood circles
Resources: *Silver Bullets*, pg. 112
Setting: Outdoors
Time Duration: All period

Day 2, 3, & 4
Activity: *Jelly Swamp*
Goal: Group cooperation
Size of Group: Whole class
Equipment: Paper cores, 4 ropes, 2 boards, 2 platforms
Resources: *Silver Bullets*, pg. 134
Setting: Indoors
Time Duration: 3 days

Day 5
Activity: *Glute Walk*
Goal: Break down inhibitions
Size of Group: All
Equipment: None
Resources: *Cowstails and Cobras*
Setting: Indoors or Outdoors
Time Duration: 10–15 min.

Activity: *Python Pentathlon*
Goal: To increase mutual support with a group;
   Good stretching and abdominal exercise
Size of Group: 4 or 5
Equipment: None
Resources: *Cowstails and Cobras*
Setting: Indoors or Outdoors
Time Duration: 10–20 min.

──────────── **Week 6** ────────────

Day 1

Activity: *Yurt Circle*
Goal: Each supporting the whole
Size of Group: All
Equipment: None
Resources: *Cowstails and Cobras*
Setting: Indoors or Outdoors
Time Duration: 10–12 min.

Activity: *Willow in the Wind*
Goal: Trust
Size of Group: 8
Equipment: None
Resources: *Cowstails and Cobras*
Setting: Indoors or Outdoors
Time Duration: 10–15 min.

Day 2

Activity: *Cookie Machine*
Goal: Group support
Size of Group: 10–14
Equipment: None
Resources: *More New Games*
Setting: Indoors or Outdoors
Time Duration: 10–12 min.

Activity: *People Pass*
Goal: Group support
Size of Group: 10–14
Equipment: None
Resources: New Games
Setting: Indoors or Outdoors
Time Duration: 10–12 min.

Day 3

Activity: *Trust Fall*
Goal: Group trust
Size of Group: 10–12
Equipment: None
Resources: *Silver Bullets,* pg. 80
Setting: Indoors or Outdoors
Time Duration: All period

Day 4 & 5

Activity: *Trust Dive*
Goal: Group trust
Size of Group: 10–12
Equipment: None
Resources: *Silver Bullets*, pg. 83
Setting: Indoors or Outdoors
Time Duration: All period

Project Adventure II

Course Description

This is a required course for all sophomores that extends the philosophy that people can expand their perceived personal limits to accomplish new goals. Through a carefully planned series of group and personal challenges, students are given an opportunity to test themselves against physical and emotional limits in order to attain higher levels of performance.

In this course students will first review and then expand upon their experiences in Project Adventure I. Once again, all students will be expected to participate in all group activities and have an option to pass on the activities which they are convinced are beyond their personal limits.

The emphasis in this course will be upon participation and will be based on student involvement in class activities, as well as the successful completion of the assessment tasks listed on the next page.

Course Objectives

Students will:

- Develop positive interpersonal relationships based on mutual respect and trust of fellow class members.
- Acquire the physical skills necessary to belay, climb, and rappel on an outdoor climbing wall.
- Develop skills that enable them to enter into the group process of debriefing a group challenge experience without feeling resentment over criticism or embarrassment over praise.
- Prepare and dismantle the necessary equipment for a class of students to participate in a climbing experience.
- Present and lead a new games activity that is new to the class.

--------------------- **Week 1** ---------------------

Day 2

Activity: *Sherpa Walk*

Goal: An activity designed to develop trust and communication skills

Size of Group: 8–15

Equipment: Blindfolds

Resources: *Silver Bullets*, pp. 89–90

Setting: Indoors or Outdoors

Time Duration: varies

Day 3

Activity: *The Unholy Alliance*

Goal: To have fun and develop strategies that help bring your group on to victory.

Size of Group: 4 teams of no more than 15

Equipment: 1) 100 foot length of 1/4" polypropalene cord. 2) 4-way tug of war ropes.

Resources: *Silver Bullets,* pg. 36.

Setting: Outdoors

Time Duration: 15 minutes

Activity: *Human Ladder*

Goal: To develop trust; to be responsible for each other's safety; to engage in a unselfconscious physical contact with members of your group

Size of Group: All in the class

Equipment: 6–10 smooth hardwood dowel rods about 3 feet long, 1-1/4" diameter

Resource: *Silver Bullets*, pg. 113

Setting: Indoors or Outdoors

Time Duration: 20 min.

Day 4

Activity: *The Maze*

Resource: *Cowstails and Cobras*

--------------------- **Week 2** ---------------------

Day 1

Activity: *Trust Falls* and *Trust Dives*

Goal: To establish a level of trust within the group that later activities can be based on.

Size of Group: 10–12 students in each group

Equipment: Wall or platform to fall or dive off from.

Resources: *Silver Bullets,* pp. 80–83.

Setting: Indoors or Outdoors

Time Duration: full period

Day 2

Activity: *The Beam*

Goal: 1) Improvement of socialization skills (communication, group interaction)

2) Improvement of emotional strengths (increased awareness of individual potential and individual strengths)

Size of Group: Min. 10–12; 20–25 is good

Equipment: One peeled and treated hardwood log horizontally supported 7'–8' high

Resources: *Cowstails and Cobras*

Setting: Indoors or Outdoors

Time Duration: varies

Day 3

Activity: *Marooned*

Day 4

Activity: *Spider's Web*

Goal: To develop group commitment and the necessity of working together

Size of Group: Whole class

Equipment: Spider's Web

Resources: *Silver Bullets,* pg. 114.

Setting: Outdoors

Time Duration: whole period

———————— **Week 3** ————————

Day 1

Activity: *Schmerltz Tag*

Goal: To have fun with an aerobic activity; To develop cooperation among group

Size of Group: Whole class

Equipment: 5–10 tennis balls and 5–10 tube socks

Resource: *New Games Book*

Setting: Outdoors

Time Duration: 15 min.

Activity: *Aerobic Tag*

Goal: Excellent physical activity to use as warm-up; Great social activity for group

Size of Group: Whole Group

Equipment: Frisbee or beanbag

Resources: *Cowstails and Cobras*

Setting: Indoors or Outdoors

Time Duration: until one team wins

Day 2

Activity: *The Giant's Ring*

Goal: Improvement of socialization skills; Improvement of physical fitness

Size of Group: 15–20

Equipment: Vertical pole about 12'–14' tall in center of auto tire

Resource: *Cowstails and Cobras*

Setting: Outdoors

Time Duration: 10–15 min.

Activity: *All Aboard*

Goal: Group participation and cooperation; Improve communications and decision making

Size of Group: 12–15

Equipment: 2'x2' elevated platform

Resources: *Silver Bullets,* pg. 106.

Setting: Indoors or Outdoors

Time Duration: 20 minutes

Day 3

Activity: *Elephant Walk*

Goal: Improvement of physical fitness; Improvement of socialization skills

Size of Group: 12

Equipment: Minimum 2 elephants; 4 or 6 are better

Resource: *Silver Bullets,* pg. 119

Setting: Outdoors

Time Duration: 20 min.

Day 4

Activity: *Cargo Net Initiative*

Goal: Group cooperation, communication, and problem solving

Size of Group: Whole class

Equipment: Cargo net

Resources: None

Setting: Outdoors

Time Duration: whole period

———————— **Week 4** ————————

Day 1

Activity: *Macro-Moonball*

Goal: To develop cooperation of fast reactions

Size of Group: Whole class

Equipment: Beach ball

Resource: *Silver Bullets,* pg. 31

Setting: Indoors or Outdoors

Time Duration: 10–15 min.

Activity: *Existential Volleyball*

Goal: Group cooperation and participation

Size of Group: Whole class

Equipment: Beach ball

Resources: Karl Rohnke

Setting: Indoors

Time Duration: 15–20 min.

Day 2

Activity: *Tire Traverse*

Goal: To get the entire group and a "bomb" over a series of suspended tires without touching the ground

Size of Group: Whole class

Equipment: "Bomb", about 30 lbs

Resource: Project Adventure

Setting: Outdoors

Time Duration: 30 min.

Activity: *Kitten Crawl*

Goal: Develop spotting and a sense of group support for the individual

Size of Group: 10–15

Equipment: Ropes or cables to cross

Resources: *Cowstails and Cobras*

Setting: Indoors or Outdoors

Time Duration: 15–20 min.

Day 3

Activity: *Mohawk Walk*

Goal: To develop team work and learn to deal with frustrations

Size of Group: 15–20

Equipment: Set up cables, ropes, and other materials for crossing

Resource: *Cowstails and Cobras*

Setting: Indoors or Outdoors

Time Duration: as long as it takes

Day 4

Activity: *The Blind Tent Initiative*

Goal: Work on problem solving, dealing with frustration, and group cooperation

Size of Group: 10–12

Equipment: 1) Tent and equipment for setting up. 2) Blindfolds

Resources: Project Adventure Supplement

Setting: Outdoors

Time Duration: 30 minutes

Week 5

Day 2

Activity: *Seagull Landing*

Goal: To have students participate in a coordination-commitment activity

Size of Group: Whole class

Equipment: Swinging rope and various perches

Resources: Hamilton-Wenham High School

Setting: Indoors or Outdoors

Time Duration: 15–20 min.

Activity: *Track Walk*

Goal: To develop confidence and commitment while participating in an activity that is unintimidating and fun

Size of Group: Whole class

Resource: Project Adventure

Setting: Indoors

Time Duration: 15–20 min.

Day 3

Activity: *Rebirth* (Spaceways)

Goal: To give students some opportunity to practice problem solving: This activity is also designed to encourage cooperation and teamwork

Size of Group: Whole class

Equipment: A truck tire suspended by 4 cables

Resources: Project Adventure

Setting: Outdoors

Time Duration: whole period

Day 4

Activity: Process questions for previous work and do group discussion Initiatives: 1.) Emergency: 2.) Breath easy

Goal: To give students practice in problem solving and some insight into their own values and behavior

Size of Group: Whole class

Equipment: Pencils, paper, watches with second hands

Resource: Project Adventure supplement

Setting: Indoors or Outdoors

Time Duration: 10–15 min.

———————— **Week 6** ————————

Day 1

Activity: Review of Knots and Seats

Goal: To assess the students' knowledge of the important knots and seats they must know to climb and rappel

Size of Group: pairs

Equipment: Ropes and webbing for each student

Resources: Refer to P.A.I. section on knots and Seats

Setting: Indoors

Time Duration: whole class

Day 2

Activity: Review of Belay Techniques

Goal: To refresh the students on proper belay techniques and give them an opportunity to practice

Size of Group: Whole class

Equipment: Ropes, webbing, figure eights, carabiners

Resource: Refer to P.A.I. section on belaying

Setting: Indoors

Time Duration: Whole period

Day 3

Activity: Review of Rappelling Techniques

Goal: To improve skills worked on in P.A.I.

Size of Group: Whole class

Equipment: Ropes, carabiners, figure eights

Resources: Refer to Rappelling section P.A.I.

Setting: Indoors

Time Duration: Whole class

Day 4

Activity: Indoor high element work: *Log Walk, Burma Bridge, Heebie Jeebie, Wall Climb*

Goal: To conquer fear and challenge the commitment of each student

Size of Group: Whole class

Equipment: Ropes, carabiners, figure eights

Resource: *Cowstails and Cobras*

Setting: Indoors

Time Duration: Whole period

———————— **Week 7** ————————

Day 1, 2, & 3

Activity: Climb and rappelling stations on west face of gymnasium

Goal: To take individuals and groups beyond their own expectations, or perceived willingness to try; By meeting the challenge we hope to break down self-imposed boundaries and become stronger in terms of self-confidence and self-awareness

Size of Group: Whole group

Equipment: Ropes, carabiners, gloves, figure eights.

Resources: none

Setting: Outdoors

Time Duration: Whole period

Day 4

Activity: *Trapeze Jump* and all other indoor elements

Goal: Challenge fears and self-imposed restrictions

Size of Group: Whole group

Equipment: Ropes, carabiners, gloves, figure eights

Setting: Indoors

Time Duration: Whole period

——————————— **Week 8** ———————————

Day 1

Activity: High Tree Climb to Rappel, *Two Line Bridge, Commando Crawl, Inclined Walk*

Goal: Challenge self-doubts, insecurity, decision making; Develop balance

Size of Group: Whole group

Equipment: Ropes, carabiners, gloves, figure eights

Resource:

Setting: Outdoors

Time Duration: Whole period

Day 2, 3, & 4

Activity: Introduction to *High Zip, Pole, High Log Walk, Vine Walk*

Goal: Challenge climbing fears; Work on balance, self-doubt; Deal with the unpredictability of a new situation; Increase confidence; trust in belayer and oneself

Size of Group: Whole group

Equipment: Ropes, carabiners, gloves, figure eight

Resources:

Setting: Outdoors

Time Duration: Whole class

——————————— **Week 9** ———————————

Day 1, 2, & 3

Activity: Continue high element work of students' choice

Goal: stated above

Size of Group: Whole group

Equipment: Ropes, carabiners, gloves, figure eights, helmets

Resources:

Setting: Outdoors

Time Duration: Whole period

Day 4

Activity: Final student evaluation and debriefing

Cambridge High School UMPA Unit Plan

Week #1

Objective	*Activity*	*Hints/Comments*

Students will:
• get to know each other
• understand course requirements
• learn cooperation and consideration techniques
• learn the proper techniques involved in falling
• be exposed to new alternative forms of stretching
• be introduced to a group initiative and begin a cooperative effort
	Introduction Activities
	
	Warm-ups
	• Coordination and Cardiovascular Movements
	  Hopping, Straddle Jump, Follow the Leader, Toe Fencing
	• Limberness and Flexibility Movements
	  Comfortable Position, Row Boat Stretch, Duo Sit, Angel
	• Activities for Covering Distance
	  Forward Jog, Forward, Backwards, and Sideways Hopping
	• Small "Apparatus" Warm-Ups
	  Hula Hoops, Jump Ropes, Tubes, Parachute
	• Aerobic Dancing
	
	Falls
	
	Group Initiative Problems:
	  High School
	  Mohawk Walk, Tube Stack, Trust Fall, Amazon, Nitro Crossing
		Stress the importance of "getting to know" each member of the group.
		Make sure students realize the necessity of spotting techniques for the various activities.
		Emphasize good cooperation and group effort.
		
		"No put-downs."

Week #2 & 3 — New Games and Initiative Problems

Objective	Activity	Hints/Comments
Students will: • develop a new awareness of themselves • strive to new and different limits • make a commitment to work with a group • overcome looking inept in front of others • overcome some sensitivity toward failure • increase ability to be an effective member of a group • develop aerobic efficiency • develop mutual trust and support • encourage other students into making a commitment to another student and group of students • develop confidence in the group	New Games: High School *Balance Broom, Group Juggling, Python Pentathlon, Getting to Know You* Initiative Problems: High School *Trust Dive, Amazon, Nitro Crossing, All Aboard, Electric Fence*	The instructor's enthusiasm will either make or break the activity. Use spotters effectively.

Week #4 — Introduction to Ropes

Objective	Activity	Hints/Comments
Students will: • understand and demonstrate proper use and care of equipment • increase confidence and knowledge • venture beyond their preconceived limits Advanced students will become skilled in belay technique.	Introduction to the Ropes Course and Its Equipment Belay techniques Gold Line Stretch Low Elements *Kitten Crawl, Hickory Jump, Tension Traverse, Swinging Log*	Emphasize spotting in Low Ropes Use retired ropes attached to eye bolts in wall for belay practice and gold line stretch. High jump pits placed under ladder climb for practice belaying. Students belay with teacher back up system at first.

Week #5–8 — High Ropes Elements

Objective	Activity	Hints/Comments
Students will: • test their commitment • develop balancing skills • test their strength • develop skills in sensible risk taking • exhibit mutual support, group cooperation and trust • respect and understanding for each other	Choose from High Elements *Two Line Bridge, Catwalk, Zip Line, Burma Bridge, Dangle Duo*	Offer elements of varying degrees of difficulties. After students have succeeded, have them try the elements blindfolded. Encourage students to make the effort and attempt. Don't let students remain on the platform too long — they can try it again. Have advanced students belay with a mechanical belay device, while another student backs up with a body belay. Student leaders can supervise one station. Instructors can supervise 2 or 3 stations.

Chapter 8
Higher Education

Nicki Hall photo

Application of Project Adventure Curriculum for Physical Education and Recreation at Radford University

by Dr. Gary G. Nussbaum

Project Adventure (PA) has been implemented and disseminated at Radford University (RU), Radford, VA, through three main channels; 1.) as an integral part of the curriculum of the Recreation and Leisure Services Department; 2.) as "teambuilding" trainings for various student groups with leadership provided by Recreation faculty/students; 3.) as "trickle down" programs where participants of previous PA trainings (1 & 2 above) program for their respective clientele.

Sample training formats are provided for each of these PA implementation channels. Before doing so, however, the following general considerations are noteworthy regarding all of the formats presented:

- The goals of PA programs at RU are consistent with the general goals of PA as articulated in the PA literature. Beyond the "generic" goals of PA, specific goals are generated for specific programs, and PA activities are adapted accordingly. An important question we ask is, "Why is this particular group doing these activities at this site at this time."

- The Challenge by Choice philosophy is the cornerstone of our PA programs. This philosophy is meaningless without the development of a genuine atmosphere of group support for the understanding of individual challenge and choice.

- Appropriate planning and sequencing of activities is crucial to PA methodology. Typically, a projected activity plan is developed for each program and these projected or initial plans are generally followed with only minor modifications. Nevertheless, no plan should preclude necessary modifications to insure a better activity format or sequence once the program begins. There are simply too many variables to perfectly predict the ideal sequence for a particular group. This is where the facilitator's "bag of tricks" comes into play. Always program for more activities than you anticipate using. In essence, our activity plans have built-in flexibility. A plan is like a mirror that tells us whether or not we have dressed properly for the curricular occasion.

- Individual and group goal-setting are an integral part of PA implementation at RU. This may simply mean the development of and adherence to a positive value contract (aka "Full Value contract"). Or, for longer or multi-day programs, it may mean periodic reevaluation and resetting of individual as well as group goals. And it's perfectly legitimate for that goal to be FUN!!!

- We feel that PA programming does not depend upon the utilization of a Low and/or High Ropes Course or the use of props. This is where the facilitator's ability to adapt and utilize his or her bag of tricks comes into play. By not relying on props, the facilitator develops a great degree of self-resourcefulness and confidence with regard to PA programming.

- Team leadership, regarding the total program process — planning, implementation, and evaluation, is encouraged and practiced wherever possible. Such leadership provides for greater safety, exposure to different leadership roles and styles, diffusion of reliance on single "authority" figures, greater total leadership energy, a more balanced sensitivity to the needs and wants of individual participants, and more personalized attention/interaction with participants. Team leadership is simply a model of shared leadership and responsibility.

- At some level it is desirable for the leaders/facilitators to model a play spirit or attitude; to infuse a certain "joie de play" into their PA programs. Play hard, play fair — but play!!!

- In reviewing the formats presented in the following pages, the reader may note that many PA activities are used again and again. Although we are always trying new activities and/or variations of "old" ones, there are certain activities that have been tried and tested over and over that have been found to work. It's reassuring to know that some activities are practically sure fire. Knowing that a good portion of a program can't fail spurs a willingness to try other activities (trial and error) that may flop.

- Both formal and informal processing of the PA experience is woven into the fabric of our programs. Consequently, processing or debriefing is not listed as a separate activity. Although processing is pervasive, it is friendly pervasiveness, rather than overwhelming.

Project Adventure and the Recreation and Leisure Services Curriculum

The RU undergraduate degree program in Recreation and Leisure Services is accredited by the National Council on Accreditation for Park, Recreation, and Leisure Services. Concentrations or emphases in recreation management (municipal), therapeutic recreation and outdoor recreation/education are also accredited. REC 417, Project Adventure (2 semester hours), was developed to enhance the outdoor emphasis within the curriculum. REC 417 is essentially the same as the five-day Adventure Programming Workshop offered by PA. We run this adventure workshop on five consecutive days (Wednesday through Sunday).

REC 417 utilizes the Dedmon Center Ropes Course, a Low and High Ropes Course along the New River (which borders the Radford campus).

Some undergraduate students go beyond REC 417 and complete the Advanced Skills and Standards Workshop (noncredit workshop where PA staff come to RU). Recently, to "graduate" and culminate such a workshop, five students helped in the implementation of an Adventure Programming Workshop for sixteen of the staff of the Nantahala Outdoor Center (NOC), Bryson City, North Carolina. We provided PA training for their river staff in exchange for instruction in canoeing, kayaking, and/or rafting for our PA staff. By assisting in the implementation of the NOC training, our students earned a trip to NOC. Although the NOC training was not for academic credit, it more or less parallels REC 417 and was therefore included as representative.

NOC — PA Training

Sunday, March 22 *(two sessions)*
Toss-A-Name Game
Wampum
Samurai
Line Up First Name Only
Everybody's It
Partner Tag/Elbow/Shoulder Tag
Team Tag (3-person)
Inch Worm
Bottoms Up
Windmill Stretch
Swaying Stretch
Knots — Nonverbal
Line Up By Number — Nonverbal
Sneakers
Monster
Hog Call
Video Tape Replay

Rope work

Monday, March 23 *(three sessions)*
Moon Ball
Swat Tag
Tusker/Blob Tag
Touch My Can
Shipwreck
Circle the Circle
Standup
Stork
Trust Sequence

Dog Shake
Squat Thrust
Texas Big Foot
Tickle-A-Pickle
TP Shuffle
Spider's Web
Mohawk Walk
Giant's Finger

Striker
5-A-Side Flatball
Quail Shooter's Delight
Polar Bears

Hands Down
I've Got the Beat
4 Letter Word
Rope work

Tuesday, March 24 *(three sessions)*
Yell
Hopping
Can-Can
Return to Soil
Cobra
Skirt Stretch
Glutewalk/Glute Thrust
Python Pentathlon
Clock
Popsicle Pushup
Aerobic Tag — "Hooper"
PDQ
Nail Trick/Porcupine Progression
Ah-So (Zen Clap)

Low and High Ropes Course

Frantic
Paper Core Massage
One/Two Person Paper Core Balance (Butt Balance)
Smokestack
Paul's Balls
Helga's Hoops (Ring Toss)
Group Blow
Pick and Choose
Wonderful Circle

Wednesday, March 25 *(two sessions)*
Pairs Tag
Hospital Tag
Needle and Thread Tag
Red Baron Stretch
Mirror Image
All Aboard in a Tree
Trust Fall (from same tree)
Low and High Ropes Course

Caving Trip (3:00–10:00 PM)

Thursday, March 26 (one long session)
5-5-5
Squat Thrust
Witches Broom
Yurt Circle
Nitro Crossing
Low and High Ropes Course

Personnel
Coordinators: Dr. Gary G. Nussbaum, Associate Professor; Jim Lustig, Graduate Assistant

Undergraduate Assistants: Todd Jones, Samia Hollinger, Thom Jones, Steve Huter, Rich Helmuth

Professional Assistants: Tom Clarke, Outdoor Recreation Supervisor, Blacksburg Parks & Recreation Department; Ricky Showalter, Outdoor Recreation Supervisor, Roanoke County Parks and Recreation Department

Dalton Intermediate Outdoor School (DIOS) — 1987

Recreation students in REC 235, Camp Counseling, are required to assist in the implementation of a three-day, two-night outdoor Adventure Education program at Camp Carysbrook, a nearby camp in Riner, Virginia. The program is built around caving, canoeing, ropes, and Initiatives as well as more traditional camp fare. The approximately fifty eighth graders are divided into three activity sites. The format below reflects a six-hour time block, including lunch.

At camp
Videotape replay
Samurai
Swat Tag
Tusker or *Add-on-Tag*
Moonball
Hike to playing field
Human Camera (during hike)
Blindfold sequence (two groups)
Trust walks
Lineup #1–8 (two groups)
Sneakers
Hopping
Circle the Circle

At playing field
Shipwreck
Bottoms Up
Inchworm
Return to the Soil/Cobra Stretch
Trust sequence
Squat thrust thrust
Partner Trust
See-saw Trust
Trolleys
Commando Crawl — (at Pond)
Fidget Ladder
Big Gulp (rope swing)
Punctured Drum
Zip Line

At ropes course
The Ropes Course activities at the pond were put up/take down activities designed specifically for this program. As part of staff training, REC 235 students "walked through," or actually played the activities in this sequence. Lastly, the program was designed and implemented by REC 235 students under faculty supervision.

Personnel
Coordinators: Steve Huter, Director, DIOS 1987; Rich Helmuth, Assistant Director, DIOS 1987

Supervisors: Dr. Richard D. McWhorter, Associate Professor; Dr. Gary G. Nussbaum.

Teambuilding Trainings for RU Student Groups

Quest, Spring 1987

Quest is an orientation program for all new students at the beginning of each semester designed so that their initial adjustment to college can be pleasant and productive. New students who are admitted for the fall semester are invited to attend a Quest session during the summer. Students attending these sessions are preregistered for fall classes. Student leaders, trained as "Quest Assistants," are an integral part of the Quest Leadership Team.

Quest Assistants undergo rigorous training, including the teambuilding session outlined below. This session went from 8:30 AM – 2:30 PM including lunch.

Toss-a-Name Game
Group Juggle/Time Warp variation
Glutewalk
PA Glute Ballet
Inchworm
Python Pentathlon
Clothes Pin Tag (version of Everybody's It)
Tusker or *Blob Tag*
Windmill Stretch
#10 Tin Can
Monster or 4x7
Do you love your neighbors?
Honey, I love ya, but I just can't make you smile
Trust Sequence
Partner Trust
Seesaw Trust
Trust Fall
Egg Drop

Personnel
Dr. Gary G. Nussbaum
Mike Dunn, Associate Dean of Students

Student Leadership Conference, Fall 1986

Each year the undergraduate Student Government Association (SGA) sponsors a leadership conference for high school leaders throughout Virginia. The weekend conference gets underway Friday evening with an initiatives session focusing on fun and group dynamics (7:00 – 9:30 PM). The activities were selected with the idea that most could be utilized by the student leaders at their respective high schools. Approximately 50 – 70 high school students attend the conference.

Quick Lineup
Everybody's it/ Asteroids/ Ankle Biters/ Team Ankle
Human Treasure Hunt
Birthdays
Pic-N-Choose

Rat-a-Tat-Tat (tennis balls thrown against black board)
Relay: Python Pentathlon
Balloon Carry
Fire-in-the-Hole
Moonball
People Pass
People-to-People
Lap Sit

Personnel
Dr. Richard M. McWhorter
Dr. Gary G. Nussbaum

Residential Life Training, Summer 1984

This training occurred in four, four-hour activity blocks over a period of two days with different groups of Residential Life Staff (resident assistants, resident directors, and area coordinators). The development of "comfortability" among staff was the general goal of these short training sessions.

Glutewalk
Inchworm
Boop
Standup
Touch My Can
Hospital Tag/Triangle Tag
Clock
Human Ladder
Human Camera
Turnstile
I trust you, but...
Blind trust walk
The Wall

Personnel
Dr. Richard M. McWhorter
Dr. Gary G. Nussbaum

"Trickle Down" Programs

Some of the participants in our PA trainings have gone on to lead PA programs in a variety of settings and leadership training situations. We asked three of our alumni to provide a sample program including a general description of program goals of the program as well as the rationale for the selection of activities. It should be noted that the leaders of these three programs all completed REC 417, Project Adventure ("Adventure Programming Workshop").

St. Alban's Hospital Chemical Dependency Staff

On March 26, 1987 Alexa Marchall and Mary Lucy Reeves, Certified Therapeutic Recreation Specialists on staff at St. Alban's Psychiatric Hospital, presented a day of group Initiatives and trust building activities. This day was planned specifically for the Chemical Dependency Program Staff. The goals established include:

1. To introduce the Chemical Dependency Staff to the philosophy of Project Adventure in the treatment facility.
2. To strengthen the ties between the Chemical Dependency Staff and the Adjunctive Therapy Department.
3. To strengthen the bond between the members of the Chemical Dependency Staff.
4. To allow each person to grow professionally and personally.
5. To allow the Chemical Dependency Staff to experience "hands-on" the process of Project Adventure.

After meeting with the Chemical Dependency Team and establishing goals, the following activities were chosen:

Discussion — PA concept and history, discussion of group as well as individual goals and expectations, discussion of leadership roles and introduction of journals.

Stretching — included *Stork*, *Red Baron* and *Inchworm*

Aerobic Tag — (increase energy and a good warm-up)

Trolley — completed easily

Monster

Three Pointer — (changed to *Monster* because we had 8 people)

Processed — began dealing with issues such as subgroups and leaders' responsibilities)

Smokestack — had difficulty

Lunch

Leisurely walk to the River — time to write in journals

Snowflake

Blindfold line up by #

Shoe Search (blindfolded)

Trust Rock (3 people)

Trust Fall

Cookie Machine Pass

Processed

Alligator Crossing

Processed — shared journals, discussed implementation at treatment facility.

From the leaders' point of view, the day itself was ideal. The weather was sunny and warm and paralleled the feeling of the group. Because these folks already knew each other, they developed a close bond, and we chose to build upon that bond. The group did struggle with leadership from time to time, and because of this struggle, the processing was quite effective. The drawback was that the day was too short to really confront those issues that began to surface. My view point as a leader is that we have started a great program that will be utilized throughout the hospital. At the end of the day I felt energized, exhilarated, and completely worn out!!!

To follow-up on our progress thus far, we are beginning to build a Low Ropes course on the hospital grounds. This course will be utilized by adolescents, Chemical Dependency Program, Women's Group Therapy, and Men's Group Therapy. The Chemical Dependency Staff is planning several day trips which will include group initiatives and team building. These are to begin June '87.

Tour Guide Training

by Nancy Murray

Project Adventure games and Initiatives were used for a Tour Guide Training Session. New tour guides (TG) are selected each year and must go through 9 intensive training sessions. These sessions are designed to provide tour guides with leadership skills as well as information about Radford University. PA had never been used before as part of TG training, but the director/coordinator of the tour guides had learned about the program through the Recreation Leisure Services Department.

I wanted to do some games and Initiatives with the new guides in order to bring the new group closer together, to try to develop leadership skills, and to have fun.

Activities

Human Bingo — done as an ice breaker and a chance for everyone to learn others' names. It also gave people a chance to learn new things about others.

Line Up by Age (without talking) — done to show everyone the importance of non-verbal communication. We processed this and talked about how non-verbal communication is important while giving tours and leading groups.

Hog Call — done to show importance of listening to others — as well as speaking out. This activity processed as well, with reference to tours.

Knots — to see how group dynamics work, how people should listen and talk at proper times — processed.

Hoops — done for group initiative and fun!

Impulse — ditto — great warm down!

Wonderful Circle — A great closing activity! Also a good outlet for what participants were thinking and expecting for their future as RU tour guides.

Note: All the other sessions which tour guides participate in are lectures. This session was a great way to break up the monotony. After already going through a training session the year before, I felt that games and Initiatives would be very applicable! It worked!!

Climb with Me — Resident Assistant Training Session

Julie Hogan, Graduate Assistant

Toss-a-Name-Game — gets people active, learning names

Circle Up — definitely learn names

Wampum — mixes group - actively learning names

Blanket Game — increases awareness, involves quick thinking

Line Up by First Name — develops communication

Hog Call — Builds trust, sense of needing help from another

Animal Sounds — same game only animal sounds

Partner Tag (Elbow Tag) and *Hospital Tag* — active games where you must work with a disability, partner of injury

Moonball — builds group cohesiveness — gets them working together

Swat Tag — FUN!

Samurai and *Kamikaze* — gets their attention, fun, makes them observe carefully

Human Camera, Trust Circle, Trust Fall and *I Trust You But...* — develops trust in new-found friends

Red Baron — chance to be silly, breaks down barriers

Touch My Can — working together

Knots (nonverbal) — working using only people's faces and non-verbal's

All Aboard and *Everybody's Up* — builds enthusiasm, teamwork

Impulse — builds group cohesiveness

Process — Goal: to break down barriers within the group of newly hired RA's and get them working as a whole unit.

Texas Big Foot and *Tickle Pickle* — Group Hug and Togetherness

Chapter 9
Camp Programs

Camps and other institutions that provide short term experiences — their programs don't normally stretch out through the school year or the hospital stay — have a special challenge. They must utilize the curriculum in such a way that they don't minimize the sequential approach and at the same time stick to their own unique curriculum. Our continual concern is that institutions utilizing Adventure activities make those activities complement what they are already doing. The American Youth Foundation does this integrating as well as any camp structure we know. This is aided by the fact that the current AYF director, Bob MacArthur, is past director of the Dartmouth Outward Bound School (now a part of the Hurricane Island Outward Bound School), and one of their camp directors, Beau Bassett (Merrowvista), is a Project Adventure National trainer. Bringing their extensive knowledge of Experiential Education to their work settings was a natural thing for them to do. The following is a discussion of their camp purposes in terms of the relationship to Project Adventure activities.

American Youth Foundation

by Beau Bassett

AYF History and Programs

The American Youth Foundation was founded in 1924 as a non-sectarian, not-for-profit organization. Its primary mission today is to promote the personal and leadership development of youth between the ages of 8 and 21.

The AYF operates two camps, located in beautiful remote settings; Camp Merrowvista, on 700 acres in the Ossipee Mountains of central New Hampshire; Camp Miniwanca, located on the eastern shore of Lake Michigan, covering close to 300 acres of wooded sand dunes. AYF camps conduct two- to seven-week programs during the summer, including ten day national leadership conferences. These programs emphasize waterfront activities, environmental education, individual and team Challenge Courses, and outdoor skills such as cycling, canoeing, backpacking, sailing, and sea kayaking.

What sets AYF camps apart is that in addition to providing a fun-filled experience for young people, the camps exist for a larger purpose — to teach campers a way of life based upon balanced living, doing your best, and serving others. William H. Danforth, one of the founders, put it this way, "You have a fourfold life to live: a body, a brain, a heart, and a soul — these are your living tools. To use and develop them is not a task. It is a golden opportunity."

Both camps dare participants to grow mentally, physically, socially, and spiritually, through a wide variety of educational and recreational activities. Offering both single sex and coed groups, the camp programs encourage each individual to be "my own self at my very best all the time." Through the pursuit of challenging activities demanding cooperation and commitment, AYF camp programs utilize Adventure-based Challenge Courses modeled after Project Adventure designs. These courses are called Challenge as opposed to Ropes Courses, in order to best achieve the AYF's core educational themes. These themes are the central focus of all AYF programs.

The Role of Adventure in AYF Camps

The intentional use of Adventure activities in the camp programs of the American Youth Foundation is consistent with the goal of daring young people to be their own best self all the time. AYF supports the premise that to be the best involves stretching and growing into new abilities, competencies, and confidence. In the camp programs, the process of becoming better involves a curriculum promoting intelligent risk-taking behavior and the willingness to try with a best effort in new situations where the outcomes are uncertain. Each Challenge in the camp curriculum calls upon the camper to look at and respond with his or her own personal resources and acknowledge as well as respect the value of different resources presented by others.

A progression of activities utilizing Adventure always begins with warm-up activities, such as new games, in order to prepare the campers for focused learning, no matter what their age and experience level. Because AYF camps serve youth between the ages of 8–21, the Adventure curriculum is tailored to the specific developmental stages of each camper group. These stages are referred to as Pioneer Campers (age 8–12), Four Trails Campers (age 13–17), and Leadership Campers (age 17–21). Depending upon the developmental readiness of the group of campers, the camp curriculum offers the following adventure activities:

1. Adventure warm-up activities: spotting techniques, stretches, new games.
2. Mobile Initiative problems: portable structured problems taking 15–45 minutes, presented to campers by their leaders.
3. Outdoor Adventure activities:
   - acclimatization and nature investigation
   - shelter building
   - outdoor skill instruction
   - orienteering
   - search and rescue
   - night experience
   - solo experience
4. Team Challenge Course Elements — structured Challenges built in area of camp that are presented to the primary social group of campers (the village of 8–12 campers who live together).
5. 1–4 day adventure trips.
6. High Challenge Course elements — structured Challenges at heights of 20–30 feet, requiring individuals belaying and being belayed to accomplish the tasks.

In order to best see the application of Project Adventure ideas and methods in the AYF camp programs, a part of the camp team Challenge Course curriculum follows. This part of the Adventure curriculum explains how AYF camps utilize Adventure activities to achieve specific learning outcomes. Most of the team Challenge Course elements are common ones used in a standard course. However, the elements are uniquely named, defined, and presented, in order to instruct campers in a manner consistent with the AYF's educational objectives. These examples are representative of the camp's overall Adventure curriculum.

American Youth Foundation Camp Adventure Curriculum

Quality Call

This activity is sometimes called *Hog Call.* In AYF camps, campers are paired up at the start of camp with someone they are meeting for the first time. This is often done within their village of 8–12 campers which is the primary small group community in camp. Campers are asked to identify one quality in themselves they would like more of and to share that quality with their partners. Once partners have disclosed the area for which they see a need to improve, they are separated across a 50–100 yd. field. Along with their village peers, the campers are blindfolded and asked to find their respective partner by calling out that quality of which their partner wanted more. Starting at an announced time, campers move across the field listening for their quality being announced while announcing their partner's. Qualities such as patience, strength, confidence, trust, joy, all find their way onto the field and create an atmosphere of commitment to personal improvement. The qualities identified by campers then become areas in which village staff leaders can help campers grow.

Living Ladder

Also called the *Fidget Ladder*, in the AYF camps the element is presented as a ladder which represents each camper's journey in life, from the low end of the ladder, early childhood, to the uppermost end, adulthood. The instability of the ladder represents the common surprises, forces, and events, that shape one's life. The campers are challenged to move individually (while others spot from the low end of the ladder) to the top rung of the upper end without falling. After a series of attempts, campers begin to master weight distribution, even pace, coordinated movement, concentration, and other skills which allow successful travel across the ladder. Parallels are drawn between real life growth and development, and the competency of getting farther along the ladder (in life). When each camper has had several tries, campers are asked to grab two rungs on the ladder that represent personal goals they have in life. As a group, they share their life goals, which sometimes are immediate (within the next month), to goals that are 5–10 years in the future. Professional goals (education, career), and personal goals (family, sports), then become the focus of group discussions about what it takes for an individual to reach his/her goals. Commonly, campers discover that taking a spill in life — having a setback (falling off the ladder) — is not unusual, but it takes courage, commitment, and thoughtful action to become more effective as a person in striving towards one's goals.

Relationship Walk

Also known as *Wild Woosey*. For AYF curriculum purposes, it is called the Relationship Walk. Again, the group of campers is asked to pair up with someone in their village that they don't know well and with whom they would like to build a better relationship. Each pair (spotted by others in the group) is asked to walk along two diverging cables, approximately 2 feet off the ground, without either of them falling off the cable. They are to get as far out along the cables as they possibly can, which will evidence the degree of development and quality of success in their relationship. The farther they get, the better the relationship. This activity highlights the important aspects of any good relationship; give and take, clear, honest, and direct communication, interdependency, and trust. After each pair has had several opportunities to try the activity and has experienced progressively more success, each camper is asked to think about an important relationship at home. They are then asked to stand at a point along the diverging cables which they think and feel best represents that relationship according to its current stage of development.

Campers are given the opportunity to share these relationships (friendships, family ties, etc.) and asked to think about ways they could act to improve and build better relationships.

Serum Crossing

Commonly referred to as the *Nitro Crossing*. In the AYF curriculum the focus of the activity is changed from a group task of transporting nitroglycerine, an explosive to blow something up, to a group task of delivering a life-saving serum that will prevent the spread of a deadly disease in an isolated community. The entire group of campers is presented the problem of swinging across an open area and onto a small platform. The platform represents the isolated community suffering from the spread of un-checked disease. Without any group member touching the ground in the open area (which is contaminated with the disease), the entire group must get themselves and the serum safely to the community (platform), and stay on the platform for a full minute in order to save the community. If any member touches the ground, or comes off the platform prema-turely, the whole group returns to their origi-nal position and treats the campers who touched with the serum. For each member that has to be treated, there is less serum for the community. This activity is used to emphasize the concept of an individual's capacity for service to others. Campers talk about what it takes to recognize the needs of others and act to help those more needy. Examples are given of the variety of needs in society that call for compassion, understanding, and response by those more fortunate.

Web of Life

This Challenge Course activity is often called the *Spider's Web*. For the AYF camp curriculum, the same net (suspended vertically 2–6 ft. off the ground) and containing 10–15 differently sized holes, is named the Web of Life. Campers are asked to make a personal decision about which hole they would like to go through. Each hole represents a different resource (land, air, wildlife, sun, water, miner-als, fuel, food, etc.), in the human and natural environments.

Once a camper has picked a hole, he or she describes which resource their hole represents. Resources can only be selected once. The group must get each member through the Web of Life without touching any part of it. If anyone touches, the resource is degraded (made less valuable, reduced), and the whole group must return and recommit to protecting each of the resources. By working together, the group begins to have more success passing individuals through the Web, and hence, succeeds in retaining the quality of the envi-ronment. In discussing this activity, campers are asked to reflect on how their personal choices impact resources.

Balance Log

Otherwise known as the *Swinging Log*, this Adventure Activity asks campers to traverse the length of an 18–20 ft. log suspended 1–2 ft. off the ground. Campers are actively spotted on either side of the log and encouraged to move across it without falling off and without touching the spotters. Campers develop their own technique, style, pace, and capability in doing this Challenge. They experience varying degrees of success at first and experiment with foot and body positions as well as speed.

Campers often talk to themselves and either help or hinder their efforts by what they say. In discussing this Adventure Element, groups compare and contrast different approaches to traversing the log. They talk about what worked best and how they felt while on the log. This reflection can lead to sharing on how one stays in balance in life's daily experience, the kinds of events that throw us off balance, how our personalities affect our approaches to life's situations, and the nature of personal wellness. Wellness is often looked at from the fourfold interpretation of mental, physical, social, and spiritual well-being. Finally, campers are asked about making a plan to better manage their personal wellness. This might include goals such as increasing physical exercise or developing more positive attitudes about one's self-image.

Human Alliance

The AYF uses this activity, commonly referred to as the *Human Knot*, to create a series of agreements and commitments between campers in a group of 10–12. Campers are asked to form a circle, reach across and connect right hands with one person, and left hands with a different person. They are then asked to untangle this community of people without letting go of their hands. The group works to organize themselves in a more comfortable, less dense configuration. The Challenge of being in this community is looked at by examining the working agreements individuals have with those they are holding hands with, the personal and group commitments to keep on the task at hand, and the frustrations of being in such a close, awkward alliance. Campers then discuss how they form agreements in real life, the importance of keeping agreements, how one appreciates and works with a diversity of people, and the role of commitment and community in today's society.

Cooperation Tarp

This activity is sometimes called *Team on a Tarp* and involves presenting to a village of 10–12 campers, the task of thinking about their own cooperative behavior. Campers are asked to individually identify two or three examples of how they act when cooperating with others. Then they pick one of these cooperative tendencies and offer it to the group to enhance the group's ability to cooperate. A 10' x 10' tarp or ground cloth is spread on the ground, and it is explained that this tarp is a symbol of the campers' ability to cooperate with each other. The group is challenged to get everyone on the tarp for five seconds with no one touching the ground around the tarp. Once the campers succeed at this task, the cooperation tarp is folded to reduce the ground area covered. It may be folded in half, or thirds, or just a small corner taken away. As the group works on each succeeding smaller section of tarp, they're asked to show their commitment and ability to collaborate by accomplishing the task on the smallest possible dimension of tarp. In discussing their efforts afterwards, campers learn a range of cooperative behaviors. They talk about how their own tendencies can be improved to better work with others in a team fashion. Cooperative learning theory and the task and maintenance functions of small groups are examined.

Spirit Jump

The AYF camp curriculum uses what is usually called the *Hickory Jump* to develop a sense of spiritual dimension in campers. Each camper is spotted by the village group when she/he leaps from a series of cut-off stumps to a trapeze suspended eight to nine feet off the ground. The group catches and supports the jumper if he or she comes up short of the trapeze. The objective of the Spirit Jump is explained so that campers are challenged to demonstrate and display the *most spirit* in leaping for the trapeze. The goal of catching the trapeze is secondary to communicating the greatest spirit possible. As campers complete this activity, a discussion ensues about the types and nature of spirit that campers chose to display. Leaders help campers focus on what inspires them in their lives, and how and why one chooses to trust others and have faith that things will work out okay. Campers are encouraged to show their respective belief systems and acknowledge the importance of spiritual guidelines and development, which can provide a source of strength, renewal, and meaning in life situations.

Learning Polygon

The Learning Polygon, or *Blind Polygon,* is used in the AYF camp curriculum to challenge campers to develop an awareness of, and range in, problem solving skills. The entire village of campers is blindfolded in an open field and a rope 100'–150' long is stretched out on the ground nearby. Without any verbal communication, the campers are to form a perfect square, using all the rope, and with each camper touching the rope at all times. As the group works to solve the problem, leaders rate the different strategies and campers who are not involved. After a period of time, it may be necessary to tell the group that they can now communicate verbally. In the discussion following the group's efforts, campers are asked to look at their own learning style preference (auditory, visual, kinesthetic), whether the exercise required and/or allowed more right brain or left brain activity, and how the problem solving strategies changed between verbal and non-verbal approaches. A wide variety of problem-solving skills are usually talked about, and campers can sometimes clearly see their strengths and areas needing improvement.

For more information on American Youth Foundation Camps and National Leadership Conferences, call or write:

American Youth Foundation
1315 Ann Avenue
St. Louis, MO 63104
(314) 772-8626

Merrowvista
Ossipee, NH 03864
(603) 539-6607

Miniwanca
Shelby, MI 49455
(616) 861-2262

Appendix A
Knots

After every PA training workshop, the staff hands out evaluation forms and one of the questions asked is, "What would you change or add to the workshop format?" It's predictable that we get the same response each time from at least one participant. "I wish there had been more time (emphasis) for knot tying."

When our staff visits schools that are currently implementing an Adventure curriculum (and which includes a High Challenge Course), a frequently heard comment is, "I wish I could remember all those knots we learned at the workshop." All those knots numbered about five.

A lot of worry and anxious moments could be alleviated by learning and practicing a FEW knots.

Knot tying at this level is not an art or even a skill; it is simply having the patience to stick with a series of digital manipulations until they become ingrained. Knot tying is a matter of teaching your fingers what to do and then performing the sequence over and over. Then,

after having put in sufficient practice time, the fingers seem to have a mind of their own and fairly dance through the twists, turns, and loops that recently seemed so mystifying. Also, remember that tying knots isn't like learning to ride a bicycle. Learn to ride a bike and the ability is yours forever. Learn to tie a bowline, then not tie another for a month, and the finger-fumbles return.

Nobody has all thumbs but some people do learn to tie knots with greater ease because they have better spatial awareness and can "see" the knot.

So, now that I have your promise to practice, here are a few basic knots for setting up safely on a ropes course.

These excellent knot sequence drawings are by Plynn Williams, who obviously sees the knots in more than one plane.

Bowline by itself

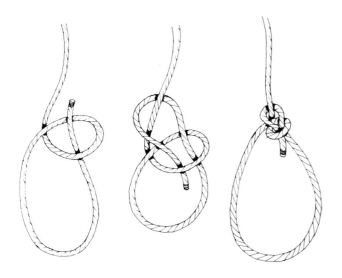

Bowline on a roundturn with backup safety knot

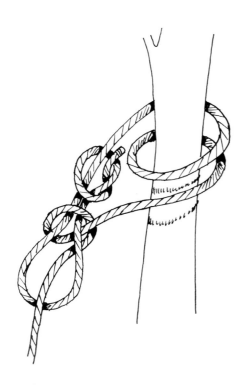

Figure 8 loop

Square knot and safety (tunnel) knots

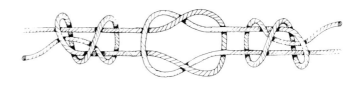

Double fisherman's knot (barrel knot)

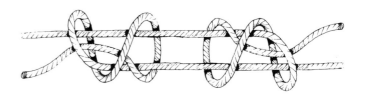

Knot Efficiency Table

The following knot and splice efficiency rating is a composite of three such comparisons. What this rating or any comparison points out is that the actual knots or splices used significantly affect the Safe Working Load (SWL = 20% of the tensile strength) of the rope. The figures also provide you with impressive statistics for your student or parent presentations.

Cordage Item	Efficiency
Full strength of rope	100% — This is the only percentage figure that everyone agrees on.
Eye splice over a thimble	90%
Short splice	87%
Bowline	60%
Square knot	50%
Overhand knot	47%

Knot tying can be an end in itself as you will see from the enthusiastic response from your students. The result of your over, under, and through efforts are aesthetic, self-satisfying, and, most importantly in this context, provide a confidence-inspiring link between belayer and climber.

There are many ways to bend a rope or throw a knot. As an organization (more than one person), you should decide on the technique that you feel is easiest to learn and meets the criteria for safety, then require that everyone on the staff teach and tie all knots the same way. Such demands may seem dictatorial (particularly to your 5.9 part-timers), but in this case, congruity is a fine safety habit and reduces the tedious and unnecessary arguments about the best way to tie a particular knot.

As with all these motor movement skills, a knowledgeable person at hand makes the learning easier. Learning any procedure that involves safety from a book is not a good idea.

As you approach your first knot tying session as teacher, think about the following hints:

- Be absolutely sure that you know how to confidently tie whatever knot or knot sequence you have chosen to present. You are attempting not only to teach a knot, but to build trust and confidence. This will not happen if you flub or fumble a tying sequence.

- Have sections of rope or webbing cut at different lengths and color-coded so that you can unobtrusively make sure that a hefty (well covered) student gets a compassionately longer rope for a swiss seat or studebaker wrap.

- Learn one or two more knots than you plan to use so that the students think you know every knot that's ever been tied. Image plays a considerable part toward building initial trust. Work on your cordage vocabulary. Learn and use the words bight, reeve, loop, working end, standing end, cowstail, etc.

- Consider learning a few "nonsense" knots. This type of knot has no real purpose except to entertain the tier and act as a come-on to encourage reluctant students to try working with cordage. Demonstrate a rope trick and then announce, "Come here and I'll show you how to do that." Develop a patter concerning these facts (and many others that can be gleaned from reading mountaineering periodicals and knot books) that exudes confidence. Nothing seems to engender confidence more than a genuinely confident approach. Remember, if someone were helping you tie a knot and was fumbling around, you probably wouldn't have much faith in their belaying ability.

- Purchase *The Knot Book*, by Geoffrey Budworth. It's the best contemporary knot book on the market. (Available from PA)

If you think you need a more visual reminder of all the workshop knots that become fuzzier the longer you don't practice, purchase the 50 min. color video tape, *Karl on Knots,* also available from Project Adventure.

Splicing — Briefly

An eye splice represents about 90% of the rope's tensile strength. A bowline allows about 60%. Why not use a splice for every loop needed? Because it takes considerably longer to perform and cannot easily be removed. However, if a rope end loop is to remain placed, a thimbled eye splice is by far the strongest and most aesthetic choice.

Learn to splice from someone who knows how. Learning from a book; i.e., attempting to learn, is the pits and terminally frustrating.

Ropes, Carabiners, etc.

A plethora of climbing gear and hardware is now available, not only to protect you in the vertical world of climbing, but also to look good (outrageous) while you're vertical. In fact, considering what you need the gear for (ropes course use), there is too much to choose from.

Most people like to mentally sift through colorful catalogs of exotic gear. I don't want to subtract from your "wish book" time, but here's what you really need:
- Locking D carabiners
- 1" tubular webbing. You need 18' for an adult swiss seat and 26' for a studebaker

wrap. Vary lengths as to your normal student size.

- You can substitute 9mm kernmantle rope for the 1" webbing — not as comfortable but somewhat stronger.
- Pre-made commercial harness. These step-into pelvic harnesses do not require knot tying ability and are ordinarily chosen when limited class time is a factor. A harness is much more expensive than a length of rope or webbing but is usually more comfortable to wear.
- Helmets are *de rigueur* on some ropes course elements. Buy the best quality available because expensive helmets adjust for size easier and last longer. A helmet might even save you a hard knock on the noggin.

All climbing gear that is UIAA (Union of International Associations of Alpinism) certified is good stuff. Look for the UIAA stamped impression or tag.

I do not agree with the notion that a Challenge Course participant needs a helmet for every element. If so, we'd better start requiring them on playgrounds, autos, physical education classes, and certainly in the home, since statistically most accidents occur there.

On the ropes course, however, if there is a chance of falling into or onto a hard unyielding object as the result of a fall, jump, or slip — wear a helmet. Examples: *Pamper Pole*, wooden block climbing walls, *Cat Walk*, *Dangle Do*.

Belay Gear Specs

Many ropes course elements can be safely spotted, but if a student climbs more than 8 feet off the ground, a rope belay becomes necessary for safety. Above 8 feet spotting becomes dangerous to both climber and spotter.

To assuage that typical and inevitable twinge of fear of performing at heights, it is useful to make a statement as to the use and breaking strengths of ropes and carabiners. Remember, at this time you are presenting these figures to ease student tension, not to pull their chain any tighter.

- 7/16" diameter skyline (nylon hawser-layered climbing rope) has a tensile strength in excess of 5,000 lbs. This same rope will stretch 35–40% of its length before breaking, providing a gut-saving cushioning effect in the event of a fall.
- 11mm kernmantle (continuous parallel nylon fibers surrounded by a woven nylon sheath) rope is also available at greater cost. Benefits of kernmantle over hawser-lay rope include suppleness of rope, controlled stretch, and availability of colors.
- 9mm kernmantle ropes and 1" tubular webbing are also used extensively for self-tied Swiss seats and Studebaker wrap pelvic harnesses.
- Carabiners, also variously referred to as "crabs," "snap links," and "biners," have varied breaking strengths as to their chosen use and price. Generally, they hold well over 3,000 lbs.

The D-shaped locking carabiner is most used in Adventure Challenge programs. Do not use non-locking carabiners for belay use, and never clip two non-locking carabiners together for any reason. If the right twisting motion is applied, a gate will be forced open, and the crabs will separate. Snap two non-locking carabiners together and without looking, twist them against one another. You will soon inadvertently find the right twisting maneuver that easily separates them.

Consideration:

Never expect a student (any individual that is in the learning phase of a potentially hazardous skill), to do the right thing. Think back to when you were first learning the esoteric and seemingly endless tricks of the trade. What knot do I tie? Does the carabiner go here and how many loops should I include? Does the rope go over or under, or does it go here at all? Oh boy! I hope this is set up right.

Check the obvious. Quite often you will find that something is wrong.

Belaying

There is nothing complicated or hard to learn about belaying on a ropes course. Belaying, in a climbing context, means to protect someone from falling to the ground from a height by means of a rope connected between the climber (person at height) and the belayer (person holding the rope).

The belaying techniques used on a ropes course are identical to and borrowed from the rope safety systems used in rock climbing. The belay techniques taught by PA have been tested and used for decades and are easy to learn. Which technique you choose for use on your ropes course is up to you and how comfortable you feel using a particular belay method or device.

Paradoxically, the higher you are, the safer you are. This loaded statement becomes more acceptable when you consider that; at height the belayer has more time to react; the longer rope involved will provide more stretch (comfort); the higher belay cable attachment will cause the support trees to bend more, taking additional strain off the entire belay system (belayer, belay rope, climber).

The following belay techniques are currently taught at PA training workshops:
- Standing Hip Belay (emphasize use of gloves and Studebaker wrap or Swiss seat clip in).
- Figure 8
- Sticht Plate
- Australian Back-Up Belay

There are other ways to belay that also do the job. If you have been using a Tuber, Cosmic Belay Plate, Munter Hitch, Ruapehu, Long Horn, or one of the many accepted belay devices on the market and you feel comfortable with that device, keep using it.

begin doing things at heights that they would have previously considered impossible. The belay builds a person's confidence in his/her ability to perform improbable tasks which in turn leads to a dramatic increase in self-confidence. True, the comment, "I would have never have tried it without a belay," is often heard, but is "trying it without a belay" the prudent choice of a reasonable person, or is the self-satisfaction and glow of success diminished by using a rope?

Nicki Hall photo

It is not the function or intent of these paragraphs to teach belaying, only to encourage you to seek skilled and competent instruction. Although the techniques are easy to learn, there is little room for error, and the consequences of a mistake can be tragic. Do not attempt any type of belay without having received instruction from a knowledgeable and responsible person. Learning to belay from text material is poor practice. Don't do it.

A recent Adventure workshop participant astutely remarked, "It appears to me that you are not only using the belay rope as a means of insuring safety but as a tool to encourage greater commitment." This is true. As a staff we generally expect more from individuals than they expect of themselves. Once participants develop trust in the belay system, they

Free solo climbing (no rope) is exciting to contemplate and read about, but is well beyond the scope or rationale of programmed Adventure activities.

Appendix B

Orienteering with Map and Compass

by Jim Schoel

"If thy goal this day is unknown even unto you, thy destination by dusk shall also remain a mystery."

— Clavidicus

The mysteries of television and computers are accepted without question by our modern culture, though it is a small number of people who can begin to explain how they work. The compass, though it also presents a mystery, is simple enough to be readily understood. This is not to say that a solution to the entire mystery of the compass is available, but rather that practical orienteering principles can be visualized quickly by a diversity of students. This feedback about one of the first and most important of our technological tools can give students a rewarding sense of accomplishment.

Why the compass? With space age technology providing light-speed navigation capabilities, we don't seem to need it any more. But the compass is a hardy instrument, one that has lasted for hundreds of years, and one that still offers a function today. As a survival tool in wilderness areas, it allows us to do one thing well: walk a straight line. Disorientation can cause such confusion that we will literally walk in circles, thinking we're going in a straight line. Many wilderness hikers have become lost because of an unreasoning trust in their own instinctual capabilities. This disorientation doesn't have to take place in the deep woods. One time I had hiked out only a half mile from an unfamiliar campsite. The undergrowth and tree and cloud cover made the sun useless as a directional guide. And it was getting dark! I got lost and panic started to set in. I walked in circles, hyperventilated, and cursed myself as a fool for not keeping better

track of where I was. I remember finally walking back into camp and acting as if nothing had happened. Following a simple compass course out, and repeating its reciprocal going back, would have prevented all of that.

We can use the compass in conjunction with a map (quadrangle maps are available for every section of the country), to aid us in taking shortcuts, or finding areas not accessible by trail (isolated lakes, rock areas, etc.). And it is certainly important for use in coastal piloting with small craft not outfitted with Loran or electronics. Hence, as an outdoor skill, knowledge of compass theory and function is a necessity. Whether or not a student has immediate plans to use the compass, knowledge of its function can open a whole vista of opportunity.

Simply as a theoretical experience, the compass offers immediate feedback in the understanding of magnetism, latitude and longitude, bearings, landmarks, topography and contour lines, measuring and pacing, true and magnetic north differences, variation (or declination), and deviation. In this way it serves as an ideal tool for cooperative learning, where small groups are given map and compass problems to solve.

Finally, expertise with map and compass offers an opportunity for some philosophizing. To orient is defined: "To place in any definite position with reference to the points of the compass or other points. To adjust with relation to, or bring into due relation to, surroundings, circumstances, facts, etc. To orient one's ideas to new conditions." (American College Dictionary, Random House, New York, N.Y., 1962.) For Western peoples, facing the east, or the Orient, has been symbolic of looking into the mystery and the source of Judeo-Christian-Islamic thought and devotion. Indeed, Islamic people pray to Mecca, and for western persons, Mecca is to the east. Readings that speak to a person of orienting, finding, or adjusting to conditions, opportunities, and insights, can be introduced along with compass activities. After all, life is a journey. It helps to know where we are, to orient ourselves along the way.

Background Material

Magnetism — The discovery of magnetism dates back at least as far as the ancient Greeks. One story tells of a Greek shepherd named Magnes who noticed that the iron head of his staff was attracted to a certain black stone. Another story is that this magnetic stone was first discovered in Magnesia, in Asia Minor. The stone was called lodestone (lode meaning to attract or lead), which we now know to be a fairly common iron ore called magnetite. For centuries after, lodestone was considered to have magical powers of healing. Its eventual use as a navigational device must have seemed magical, too.

In 1600 a treatise called De Magnete (on the Nature of Magnetism) was published by William Gilbert, court physician to Queen Elizabeth I. In this treatise, which proved to be a milestone in the history of science, the idea was first proposed that the earth itself was a giant magnet. Lodestone apparently had become magnetized in the earth's magnetic field. Until 1820, when it was discovered that an electric current could induce magnetism, such natural magnets as lodestone were the only source of magnetism.

Why does the earth behave like a magnet?

Scientists are not entirely sure. One theory suggests that the earth's magnetic field originates in electric currents generated in the planet's core of molten iron.

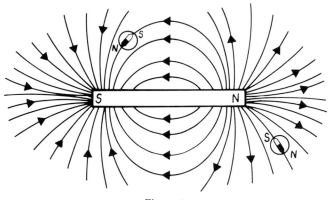

Figure 1

What does it mean when we say the earth behaves like a giant magnet? It means that there are North and South Polar regions which produce a magnetic field with lines of force such as pictured in Figure 1. It should be remembered that these lines of force do not actually exist but are convenient representations to show how a compass or metallic object behaves when near enough to the magnet to be affected by it. In no magnet, the earth included, is there a specific point which one can call *the* North Pole, but only a general region from which the lines of force seem to originate. Because of the size of the earth, you can imagine that the polar regions are rather large. It is also known that on the earth the polar regions wander extensively. These variations are measurable and are somewhat predictable from year to year, but no really satisfactory explanation has been found for this wandering. Although magnetism is one of the oldest areas in science, there are still a lot of unanswered questions.

The Compass — The functioning principle of the compass is that the compass needle aligns itself with the earth's magnetic field, pointing toward the region we call the North

Magnetic Pole. This pole is not very near the geographical North Pole, or True North Pole (which is the end of the imaginary axis about which the earth rotates and upon which all our globes, maps and charts are based). At present, the North Magnetic Pole is over 1000 miles south of the True North Pole and situated to the north of Hudson Bay. The South Magnetic Pole is south of Australia and north of Antarctica.

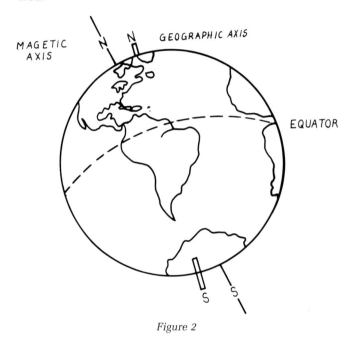

Figure 2

The operation of a compass is complicated by the Magnetic Poles not coinciding with the Geographic Poles. This causes what is known as compass *variation* (on sea), or *declination* (on land) — two different terms for the same thing. On the following map (Fig. 3), you will see that on only one line of declination in the U.S. will a magnet point to the True North Pole. To the east of this line the compass tends to point west of True North, and in the western part of the United States it points east of True North. The exact variation of a magnet is determined for each location and is indicated on the compass rose on many maps and navigational charts along with any yearly change in variation.

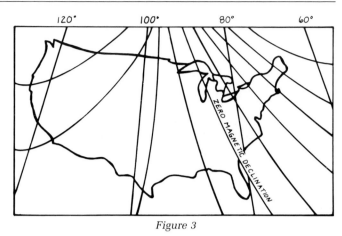

Figure 3

Another compass error, called *deviation,* is caused by magnetic materials being too near the compass. It is important that the compass be held away from magnetic materials (belt buckles, watches, etc.), which will cause fluctuations of the needle.

Did you know that:

The word compass comes from the Latin "cum passus" meaning "with step." In ancient days, distance was measured by pacing or stepping it off. Both the compass divider and the magnetic compass measure distances.

The Romans used the double pace (two steps or strides) as a means of measurement. Our present word mile comes from a distance, "milia passum" (1000 paces), which happens to be 5,280 ft. — the length on one statute or land mile.

The Nautical Mile is defined as being equivalent to 1 minute of latitude, which is 6080 feet. Thus, a nautical mile equals 1.15 statute miles, or 7 nautical miles equal almost 8 statute miles.

This background information is supplied with the permission of Emily Cassidy, former Chemistry and Project Adventure teacher at Gloucester High School, Gloucester, Mass., from her unpublished paper "The Compass: Charting Courses and Taking Bearings," July 12, 1974.

Map and Compass Activities

1. Teach the nomenclature of the compass.

(We use the Silva Polaris because it provides a liquid filled compass at a reasonable cost.)
   A. Base plate (inch and mm. gradations)
   B. Bezel (upon which the degrees are stamped)
   C. Travel arrow
   D. Orienting arrow
   E. Compass needle

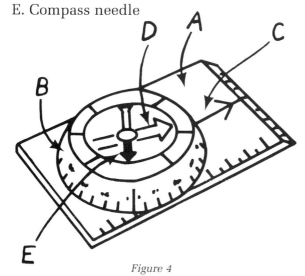

Figure 4

Review material is available in the directions for the Silva compass and in a number of books, such as Bjorn Kjellstrom's *Be Expert with Map and Compass.*

2. Teach how to take a bearing (finding the magnetic compass heading for any distant object).

This is an excellent beginning activity and should be done out-of-doors if possible, though it can also be accomplished in a gym area or even a classroom.
- Take the *base plate* (A) and line up the *travel arrow* (C) with the object you want to "shoot."
- Turn the *bezel* (B) so that the *orienting arrow* (D) is under the *compass needle* (E).
- The bearing can be read on the bezel where it intersects the direction of travel arrow (C).

- Cross bearings can be utilized in order to find out where you are on the map. Take two bearings from known landmarks and draw a line along the compass bearing from each landmark. Where the two lines intersect, there you are (or close by).

3. Teach the setting of a compass course on a map, the use of contour lines, measuring distances, and the identification of landmarks (roads, churches, quarries).

A. Follow the "Three Step System":
   1. Locate where you are on the map (it needs to be a topographic map). Draw a line to where you want to go, and lay the edge of the compass base plate on that line.
   2. Turn the Bezel arrow so that it faces to the top of the map. The "up" side of the map represents true north.
   3. Read at the bottom of the topo map where it says "declination," and add or subtract that number to or from the true north reading. For example, in the Eastern part of the United States, you would add the declination to the true north reading.

   In order to follow the course produced from this process, you "put the red in the shed and follow Fred." This ditty means that the red magnetic arrow (the "red") is lined up with the arrow on the Bezel (the "shed"). You then follow in the direction the base plate arrow is pointing (or "Fred"). If the "red" comes out of the "shed," then you are off course, of course!
B. Contour lines indicate the shape of the land. The closer together the lines are, the steeper the indicated hill or mountain. A number will be placed somewhere along the darker contour lines indicating the height above sea level. The amount of rise or decline between each line is indicated on the bottom of most maps, though it can be figured by studying a series of lines. The

distance between lines is called the "contour interval." You can ask students to find the lowest areas, where water would likely be (marshy), what the tallest areas are, and where the streams are and where they flow (and why).

C. Measuring distances: Most topographic maps will have a graph at the bottom indicating miles, feet, and kilometers. Utilizing the ruler on the side of the compass plate, you can measure the distance between destinations.

D. Landmarks are indicated by symbols and pose an interesting scavenger hunt and history lesson. Quarries, churches, houses, and land survey markers, are just some of a broad range of landmarks that can be "discovered."

E. To take Cross Bearings you need to know what distant objects you are shooting (a church steeple, a mountain top, a water tower). Take the magnetic bearings for the two objects (or three for even more accuracy), and write them down. Then find the landmark on the map. Adjusting for the declination, so that you come up with true north, lay the compass down on the map with north on the bezel pointing to the top of the map and the plate lined up with the landmark. Draw a line on the map. Repeat this for all the bearings. The point where the lines cross indicates your position on the map. This has a practical use for sailors or hikers who don't know where they are but who are able to identify distant landmarks.

4. Take the students to a large area (a gymnasium or football field will do).

Have each of them measure their own double pace (two average walking steps), by counting how many double paces it takes to walk 100–200'. Through division, the students can determine the length of their double pace. This useful measurement allows them to step

off distances with reasonable accuracy.

5. While in the same large area, students can do a "Compass Walk." (See p. 176 of *Silver Bullets* for this Initiative.)

6. The "Three Legged Compass Walk" or "Silver Dollar Game" can also be introduced.

Construct a course where a small group starts from a place marked by a flat object (a coin or small disc will do). Have the group walk out on virtually any compass course (say 224 degrees) for any distance (say 130 feet). When they get that far, their course changes to 354 degrees for the second leg of the journey, again walking 130 feet. At that destination, the course is changed to 114 degrees, while again walking 130 feet. If the group does all of this properly, they will return to their starting point having made a triangle! The trick in constructing this game is to add 120 degrees to each leg, and to keep the distance for each leg the same. (If you have a copy of Kjellstrom's book, look at the illustration on pg. 81.) You can use this game with a large class simply by breaking them down into small groups (an ideal cooperative learning activity). By giving each group a separate instruction card, you can come up with different starting directions and distances for each group. The point is to see how close each group gets to their original point (don't tell them this or, of course, they will walk right over to it). The group that gets the closest to their starting point gets hearty kudos and whatever minor reward you can think up.

7. Small out and back or destination orienteering courses can be set up, even in small areas.

Simply construct the course in such a way that it weaves around itself and the obstacles in such a manner that it can be contained by that area. You can place little sayings on destination objects that, when assembled, make up a story or a poem. Any shortcutting means an incomplete message. Tell the students that they shouldn't read their compass while walking. Take a reading, sight on a landmark, then walk to it. Take the compass out and repeat the process.

8. Longer distance bushwhacks and forest exercises are the next step.

The same principles are followed, but the compass and map are now used together as aids in getting the group from one place to another. It is good to pick major destination points, like a pond or road at least for beginning groups. For years I've used the derricks in an old quarry. If the students get disoriented, they simply climb up and take a bearing on the derrick poles.

When there is an obstacle that cannot be gone through, pick out a landmark on the other side of it, then simply walk around to it. One member of the party can be a messenger who goes around that obstacle, leaving behind the compass person. The messenger comes to the other side of the obstacle and lines up with the compass bearing of the person left behind. The whole party can then go around, meet up with the messenger, and continue on their way. When in a deep forest situation, where no practical bearings can be taken, a member of the party can climb a hill or a tree and take bearings on landmarks, shouting them down to the map-bearer.

Final Note

After you have done all this, it is important that the students be given some situations in which they can practice their new skills. Certain Initiatives and games can be done in and around a school. Nevertheless, a woodland trip provides the needed real experience.

Appendix C
Evaluation

by Dick Prouty

Mary Ladd Smith wrote an extensive evaluation of the original Project Adventure program at Hamilton-Wenham Regional High School. Completed in 1974, during the third year of the program, the evaluation covered the full sophomore class that took the program each year — 224 in 1971, and 231 in 1972. Six instruments were administered pre- and post-program application. These instruments were: the Tennessee Self-Concept Scale, the School Climate Survey (based on David McClelland's Classroom Climate Survey), two different types of student surveys, the AAHPERD physical fitness test, and the Rotter Scale of Internal vs. External Control. The specific goals addressed by the evaluation were stated as follows:

- to improve self-concept, confidence, and sense of personal competence among participants
- to increase psycho-motor skills especially in the areas of balance and coordination
- to overcome pervasive passivity, apathy, and uninvolvement among students

The full report showed a large degree of positive results and was responsible for the awarding, by the federal Office of Education, of National Demonstration Site Status, subsequent National Diffusion Network Model Program status, and funding for dissemination. The statistics are important in order to assure ourselves and others that the so called anecdotal data of student reports and comments aren't simply the result of enthusiasm or are not representative of a significant group. The

typical type of soft anecdotal data used in the evaluation write-up, in addition to the statistics, *is* helpful, though, in order to get a sense of the real life decisions which the program can affect. The following exchange is from the qualitative section of the 1974 report:

The **pre-question** asked, "How do you feel about participating in Project Adventure?"

Girl, pre-question: *"I don't think I am too thrilled about participating in the gym part. I am really scared about swinging on ropes out in the woods and walking on those ropes and jumping from the tree down on the stumps. Even when I was just watching Jim do it and he told us to spot in case he fell...I shook all over and my hand turned icy cold."*

The **post-question** was, "In what ways has Project Adventure changed your school experience this year as compared to last year?"

Same girl, post-question: *"I am not as shy as I used to be but I am still quite shy. I've stayed after school more to get involved in other things. I got up enough courage to stand in front of about 20 sixth grade kids and conduct a lesson."*

The change in self-concept, and the decrease in apathy somehow make more sense, through this girl's comments, than the dry numbers.

The replicability of the original evaluation of Project Adventure has been somewhat of a problem because of the large scope of the evaluation and the amount of grant money that it took to accomplish the original evaluation. There have, however, been some significant evaluations of the Project Adventure Physical Education model. In 1983, Tom Quimby finished his doctoral thesis from Boston University with a dissertation that again used the Tennessee Self-Concept Scale, and the PABS (Platt Affective Behavior Scales) with students in the Project Adventure physical education class at North Conway, New Hampshire. Tom replicated the original Hamilton study in that he also found statistically significant change on the Tennessee, but he did it with a control group, something that was missing from the original study. Tom (now a Professor at Plymouth State College in Plymouth, New Hampshire where he runs his own PA program), used the PABS to back up the Tennessee. The PABS describes itself as a "Self-Concept Observer System" and uses a series of observer rating scales to pre- and post-test a PA type participant group. The scales have titles such as Expression of Opinion, Other Orientation, and Perseverance. It is somewhat cumbersome to use the PABS and go through the process of training observers, but it is designed to measure what we in the program "know" changes during the course of the program. It can also be used as a helpful teacher diagnostic aid for program modification. When a student goes on the PABS from a one rating (makes excuses for not taking responsibility), to a five (gives support to all group members), the teacher is able to learn from the evaluation and make adjustments accordingly. The results also provide a nice way to describe the positive results of a class in a targeted manner, to students, parents, or other audiences.

Another evaluation of the Physical Education PA model is the 1984 study of the Cambridge Public School's UMPA (Urban Modification of Project Adventure). This evaluation used the Piers-Harris Self-Concept Test and the Selman Inventory, a cognitive-development measure of Interpersonal awareness, as developed by Dr. Selman of Harvard University. This study measured students in the eight-week UMPA middle elementary school program. It showed positive gain on both tests for the experimental groups as opposed to the control group, but only in the Selman was the gain large enough to be statistically significant. The Selman is an interesting inventory that measure gains in the *intellectual* understanding of issues of trust/reciprocity, conflict resolution, group cohesion, decision making/ organization, and leadership. These were seen as especially important to UMPA, as the original rationale for the program was to enhance the chances for success of the Cambridge Magnet School Desegregation program.

Another evaluation worth noting is the 1982 study of the Adventure Based Counseling development grant subjects. This study looked at students in counseling groups in the Massachusetts schools of Gloucester, Manchester, and Hamilton using the Tennessee and the Piers-Harris scale. The students were in the program for at least one weekly meeting for a year. Control groups were used, and the pre- and post-test results showed strong statistical significance.

The question of effective evaluation is crucial to the on-going success of any program such as Project Adventure that concerns educational change. The question of resources is always critical in trying to get the scale of evaluation that produces the scope of evaluation described previously. We strongly advocate that all teachers do at least a soft data questionnaire evaluation of the type described in the curriculum chapter of this book. Copies of the four evaluations described here are available from Project Adventure, Inc., and are often used by people in the early stages of program design and planning.

Appendix D

Outdoor Adventure Activities in the Elementary Physical Education Curriculum

by Gary Moore, Ph.D.
Worthington City Schools
Ohio State University
February 15, 1986

Outdoor Adventure programs and activities have grown tremendously in the past decade. There are several possible explanations for this phenomenon:

- Youngsters today have been exposed to a variety of risk recreation sports.
- The Outward Bound movement is prevalent.
- The New Games approach to physical education is leaving its mark.
- Project Adventure is an influential force. (Rohnke, 1984).

Initially envisioned strictly as a part of junior high and senior high school programs, the Adventure philosophy is slowly becoming evident even in elementary physical education programs. Siedentop (1984) suggests several possible explanations for the popularity of these Adventure activities so early in the educational process. He insists that they allow for the following:

- active participation regardless of skill level, which encourages involvement from all students.
- success in challenging activities, which can be just as rewarding as blasting the kickball over the outfielder's head...and which carries with it a greater probability for success. Farrington (1976) agrees:

"Games...[that develop trust and cooperation] are not so much a way to compare our abilities as a way to celebrate them."
- experience in a different, non-competitive atmosphere; Orlick (1982) writes, "...[Adventure] games are designed so that cooperation among players is necessary to achieve the objectives of the game; children play together for common ends rather than against one another..."

Just as pyramids provide an opportunity for children to use basic gymnastic skills learned in a tumbling program, Adventure activities offer children the opportunity to develop cooperative, trust, and problem solving skills. These skills, in turn, may enhance the caliber of children's performance in organized sports.

Furthermore, in a recent JOHPER article on team dynamics, Freischlag (1986) stated that the more students are permitted to participate in problem solving games, the more they are likely to demonstrate high levels of positive involvement in team tasks assigned to them. For physical educators, this has real implications for lead-ups to team sports. According to Bunker and Rotella (1977), a common bond exists between the objectives of these youth team sports and those of Adventure curriculums:

- "... situations should be planned to make the young athlete feel successful."
- "... what athletes feel about themselves is often more important than actual ability."
- "it is extremely important to create positive team morale."

Cooperative teammates can help each other in learning new skills as well as providing a desirable social environment." [Freischlag, 1986]

One such Adventure program at the elementary school level is operating at the Worthington Hills Elementary School near Columbus, Ohio. Adventure activities have been a part of this program for ten years. At Worthington Hills Elementary, Adventure games and activities are incorporated into four different aspects of the school curriculum. First, Adventure activities are woven into the basic instructional program. Three concentrated weeks of Adventure activities are offered during the school year, and some additional Adventure activities are taught all year long. When introducing team sports, for example, cooperative games, a kind of Adventure activity, are used as a lead up.

One of these three "Adventure weeks" is a particular highlight. During this time, students in grades four through six have the opportunity to scale three indoor climbing walls. The horizontal traverse wall, which progresses sixty feet along the gymnasium, introduces students to some basic climbing and spotting techniques. This teaching station requires a minimal amount of floor space and utilizes an often neglected segment of the physical education classroom — the walls. Blocks of different sizes and configurations are bolted to the wall at heights ranging from a few inches to five feet. The children traverse along the wall using a variety of hand and foot holds; they are never farther from the floor than the height of a balance beam. This one activity has tremendous value, for it offers an activity which can be made either more or less challenging using special color-coded blocks. Thanks to some clever paintings by the school's art teacher, students scramble along the simulated mountain ridge in the company of rock climbers, mountain goats, snakes, vipers, and other fantasy friends. Near the end of the traverse are wall charts where students can indicate their level of success by signing their names under appropriate classifications. This simple traverse wall can be constructed for less than one hundred dollars, provided you find a local lumber yard to donate fifty to sixty mahogany wood blocks. The paint comes from the students. This kind of statement yields plenty of paint: "Anyone who brings in a gallon of latex house paint is the first one to get to climb the wall!" A talented and willing art teacher can mix the paint to form the necessary colors and create a very attractive scene. At the same time, you've come up with an extremely effective public relations tool.

From the traverse wall, the students progress to one of the two vertical climbing walls which reach twenty three feet to the top of the gymnasium. Once on top, the students can sign their names on the "snow covered" simulated peak, Mount Hawkeye, or they can honk the horn and touch the "golden egg" at the top of the "bean stalk." An "I can" feeling soon prevails — it comes when students reach the top or even when they manage to extend their range to the next block. These vertical climbing walls are somewhat more difficult to construct than the traverse wall and involve more expense since this activity must depend upon "bomb proof" overhead belay anchors and specialized safety equipment. However, the vertical wall is still within the reach of the creative, energetic physical education instructor. You must, however, get expert construction advice before sending your students to the top. Otherwise, they may come down considerably faster than you would like.

As in most individual sports and activities at the elementary level, teachers must constantly be in a position to adequately supervise the children. So how does the physical educator offer a variety of Adventure activities and a large percentage of activity time while maintaining an adequate level of supervision? The answer lies in the "rotation method." The instructor simultaneously conducts a high risk climbing wall Challenge and several low risk activities. Students receive close supervision while on the high risk climbing wall but only limited supervision during the low risk activities. The instructor is quite free, however, to give plenty of *verbal* feedback to the low-risk group.

The second aspect of the school curriculum which contains some element of Adventure is the intramural program. As with all skills, children need an opportunity to practice Adventure activities, and the instructor must give the youngsters an adequate number of those practice opportunities. Therefore, Adventure games are included in all field day and special event days, which also helps to achieve a comfortable balance between competitive and non-competitive events.

The third aspect of the curriculum which exposes youngsters to Adventure experiences is the resident camp program. Sixth grade children have the opportunity to test these newly acquired Adventure skills during a three day camping session. Approximately 50% of the camp curriculum is devoted to extending the Adventure program into a natural, outdoor environment.

The final aspect of the curriculum that allows for Adventure instruction is the series of one-day field trips to the Adventure Education Center. This experientially based Center offers a variety of Adventure and outdoor activities for area youth. Here, public school teachers become trained Adventure Education leaders. The Center represents a cooperative effort among three agencies; the Ohio State University, School of Health, Physical Education and Recreation; the Godman Guild Association, which is an area social service agency; and International Field Studies, Inc., which offers logistical and program support to field trip leaders. Here, area schools have the opportunity to provide for students many new and exciting activities which are not normally available to them. Students use the facility as the site of culminating activities for the Adventure Unit. At the Center, they have the opportunity to participate in a variety of Adventure activities. For example, they can try the low level Challenge course and then progress to a twenty foot high ropes course. In addition, selected archery students can compete in the annual "Robin Hood Games." Thirty to forty students learn to use first-rate archery equipment and shoot at three different archery ranges located at the Center. Incidentally, the local parks and recreation department has picked up on the idea and is now offering classes and more practice opportunities for students who are really turned on to archery. The concept has been working quite well. Over ninety trained area teachers are becoming actively involved in the program.

Indeed, Adventure activities are becoming a popular part of quality elementary physical education curriculums. Challenging Adventure activities develop not only the body but one's inner being as well. Aristotle issued a challenge to physical educators as early as 350 B.C.:

"The results of good physical education are not limited to the body alone, but they extend to the soul itself."

If, in 1986, we wish to use Aristotle's challenge, if we wish to develop both body and soul, then the importance of creative, challenging Adventure activities in the elementary physical education curriculum cannot be ignored.

References

Bunker, L. & Rotella, R. *Getting Them Up, Not Uptight.* In Jerry R. Thomas (Ed.), Youth Sports Guide for Coaches and Parents. Washington, D.C. Manufacturers' Life Insurance and the National Association for Sport and Physical Education, 1977.

Farrington, P. Games. Fluegelman, A. (Ed.), *The New Games Book.* Garden City: Dolphin Books/Doubleday & Company Inc., 1976.

Freischlag, Jerry. *Team Dynamics — Implications for Coaching.* Journal of Health, Physical Education and Recreation, 56, 67-71.

Orlick, T. *The Second Cooperative Sports and Games Book.* New York: Pantheon Books, 1982.

Rohnke, Karl. *Silver Bullets.* Hamilton, Massachusetts: Project Adventure, 1984.

Siedentap, D., Herkowitz, J. & Rink, J. *Elementary Physical Education Methods.* Englewood Cliffs, New Jersey: Prentice Hall, 1984.

For more information write to the author at:

Ohio State University
School of Health, Physical Education and Recreation
337 W. 17th Ave.
Columbus, Ohio   43210

Index

▼ = Spotting Issues discussed
✔ = Leadership Issues discussed

Project Adventure Services

Since 1971 Project Adventure has been creating learning programs that challenge people to go beyond their perceived boundaries, to work with others to solve problems and to experience success. Over 1 million people have used our approach to realize increased self-confidence, develop leadership skills, discover the power of group cooperation, and learn to view obstacles as opportunities for growth.

The Project Adventure concept is characterized by an atmosphere that is fun, supportive and challenging. Non-competitive games, group problem solving Initiatives and ropes course events are the principal activities we use to help individuals reach their goals; to improve self-esteem, to develop strategies that enhance decision-making, and to respect differences within a group.

We offer the following services:

Project Adventure Workshops

Through a network of national certified trainers, Project Adventure conducts workshops for teachers, counselors, youth workers and other professionals who work with people. These workshops are given in various sections of the country. Separate workshops are given in Challenge Ropes Course Skills, Counseling Skills for Adventure Based Programs, Project Adventure Games and Initiatives, and Interdisciplinary Academic Curriculum.

Program Accreditation

The Accreditation process is an outside review of a program by PA staff. Programs that undertake the accreditation process are seeking outside evaluation with regard to quality and safety. The term accreditation means "formal written confirmation." Programs seeking confirmation are looking to ensure that they are within the current standards of safety and risk management. This assurance may be useful for making changes in program equipment and/or design, and in providing information on program quality to third parties such as administrators, insurance companies and the public.

Challenge Course Design and Installation

Project Adventure has been designing and installing ropes courses (a series of individual and group challenge elements situated indoors in a gymnasium or outdoors in a grove of trees) since 1971. PA Staff can travel to your site and design/install a course appropriate for your needs and budget.

Challenge Course Equipment Catalog

A catalog service of hard-to-find materials and tools used in the installation of Challenge Ropes Courses. This catalog also contains climbing rope and a variety of items useful to Adventure programs.

Professional Development

Management workshops for business and professional persons. These workshops are designed for increasing efficiency of team members in the workplace. The trust, communication, and risk-taking ability learned in the executive programs translate into a more cohesive and productive team at work.

Publications

Project Adventure, Inc. publishes books and other material for the field of Experiential and Adventure Education. Our titles cover such diverse subjects as: games, Initiatives and Adventure activities, theory, leadership, and safety. An order form is provided on the next page that includes some our best sellers, which are described below. Call or write Project Adventure for a compete publications list.

Cowstails and Cobras II

The 1989 revision of Karl Rohnke's classic guide to games, Initiatives and Adventure activities contains much of what made the original a classic in the field. This expanded edition includes sections on leadership issues and curriculum outlines from model programs.

QuickSilver

In the tradition of *Cowstails and Cobras II* and *Silver Bullets*, *QuickSilver* promises to become an instant classic in the field of Adventure and Experiential Education. Karl continues to crank out new games, refine and adapt old ones, and collect ideas from other Adventure practitioners. This latest offering contains over 150 new Games, Initiatives, Ice Breakers, Variations on old standards, Trust, Closures and more.

Karl and co-author Steve Butler also have included valuable information on just what it takes to be an effective Adventure leader. Their collaboration on the activities and on the leadership section make *QuickSilver* a truly unique and invaluable resource. More games, especially as presented by Karl, are always eagerly anticipated, but the real value of this book is in the presentation of the leadership information. Karl and Steve impart many of the *secrets* that they use when leading and designing programs. *QuickSilver* is destined to become a standard item in any leaders bag of tricks. By Karl Rohnke and Steve Butler

Islands Of Healing

Subtitled *A Guide to Adventure Based Counseling*, *Islands* presents a comprehensive discussion of this rapidly growing counseling approach. Started in 1974, ABC is an innovative, group counseling model that uses cooperative games, Initiative problem solving, low and high Challenge Ropes Course elements, and other Adventure activities. The book contains extensive "how-to" information on group selection, training, goal setting, sequencing, and leading and debriefing activities. Also included are explorations of model ABC programs at several representative sites — junior and senior high schools, a psychiatric hospital, and court referred programs. By Jim Schoel, Dick Prouty, and Paul Radcliffe.

Youth Leadership In Action

Youth Leadership In Action is a compilation of Project Adventure's best games and activities written not only for youth leaders but written *by* youth leaders. A group of eight young authors has rewritten 54 activities in their own language and from their own perspective. They also provide information on leading Adventure programs and how to train and practice the activities before going out to lead them.

Along with the write-ups, instructions, and rules to the activities, there is a whole section on leadership that includes some basic PA concepts like • Challenge By Choice • Full Value Contract, and such topics as • sequencing • debriefing • goal setting • planning • designing different types of programs — and all written in language for the youth leaders themselves.

Project Adventure Safety Manual

An Instructor's guide for Initiatives and High and Low Elements, this practical, hands-on and detailed manual is designed to aid those in the field running Adventure programs that utilize a challenge ropes course. The manual provides, in outline form, the standards needed for Project Adventure's program accreditation but presents the information in such a way that it can be used by anyone working with a ropes course in their program. Included are task descriptions and instructor's, participant's and spotter's roles for 14 Initiatives, 11 Low Elements and 14 High Elements. Also included are sections detailing standards for belaying, ropes course set-up, accepted equipment and more. Use of this manual ensures that all persons involved in the running of a ropes course are doing so in an accepted and consistent manner.

To get further information about Project Adventure services and programs, contact one of the following offices:

Project Adventure, Inc

P.O. Box 100
Hamilton, MA 01936
508/468-7981
FAX 508/468-7605

P.O. Box 2447
Covington, GA 30209
770/784-9310
FAX 770/787-7764

P.O. Box 1640
Brattleboro, VT 05301
802/254-5054
FAX 802/254-5182

P.O. Box 14171
Portland, OR 97293
503/239-0169
FAX 503/236-6765

In New Zealand:

Project Adventure New Zealand
P.O. Box 5303
Welington, New Zealand
04/384-8096
fax 04/384-8146

In Australia:

Project Adventure Australia
332 Banyule Rd.
View Bank, Australia
03/457-6494
fax 03/457-5438

Order/Request Form

Please send information on the following programs:

o *Project Adventure Training Workshops*
o *Challenge Course Design and Installation*
o *Ropes Course Equipment Catalog*
o *Executive Reach Programs*
o *Publications List*
o *Program Accreditation*
o *Please add my name to your mailing list*

Please send the Following Books

Qty	Title	Price	Total
	Cowstails and Cobras II	18.50	
	Silver Bullets	18.50	
	QuickSilver	23.50	
	Youth Leadership	10.00	
	Islands of Healing	20.50	
	Safety Manual	12.00	

Subtotal _____

5% tax (Mass. residents only) _____

Shipping (instructions below) _____

TOTAL _____

Shipping Instructions

Orders up to $35.00 — add $3.50
Orders over $35.00 — add 10% of total
(Canada & overseas, add additional $2.00 to total)

Ship to:

Name _____

Address _____

City _____ State _____ Zip _____

Phone (_____) _____

Payment:

❏ Check enclosed   ❏ Purchase Order

Charge to: ❏ Visa ❏ MasterCard

Card # _____ Exp. _____

Signature _____

(Signature required for all charge orders.)

Copy or detach this form and return to:
Project Adventure, Inc.

P.O. Box 100
Hamilton, MA 01936
508/468-7981
FAX: 508/468-7605

or

P.O. Box 2447
Covington, GA 30209
770/784-9310
FAX: 770/787-7764

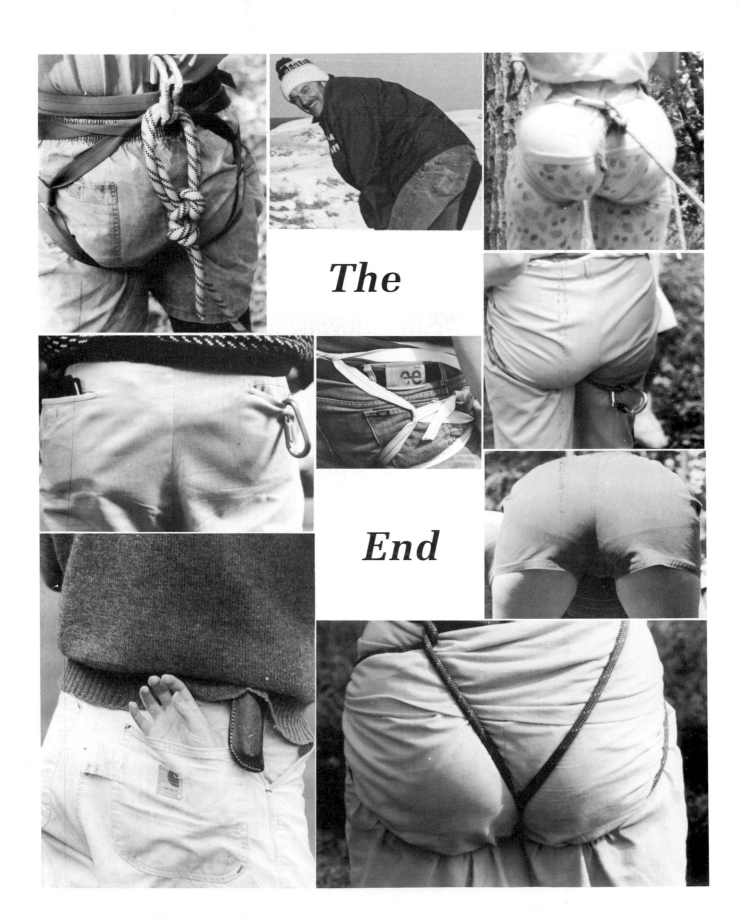

The

End